BANKS MILLER
JENNIFER S. HOLMES

READINGS IN **AMERICAN**
STATE AND LOCAL GOVERNMENT

Kendall Hunt
publishing company

CONTENTS

CHAPTER 1
FUNDAMENTALS

MCCULLOCH V. MARYLAND

SUPREME COURT OF THE UNITED STATES
17 U.S. 316 (1819)

[Congress charted a bank that Maryland subsequently decided to tax. There are two major questions arising in this case: (1) does Congress have the power to create a federal bank?, and (2) does Maryland have the authority to tax a federal bank if Congress has the power to create one?]

MARSHALL, Chief Justice, delivered the opinion of the Court.

In the case now to be determined, the defendant, a sovereign State, denies the obligation of a law enacted by the legislature of the Union, and the plaintiff, on his part, contests the validity of an act which has been passed by the legislature of that State. The Constitution of our country, in its most interesting and vital parts, is to be considered, the conflicting powers of the Government of the Union and of its members, as marked in that Constitution, are to be discussed, and an opinion given which may essentially influence the great operations of the Government. No tribunal can approach such a question without a deep sense of its importance, and of the awful responsibility involved in its decision. But it must be decided peacefully, or remain a source of hostile legislation, perhaps, of hostility of a still more serious nature; and if it is to be so decided, by this tribunal alone can the decision be made. On the Supreme Court of the United States has the Constitution of our country devolved this important duty.

The first question made in the cause is—has Congress power to incorporate a bank?

It has been truly said that this can scarcely be considered as an open question entirely unprejudiced by the former proceedings of the Nation respecting it. The principle now contested was introduced at a very early period of our history, has been recognised by many successive legislatures, and has been acted upon by the Judicial Department, in cases of peculiar delicacy, as a law of undoubted obligation.

It will not be denied that a bold and daring usurpation might be resisted after an acquiescence still longer and more complete than this. But it is conceived that a doubtful question, one on which human reason may pause and the human judgment be suspended, in the decision of which the great principles of liberty are not concerned, but the respective powers of those who are equally the representatives of the people, are to be adjusted, if not put at rest by the practice of the Government, ought to receive a considerable impression from that practice. An exposition of the Constitution, deliberately established by legislative acts, on the faith of which an immense property has been advanced, ought not to be lightly disregarded.

The power now contested was exercised by the first Congress elected under the present Constitution.

The bill for incorporating the Bank of the United States did not steal upon an unsuspecting legislature and pass unobserved. Its principle was completely understood, and was opposed with equal zeal and ability. After being resisted first in the fair and open field of debate, and afterwards in the executive cabinet, with as much persevering talent as any measure has ever experienced, and being supported by arguments which convinced minds as pure and as intelligent as this country can boast, it became a law. The original act was permitted to expire, but a short experience of the embarrassments to which the refusal to revive it exposed the Government convinced those who were most prejudiced against the measure of its necessity, and induced the passage of the present law. It would require no ordinary share of intrepidity to assert that a measure adopted under these circumstances was a bold and plain usurpation to which the Constitution gave no countenance. These observations belong to the cause; but they are not made under the impression that, were the question entirely new, the law would be found irreconcilable with the Constitution.

In discussing this question, the counsel for the State of Maryland have deemed it of some importance, in the construction of the Constitution, to consider that instrument not as emanating from the people, but as the act of sovereign and independent States. The powers of the General Government, it has been said, are delegated by the States, who alone are truly sovereign, and must be exercised in subordination to the States, who alone possess supreme dominion.

It would be difficult to sustain this proposition. The convention which framed the Constitution was indeed elected by the State legislatures. But the instrument, when it came from their hands, was a mere proposal, without obligation or pretensions to it. It was reported to the then existing Congress of the United States with a request that it might "be submitted to a convention of delegates, chosen in each State by the people thereof, under the recommendation of its legislature, for their assent and ratification."

This mode of proceeding was adopted, and by the convention, by Congress, and by the State legislatures, the instrument was submitted to the people. They acted upon it in the only manner in which they can act safely, effectively and wisely, on such a subject—by assembling in convention. It is true, they assembled in their several States—and where else should they have assembled? No political dreamer was ever wild enough to think of breaking down the lines which separate the States, and of compounding the American people into one common mass. Of consequence, when they act, they act in their States. But the measures they adopt do not, on that account, cease to be the measures of the people themselves, or become the measures of the State governments.

From these conventions the Constitution derives its whole authority. The government proceeds directly from the people; is "ordained and established" in the name of the people, and is declared to be ordained, "in order to form a more perfect union, establish justice, insure domestic tranquillity, and secure the blessings of liberty to themselves and to their posterity."

The assent of the States in their sovereign capacity is implied in calling a convention, and thus submitting that instrument to the people. But the people were at perfect liberty to accept or reject it, and their act was final. It required not the affirmance, and could not be negatived, by the State Governments. The Constitution, when thus adopted, was of complete obligation, and bound the State sovereignties.

It has been said that the people had already surrendered all their powers to the State sovereignties, and had nothing more to give. But surely the question whether they may resume and modify the powers granted to Government does not remain to be settled in this country. Much more might the legitimacy of the General Government be doubted had it been created by the States. The powers delegated to the State sovereignties were to be exercised by themselves, not by a distinct and independent sovereignty created by themselves. To the formation of a league such as was the Confederation, the State sovereignties were certainly competent. But when, "in order to form a more perfect union," it was deemed necessary to change this alliance into an effective Government, possessing great and sovereign powers and acting directly on the people, the necessity of referring it to the people, and of deriving its powers directly from them, was felt and acknowledged by all. The Government of the Union then (whatever may be the influence of this fact on the case) is, emphatically and truly, a Government of the people. In form and in substance, it emanates from them. Its powers are granted by them, and are to be exercised directly on them, and for their benefit.

This Government is acknowledged by all to be one of enumerated powers. The principle that it can exercise only the powers granted to it would seem too apparent to have required to be enforced by all those arguments which its enlightened friends, while it was depending before the people, found it necessary to urge; that principle is now universally admitted. But the question respecting the extent of the powers actually granted is perpetually arising, and will probably continue to arise so long as our system shall exist. In discussing these questions, the conflicting powers of the General and State Governments must be brought into view, and the supremacy of their respective laws, when they are in opposition, must be settled.

If any one proposition could command the universal assent of mankind, we might expect it would be this—that the Government of the Union, though limited in its powers, is supreme within its sphere of action. This would seem to result necessarily from its nature. It is the Government of all; its powers are delegated by all; it represents all, and acts for all. Though any one State may be willing to control its operations, no State is willing to allow others to control them. The nation, on those subjects on which it can act, must necessarily bind its component parts. But this question is not left to mere reason; the people have, in express terms, decided it by saying, "this Constitution, and the laws of the United States, which shall be made in pursuance thereof," "shall be the supreme law of the land," and by requiring that the members of the State legislatures and the officers of the executive and judicial departments of the States shall take the oath of fidelity to it. The Government of the United States, then, though limited in its powers, is supreme, and its laws, when made in pursuance of the Constitution, form the supreme law of the land, "anything in the Constitution or laws of any State to the contrary notwithstanding."

[. . .]

Although, among the enumerated powers of Government, we do not find the word "bank" or "incorporation," we find the great powers, to lay and collect taxes; to borrow money; to regulate commerce; to declare and conduct a war; and to raise and support armies and navies. The sword and the purse, all the external relations, and no inconsiderable portion of the industry of the nation are intrusted to its Government. It can never be pretended that these vast powers draw after them others of inferior importance merely because they are inferior. Such an idea can never be advanced. But it may with great reason be contended that a Government intrusted with such ample powers, on the due execution of which the happiness and prosperity of the Nation so vitally depends, must also be intrusted with ample means for their execution. The power being given, it is the interest of the Nation to facilitate its execution. It can never be their interest, and cannot be presumed to have been their intention, to clog and embarrass its execution by withholding the most appropriate means.

[. . .]

It is not denied that the powers given to the Government imply the ordinary means of execution. That, for example, of raising revenue and applying it to national purposes is admitted to imply the power of conveying money from place to place as the exigencies of the Nation may require, and of employing the usual means of conveyance. But it is denied that the Government has its choice of means, or that it may employ the most convenient means if, to employ them, it be necessary to erect a corporation. On what foundation does this argument rest? On this alone: the power of creating a corporation is one appertaining to sovereignty, and is not expressly conferred on Congress. This is true. But all legislative powers appertain to sovereignty. The original power of giving the law on any subject whatever is a sovereign power, and if the Government of the Union is restrained from creating a corporation as a means for performing its functions, on the single reason that the creation of a corporation is an act of sovereignty, if the sufficiency of this reason be acknowledged, there would be some difficulty in sustaining the authority of Congress to pass other laws for the accomplishment of the same objects. The Government which has a right to do an act and has imposed on it the duty of performing that act must, according to the dictates of reason, be allowed to select the means, and those who contend that it may not select any appropriate means that one particular mode of effecting the object is excepted take upon themselves the burden of establishing that exception.

[. . .]

[T]he Constitution of the United States has not left the right of Congress to employ the necessary means for the execution of the powers conferred on the Government to general reasoning. To its enumeration of powers is added that of making "all laws which shall be necessary and proper for carrying into execution the foregoing powers, and all other powers vested by this Constitution in the Government of the United States or in any department thereof."

The counsel for the State of Maryland have urged various arguments to prove that this clause, . . . the argument on which most reliance is placed is drawn from that peculiar language of this clause. Congress is not empowered by it to make all laws which may have relation to the powers conferred on the Government, but such only as may be "necessary and proper" for carrying them into execution. The word "necessary" is considered as controlling the whole sentence, and as limiting the right to pass laws for the execution of the granted powers to such as are indispensable, and without which the power would be nugatory. That it excludes the choice of means, and leaves to Congress in each case that only which is most direct and simple.

Is it true that this is the sense in which the word "necessary" is always used? Does it always import an absolute physical necessity so strong that one thing to which another may be termed necessary cannot exist without that other? We think it does not. If reference be had to its use in the common affairs of the world or in approved authors, we find that it frequently imports no more than that one thing is convenient, or useful, or essential to another. To employ the means necessary to an end is generally understood as employing any means calculated to produce the end, and not as being confined to those single means without which the end would be entirely unattainable. Such is the character of human language that no word conveys to the mind in all situations one single definite idea, and nothing is more common than to use words in a figurative sense. Almost all compositions contain words which, taken in a their rigorous sense, would convey a meaning different from that which is obviously intended. It is essential to just construction that many words which import something excessive should be understood in a more mitigated sense—in that sense which common usage justifies. The word "necessary" is of this description. It has not a fixed character peculiar to itself. It admits of all degrees of comparison, and is often connected with other words which increase or diminish the impression the mind receives of the urgency it imports. A thing may be necessary, very necessary, absolutely or indispensably necessary. To no mind would the same idea be conveyed by these several phrases. The comment on the word is well illustrated by the passage cited at the bar from the 10th section of the 1st article of the Constitution. It is, we think, impossible to compare the sentence which prohibits a State from laying "imposts, or duties on imports or exports, except what may be absolutely necessary for executing its inspection laws," with that which authorizes Congress "to make all laws which shall be necessary and proper for carrying into execution" the powers of the General Government without feeling a conviction that the convention understood itself to change materially the meaning of the word "necessary," by prefixing the word "absolutely." This word, then, like others, is used in various senses, and, in its construction, the subject, the context, the intention of the person using them are all to be taken into view.

Let this be done in the case under consideration. The subject is the execution of those great powers on which the welfare of a Nation essentially depends. It must have been the intention of those who gave these powers to insure, so far as human prudence could insure, their beneficial execution. This could not be done by confiding the choice of means to such narrow limits as not to leave it in the power of Congress to adopt any which might be appropriate, and which were conducive to the end. This provision is made in a Constitution intended to endure for ages to come, and consequently to be adapted to the various crises of human affairs. To have prescribed the means by which Government should, in all future time, execute its powers would have been to change entirely the character of the instrument and give it the properties of a legal code. It would have been an unwise attempt to provide by immutable rules for exigencies which, if foreseen at all, must have been seen dimly, and which can be best provided for as they occur. To have declared that the best means shall not be used, but those alone without which the power given would be nugatory, would have been to deprive the legislature of the capacity to avail itself of experience, to exercise its reason, and to accommodate its legislation to circumstances.

[. . .]

In ascertaining the sense in which the word "necessary" is used in this clause of the Constitution, we may derive some aid from that with which it is associated. Congress shall have power "to make all laws which shall be necessary and proper to carry into execution" the powers of the Government. If the word "necessary" was used in that strict and rigorous sense for which the counsel for the State of Maryland contend, it would be an extraordinary departure from the usual course of the human mind, as exhibited in composition, to add a word the only possible effect of which is to qualify that strict and rigorous meaning, to present to the mind the idea of some choice of means of legislation not strained and compressed within the narrow limits for which gentlemen contend.

But the argument which most conclusively demonstrates the error of the construction contended for by the counsel for the State of Maryland is founded on the intention of the convention as manifested in the whole clause. To waste time and argument in proving that, without it, Congress might carry its powers into execution would be not much less idle than to hold a lighted taper to the sun. As little can it be required to prove that, in the absence of this clause, Congress would have some choice of means. That it might employ those which, in its judgment, would most advantageously effect the object to be accomplished. That any means adapted to the end, any means which tended directly to the execution of the Constitutional powers of the Government, were in themselves Constitutional.

This clause, as construed by the State of Maryland, would abridge, and almost annihilate, this useful and necessary right of the legislature to select its means. That this could not be intended is, we should think, had it not been already controverted, too apparent for controversy.

[. . .]

The result of the most careful and attentive consideration bestowed upon this clause is that, if it does not enlarge, it cannot be construed to restrain, the powers of Congress, or to impair the right of the legislature to exercise its best judgment in the selection of measures to carry into execution the Constitutional powers of the Government. If no other motive for its insertion can be suggested, a sufficient one is found in the desire to remove all doubts respecting the right to legislate on that vast mass of incidental powers which must be involved in the Constitution if that instrument be not a splendid bauble.

We admit, as all must admit, that the powers of the Government are limited, and that its limits are not to be transcended. But we think the sound construction of the Constitution must allow to the national legislature that discretion with respect to the means by which the powers it confers are to be carried into execution which will enable that body to perform the high duties assigned to it in the manner most beneficial to the people. Let the end be legitimate, let it be within the scope of the Constitution, and all means which are appropriate, which are plainly adapted to that end, which are not prohibited, but consist with the letter and spirit of the Constitution, are Constitutional.

[. . .]

After the most deliberate consideration, it is the unanimous and decided opinion of this Court that the act to incorporate the Bank of the United States is a law made in pursuance of the Constitution, and is a part of the supreme law of the land.

[. . .]

It being the opinion of the Court that the act incorporating the bank is constitutional, and that the power of establishing a branch in the State of Maryland might be properly exercised by the bank itself, we proceed to inquire:

2. Whether the State of Maryland may, without violating the Constitution, tax that branch?

That the power of taxation is one of vital importance; that it is retained by the States; that it is not abridged by the grant of a similar power to the Government of the Union; that it is to be concurrently exercised by the two Governments—are truths which have never been denied. But such is the paramount character of the Constitution that its capacity to withdraw any subject from the action of even this power is admitted.

[. . .]

This great principle is that the Constitution and the laws made in pursuance thereof are supreme; that they control the Constitution and laws of the respective States, and cannot be controlled by them.

[. . .]

That the power of taxing it by the States may be exercised so as to destroy it is too obvious to be denied. But taxation is said to be an absolute power which acknowledges no other limits than those expressly prescribed in the Constitution, and, like sovereign power of every other description, is intrusted to the discretion of those who use it. But the very terms of this argument admit that the sovereignty of the State, in the article of taxation itself, is subordinate to, and may be controlled by, the Constitution of the United States. How far it has been controlled by that instrument must be a question of construction. In making this construction, no principle, not declared, can be admissible which would defeat the legitimate operations of a supreme Government. It is of the very essence of supremacy to remove all obstacles to its action within its own sphere, and so to modify every power vested in subordinate governments as to exempt its own operations from their own influence.

[. . .]

The argument on the part of the State of Maryland is not that the States may directly resist a law of Congress, but that they may exercise their acknowledged powers upon it, and that the Constitution leaves them this right, in the confidence that they will not abuse it.

[. . .]

The sovereignty of a State extends to everything which exists by its own authority or is introduced by its permission, but does it extend to those means which are employed by Congress to carry into execution powers conferred on that body by the people of the United States? We think it demonstrable that it does not. Those powers are not given by the people of a single State. They are given by the people of the United States, to a Government whose laws, made in pursuance of the Constitution, are declared to be supreme. Consequently, the people of a single State cannot confer a sovereignty which will extend over them.

[. . .]

That the power to tax involves the power to destroy; that the power to destroy may defeat and render useless the power to create; that there is a plain repugnance in conferring on one Government a power to control the constitutional measures of another, which other, with respect to those very measures, is declared to be supreme over that which exerts the control, are propositions not to be denied.

[. . .]

If the States may tax one instrument, employed by the Government in the execution of its powers, they may tax any and every other instrument. They may tax the mail; they may tax the mint; they may tax patent rights; they may tax the papers of the custom house; they may tax judicial process; they may tax all the means employed by the Government to an excess which would defeat all the ends of Government. This was not intended by the American people. They did not design to make their Government dependent on the States.

[. . .]

We are unanimously of opinion that the law passed by the Legislature of Maryland, imposing a tax on the Bank of the United States is unconstitutional and void.

This opinion does not deprive the States of any resources which they originally possessed. It does not extend to a tax paid by the real property of the bank, in common with the other real property within the State, nor to a tax imposed on the interest which the citizens of Maryland may hold in this institution, in common with other property of the same description throughout the State. But this is a tax on the operations of the bank, and is, consequently, a tax on the operation of an instrument employed by the Government of the Union to carry its powers into execution. Such a tax must be unconstitutional.

CHAPTER 2
FEDERALISM

UNITED STATES V. LOPEZ

SUPREME COURT OF THE UNITED STATES

514 U.S. 549 (1995)

CHIEF JUSTICE **REHNQUIST** delivered the opinion of the Court.

In the Gun-Free School Zones Act of 1990, Congress made it a federal offense "for any individual knowingly to possess a firearm at a place that the individual knows, or has reasonable cause to believe, is a school zone." 18 U.S.C. § 922 (q)(1)(A). The Act neither regulates a commercial activity nor contains a requirement that the possession be connected in any way to interstate commerce. We hold that the Act exceeds the authority of Congress "to regulate Commerce . . . among the several States . . . ." U.S. Const., Art. I, § 8, cl. 3.

On March 10, 1992, respondent, who was then a 12th-grade student, arrived at Edison High School in San Antonio, Texas, carrying a concealed .38 caliber handgun and five bullets. Acting upon an anonymous tip, school authorities confronted respondent, who admitted that he was carrying the . . . The next day, the state charges were dismissed after federal agents charged respondent by complaint with violating the Gun-Free School Zones Act of 1990. 18 U.S.C. § 922(q)(1)(A).

[. . .]

The District Court conducted a bench trial, found him guilty of violating § 922(q), and sentenced him to six months' imprisonment and two years' supervised release.

On appeal, respondent challenged his conviction based on his claim that § 922(q) exceeded Congress' power to legislate under the Commerce Clause. The Court of Appeals for the Fifth Circuit agreed and reversed respondent's conviction.

[. . .]

We start with first principles. The Constitution creates a Federal Government of enumerated powers. See Art. I, § 8. As James Madison wrote, "the powers delegated by the proposed Constitution to the federal government are few and defined. Those which are to remain in the State governments are numerous and indefinite." The Federalist No. 45, pp. 292–293 (C. Rossiter ed. 1961). This constitutionally mandated division of authority "was adopted by the Framers to ensure protection of our fundamental liberties." *Gregory* v. *Ashcroft*, 501 U.S. 452, 458. "Just as the separation and independence of the coordinate branches of the Federal Government serve to prevent the accumulation of excessive power in any one branch, a healthy balance of power between the States and the Federal Government will reduce the risk of tyranny and abuse from either front." *Ibid.*

The Constitution delegates to Congress the power "to regulate Commerce with foreign Nations, and among the several States, and with the Indian Tribes." Art. I, § 8, cl. 3. The Court, through Chief Justice Marshall, first defined the nature of Congress' commerce power in *Gibbons v. Ogden*, 22 U.S. 1:

> "Commerce, undoubtedly, is traffic, but it is something more: it is intercourse. It describes the commercial intercourse between nations, and parts of nations, in all its branches, and is regulated by prescribing rules for carrying on that intercourse."

The commerce power "is the power to regulate; that is, to prescribe the rule by which commerce is to be governed. This power, like all others vested in congress, is complete in itself, may be exercised to its utmost extent, and acknowledges no limitations, other than are prescribed in the constitution." *Id.*, at 196. The *Gibbons* Court, however, acknowledged that limitations on the commerce power are inherent in the very language of the Commerce Clause.

> "It is not intended to say that these words comprehend that commerce, which is completely internal, which is carried on between man and man in a State, or between different parts of the same State, and which does not extend to or affect other States. Such a power would be inconvenient, and is certainly unnecessary.

> "Comprehensive as the word 'among' is, it may very properly be restricted to that commerce which concerns more States than one. . . . The enumeration presupposes something not enumerated; and that something, if we regard the language, or the subject of the sentence, must be the exclusively internal commerce of a State." *Id.*, at 194–195.

[. . .]

In *Wickard* v. *Filburn*, the Court upheld the application of amendments to the Agricultural Adjustment Act of 1938 to the production and consumption of homegrown wheat. 317 U.S. at 128–129. The *Wickard* Court explicitly rejected earlier distinctions between direct and indirect effects on interstate commerce, stating:

> "Even if appellee's activity be local and though it may not be regarded as commerce, it may still, whatever its nature, be reached by Congress if it exerts a substantial economic effect on interstate commerce, and this irrespective of whether such effect is what might at some earlier time have been defined as 'direct' or 'indirect.'" *Id.*, at 125.

The *Wickard* Court emphasized that although Filburn's own contribution to the demand for wheat may have been trivial by itself, that was not "enough to remove him from the scope of federal regulation where, as here, his contribution, taken together with that of many others similarly situated, is far from trivial." *Id.*, at 127–128.

[. . .]

Consistent with this structure, we have identified three broad categories of activity that Congress may regulate under its commerce power. . . . First, Congress may regulate the use of the channels of interstate commerce . . . Second, Congress is empowered to regulate and protect the instrumentalities of interstate commerce, or persons or things in interstate commerce, even though the threat may come only from intrastate activities. . . . Finally, Congress' commerce authority includes the power to regulate those activities having a substantial relation to interstate commerce. . . .

[. . .]

We now turn to consider the power of Congress, in the light of this framework, to enact § 922(q). The first two categories of authority may be quickly disposed of: § 922(q) is not a regulation of the use of the channels of interstate commerce, nor is it an attempt to prohibit the interstate transportation of a commodity through the channels of commerce; nor can § 922(q) be justified as a regulation by which Congress has sought to protect an instrumentality of interstate commerce or a thing in interstate commerce. Thus, if § 922(q) is to be sustained, it must be under the third category as a regulation of an activity that substantially affects interstate commerce.

First, we have upheld a wide variety of congressional Acts regulating intrastate economic activity where we have concluded that the activity substantially affected interstate commerce. . . . Where economic activity substantially affects interstate commerce, legislation regulating that activity will be sustained.

Even *Wickard*, which is perhaps the most far reaching example of Commerce Clause authority over intrastate activity, involved economic activity in a way that the possession of a gun in a school zone does not. Roscoe Filburn operated a small farm in Ohio, on which, in the year involved, he raised 23 acres of wheat. It was his practice to sow winter wheat in the fall, and after harvesting it in July to sell a portion of the crop, to feed part of it to poultry and livestock on the farm, to use some in making flour for home consumption, and to keep the remainder for seeding future crops. The Secretary of Agriculture assessed a penalty against him under the Agricultural Adjustment Act of 1938 because he harvested about 12 acres more wheat than his allotment under the Act permitted. The Act was designed to regulate the volume of wheat moving in interstate and foreign commerce in order to avoid surpluses and shortages, and concomitant fluctuation in wheat prices, which had previously obtained.

[. . .]

Section 922(q) is a criminal statute that by its terms has nothing to do with "commerce" or any sort of economic enterprise, however broadly one might define those terms. Section 922(q) is not an essential part of a larger regulation of economic activity, in which the regulatory scheme could be undercut unless the intrastate activity were regulated. It cannot, therefore, be sustained under our cases upholding regulations of activities that arise out of or are connected with a commercial transaction, which viewed in the aggregate, substantially affects interstate commerce.

[. . .]

The Government's essential contention, *in fine*, is that we may determine here that § 922(q) is valid because possession of a firearm in a local school zone does indeed substantially affect interstate commerce. . . . The Government argues that possession of a firearm in a school zone may result in violent crime and that violent crime can be expected to affect the functioning of the national economy in two ways. First, the costs of violent crime are substantial, and, through the mechanism of insurance, those costs are spread throughout the population. . . . Second, violent crime reduces the willingness of individuals to travel to areas within the country that are perceived to be unsafe. . . . The Government also argues that the presence of guns in schools poses a substantial threat to the educational process by threatening the learning environment. A handicapped educational process, in turn, will result in a less productive citizenry. That, in turn, would have an adverse effect on the Nation's economic well-being. As a result, the Government argues that Congress could rationally have concluded that § 922(q) substantially affects interstate commerce.

We pause to consider the implications of the Government's arguments. The Government admits, under its "costs of crime" reasoning, that Congress could regulate not only all violent crime, but all activities that might lead to violent crime, regardless of how tenuously they relate to interstate commerce. . . . Similarly, under the Government's "national productivity" reasoning, Congress could regulate any activity that it found was related to the economic productivity of individual citizens: family law (including marriage, divorce, and child custody), for example. Under the theories that the Government presents in support of § 922(q), it is difficult to perceive any limitation on federal power, even in areas such as criminal law enforcement or education where States historically have been sovereign. Thus, if we were to accept the Government's arguments, we are hard pressed to posit any activity by an individual that Congress is without power to regulate.

[. . .]

JUSTICE **BREYER** focuses, for the most part, on the threat that firearm possession in and near schools poses to the educational process and the potential economic consequences flowing from that threat. . . . This analysis would be equally applicable, if not more so, to subjects such as family law and direct regulation of education.

For instance, if Congress can, pursuant to its Commerce Clause power, regulate activities that adversely affect the learning environment, then, *a fortiori*, it also can regulate the educational process directly. Congress could determine that a school's curriculum has a "significant" effect on the extent of classroom learning. As a result, Congress could mandate a federal curriculum for local elementary and secondary schools because what is taught in local schools has a significant "effect on classroom learning," and that, in turn, has a substantial effect on interstate commerce.

[. . .]

Admittedly, a determination whether an intrastate activity is commercial or noncommercial may in some cases result in legal uncertainty. But, so long as Congress' authority is limited to those powers enumerated in the Constitution, and so long as those enumerated powers are interpreted as having judicially enforceable outer limits, congressional legislation under the Commerce Clause always will engender "legal uncertainty."

[. . .]

These are not precise formulations, and in the nature of things they cannot be. But we think they point the way to a correct decision of this case. The possession of a gun in a local school zone is in no sense an economic activity that might, through repetition elsewhere, substantially affect any sort of interstate commerce. Respondent was a local student at a local school; there is no indication that he had recently moved in interstate commerce, and there is no requirement that his possession of the firearm have any concrete tie to interstate commerce.

[. . .]

JUSTICE **BREYER**, with whom JUSTICE STEVENS, JUSTICE SOUTER, and JUSTICE GINS-BURG join, dissenting.

The issue in this case is whether the Commerce Clause authorizes Congress to enact a statute that makes it a crime to possess a gun in, or near, a school. 18 U.S.C. § 922(q)(1)(A). . . . In my view, the statute falls well within the scope of the commerce power as this Court has understood that power over the last half century.

[. . .]

[I]n determining whether a local activity will likely have a significant effect upon interstate commerce, a court must consider, not the effect of an individual act (a single instance of gun possession), but rather the cumulative effect of all similar instances (*i. e.*, the effect of all guns possessed in or near schools). . . .

[T]he Constitution requires us to judge the connection between a regulated activity and interstate commerce, not directly, but at one remove. Courts must give Congress a degree of leeway in determining the existence of a significant factual connection between the regulated activity and interstate commerce—both because the Constitution delegates the commerce power directly to Congress and because the determination requires an empirical judgment of a kind that a legislature is more likely than a court to make with accuracy. . . . Thus, the specific question before us, as the Court recognizes, is not whether the "regulated activity sufficiently affected interstate commerce," but, rather, whether Congress could have had "*a rational basis*" for so concluding.

[. . .]

Applying these principles to the case at hand, we must ask whether Congress could have had a *rational basis* for finding a significant (or substantial) connection between gun-related school violence and interstate commerce. Or, to put the question in the language of the *explicit* finding that Congress made when it amended this law in 1994: Could Congress rationally have found that "violent crime in school zones," through its effect on the "quality of education," significantly (or substantially) affects "interstate" or "foreign commerce"?. . . Numerous reports and studies—generated both inside and outside government—make clear that Congress could reasonably have found the empirical connection that its law, implicitly or explicitly, asserts. . . .

[. . .]

Having found that guns in schools significantly undermine the quality of education in our Nation's classrooms, Congress could also have found, given the effect of education upon interstate and foreign commerce, that gun-related violence in and around schools is a commercial, as well as a human, problem. Education, although far more than a matter of economics, has long been inextricably intertwined with the Nation's economy.

[. . .]

In recent years the link between secondary education and business has strengthened, becoming both more direct and more important. Scholars on the subject report that technological changes and innovations in management techniques have altered the nature of the workplace so that more jobs now demand greater educational skills. . . .

Finally, there is evidence that, today more than ever, many firms base their location decisions upon the presence, or absence, of a work force with a basic education.

[. . .]

The economic links I have just sketched seem fairly obvious. Why then is it not equally obvious, in light of those links, that a widespread, serious, and substantial physical threat to teaching and learning *also* substantially threatens the commerce to which that teaching and learning is inextricably tied? That is to say, guns in the hands of six percent of inner-city high school students and gun-related violence throughout a city's schools must threaten the trade and commerce that those schools support. The only question, then, is whether the latter threat is (to use the majority's terminology) "substantial." The evidence of (1) the *extent* of the gun-related violence problem, see *supra*, at 619, (2) the *extent* of the resulting negative effect on classroom learning, see *ibid.*, and (3) the *extent* of the consequent negative commercial effects, see *supra*, at 620–622, when taken together, indicate a threat to trade and commerce that is "substantial." At the very least, Congress could rationally have concluded that the links are "substantial."

[. . .]

In sum, a holding that the particular statute before us falls within the commerce power would not expand the scope of that Clause. Rather, it simply would apply pre-existing law to changing economic circumstances. . . . It would recognize that, in today's economic world, gun-related violence near the classroom makes a significant difference to our economic, as well as our social, well-being.

[. . .]

Respectfully, I dissent.

THE STATES AND THE POLITICAL SETTING

DANIEL J. ELAZAR
Temple University

The Cooperative System and the Political Setting

While the practice of cooperative federalism is nationwide, the fifty states respond to the cooperative system in different ways. Understanding their responses requires an appreciation of two sets of relationships: (1) the way in which the states functioning as political systems influence the operations of the general government and (2) the way in which the states—still functioning as political systems—adapt national programs to their own needs and interests. To appreciate those relationships, it is first necessary to understand the fundamental social and political factors that serve to shape them and the political setting in which they operate.

Because the states function to divide a nationwide socioeconomic system along territorial lines, the primary socioeconomic influences on their political systems are those most clearly expressed through territorial manifestations. In this light, three overarching factors appear to be especially important in shaping the individual states' political structures, electoral behavior, and modes of organization for political action. They are *political culture*—the particular pattern of orientation to political action in which each political system is imbedded; *sectionalism*—the more or less permanent political ties that link together groups of contiguous states or segments of states with bonds of shared interests; and the continuing *frontier*—the constant effort of Americans to extend their control over their environment for human benefit and the consequent periodic reorganization of American social and settlement patterns as a result of the impact of that effort. All three of these factors represent dynamic processes that generally act upon the states and the federal system and interact with one another in everchanging ways. Between them, the three factors embrace and shape the primary social, economic, and psychological thrusts that influence American politics. Indeed, it is suggested here that other factors, often considered basic to the shaping of political systems, ranging from the class system to urbanization, are embraced within these three factors in the United States and are accordingly secondary in their influence.

Political culture is particularly important as the historical source of such differences in habits, perspectives, and attitudes that exist to influence political life in the various states. Sectionalism is particularly important as a major source of geographical variations that influence state by state differences in responding to nationwide political, economic, and social developments. The frontier is particularly important as the generator of the forces of change that influence patterns of settlement and human (economic, social, and political) organization throughout the federal system; that stimulate governmental action in new fields on all planes; and that consequently force the continual readjustment of the federal balance.

In this chapter and in Chapter Five we will be concerned with these three factors as dynamic processes affecting the states through their particular pattern of interaction with each. An attempt will be made to (1) outline the particular characteristics of political culture and sectionalism in the United States and the relationship of both to the continuing frontier, (2) relate all three to the varying responses of the states to the co-operative system, and (3) suggest ways in which the three factors influence the states as political systems.[1]

Federalism and Political Culture

One of the observations coming out of the several studies of federal-state relations conducted in the 1950's was that the states themselves (or their local subdivisions) could virtually dictate the impact of federally-aided activities within their boundaries.[2] Take the case of the impact of federal aid on the administration of state government. In those states where administration is concentrated at the executive level and the governor is usually strong, federal aid has tended to strengthen executive powers by giving the governor more and better tools to wield.[3] In those states where power is widely diffused among the separate executive departments, federal aid has tended to add to the diffusion by giving the individual departments new sources of funds outside of the normal channels of state control that can even be used to obtain more money and power from the legislature. In those states where earmarked funds reflect legislature or lobby domination over programs, earmarked federal funds have had the same effect. Despite many protestations to the contrary, only in rare situations have federal grant programs served to alter state administrative patterns in ways that did not coincide with already established state policies, though such grants have often sharpened certain tendencies in state administration.

The major governmental structural changes made in many states during the 1960's only served to confirm the lessons of the 1950's. In state after state, constitutions were revised, gubernatorial tenure and powers were strengthened, legislative sessions were lengthened, legislators' salaries were increased, and state tax systems were overhauled. While indirect federal influence, in the sense that the threat of federal encroachment on their prerogatives strengthened the states' desire to maintain their position in the Union by "modernizing," should not be ignored, there is no evidence of any direct influence on the part of the federal authorities or federal programs on state reorganization.

Or, in the case of federal merit system requirements, states dominated by political attitudes conducive to notions of professionalization and the isolation of certain forms of government activity from the pressures of partisan politics have had little problem adjusting their programs to meet federal standards, since they had either adopted similar standards earlier or were quite in sympathy with the standards when proposed. Minnesota, for example, has tighter merit system requirements than those applicable to its federally-aided programs under the Hatch Act. On the other hand, states dominated by a political outlook that has little sympathy for nonpartisanship in government administration (Kentucky and West Virginia, for example) have had a more difficult time adjusting to federal requirements of this sort and have often worked to find ways to circumvent them, even while conforming to them superficially. States with a similar lack of interest in civil service reform whose environment is also shaped by advanced industrial and commercial organization are generally open to the organizational aspects of the federal requirements if only because their dominant economic organizations already reflect the modern organizational approach. So, even if the dominant political interests in states like Massachusetts, Pennsylvania, or Illinois object to the *political* aspects of Hatch Act requirements, they are in reasonable harmony with their *organizational* demands.[4]

A parallel situation exists in regard to the substance of the federal programs. Every state has certain dominant traditions about what constitutes proper government action and every state is generally predisposed toward the federal programs it can accept as consistent with those traditions. Many states have pioneered programs that fit into their traditions before the initiation of similar ones on the federal plane or on a nationwide basis through federal aid. This, too, tends to lessen the impact of federal action on the political systems of those states and also to lessen any negative state reaction to federal entrance into particular fields.

Wisconsin's pioneering efforts in social welfare before the New Deal are well known. They became the models for many of the new federal aid programs that were often drawn so as to minimize the dislocation to that state's established programs. The majority of Minnesota's congressional delegation is continually at the forefront in supporting new federal-aid education, welfare and internal improvement programs because as a state, Minnesota is predisposed toward positive government action and finds such programs useful in supporting its own goals. In matters of national defense, the southern states have a long tradition of supporting state militia and National Guard units so that over the years they have taken greater advantage of federal subventions for the maintenance of military reserve units than have most of their sister states.[5]

Today states like California accept federal aid for mental health programs not as an innovative device but as a reenforcement of existing programs. On the other hand, professional mental health workers in states like New Jersey rely upon the same federal grants to keep their programs free of internally generated political pressures, arguing with the patronage-inclined legislatures that federal regulations demand that professional standards be maintained. Their colleagues in states like Illinois use federal aid to force the hands of their legislatures to expand state activities in new directions. Reformers interested in mental health in states like Mississippi are interested in federal aid to inaugurate new programs.

Many of these and other differences in state responses within the federal system appear to be stimulated by differences in political culture among the states. We have already defined political culture as the particular pattern of orientation to political action in which each political system is imbedded. Political culture, like all culture, is rooted in the cumulative historical experiences of particular groups of people. Indeed, the origins of particular patterns of political culture are often lost in the mists of time. Patterns of political culture frequently overlap several political systems, and two or more political cultures may coexist within the same political system.[6] Though little is known about the precise ways in which political culture is influential, it is possible to suggest some ways in which the differences in political culture are likely to be significant.

Three aspects of political culture stand out as particularly influential in shaping the operations of the state political systems within the context of American federalism. They are (1) the set of perceptions of what politics is and what can be expected from government, held by both the general public and the politicians; (2) the kinds of people who become active in government and politics, as holders of elective offices, members of the bureaucracy, and active political workers; and (3) the actual way in which the art of government is practiced by citizens, politicians, and public officials in the light of their perceptions. In turn, the cultural components of individual and group behavior in the various political systems make themselves felt at three levels: in the kind of civic behavior dictated by conscience and internalized ethical standards; in the character of law-abidingness displayed by citizens and officials; and, to a degree, in the positive actions of government.

Marketplace and Commonwealth—The American Cultural Matrix

The United States as a whole shares a general political culture that is rooted in two contrasting conceptions of the American political order, both of which can be traced back to the earliest settlement of the country.[7] In the first, the political order is conceived as a marketplace in which the primary public relationships are products of bargaining among individuals and groups acting out of self-interest. In the second, the political order is conceived to be a commonwealth—a state in which the whole people have an undivided interest—in which the citizens cooperate in an effort to create and maintain the best government in order to implement certain shared moral principles. These two conceptions have exercised an influence on government and politics throughout American history, sometimes in conflict and sometimes by complementing each other.

The two conceptions are reflected in the matrix of value concepts that forms the larger cultural basis—general as well as political—of American civilization. This matrix is portrayed in Figure 2.1. Its component value concepts together provide the framework within which the value orientations of the American people are shaped while the differences in emphasis in the interrelationships among them reflect the various sub-cultures in the United States.

The four elements of the matrix are located between *Power* and *Justice,* the two poles of politics that between them encompass the basic political concerns of all civil societies, namely, "who gets what, when, and how" (*Power*), on the one hand, and the development of the good society (*Justice*), on the other. The major continuing task of every civil society is to shape an immediately practical relationship between the two poles in a manner that best fits its situation. Indeed the character of any civil society is in large measure determined by the relationship between power and justice that shapes its political order. Consequently, a particular civil society's conceptions of the uses of power and the nature of justice are important aspects of its political culture.

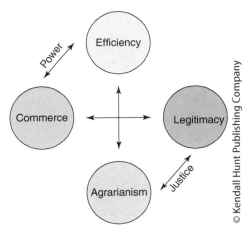

© Kendall Hunt Publishing Company

Figure 2.1 Value Concepts in American Culture

Efficiency may be defined operationally in this context as the achievement of goals in a manner that involves the least wasteful or minimum expenditure of resources. *Legitimacy* refers to those aspects of a polity that are believed to be supported by the underlying values of its citizenry particularly as embodied in its constitutional system. Both represent tendencies found in every civil society that are given meaning by each society's culture (general and political).

In the United States, *Efficiency* is measured in predominantly commercial terms as befits a civil society which *The Federalist* correctly described as a commercial republic. *Commerce,* in America, embodies the exchange of goods, services, *and ideas.* A cardinal feature of American civilization, a good case can be made that the federal republic was founded to advance and protect commerce and that it has adhered quite closely to that original purpose. *Commerce* is particularly valued because it is an efficient means of organizing, harnessing, and diffusing *Power* in light of American values. Americans characteristically rely upon various kinds of marketplaces (the economic marketplace, the "marketplace of ideas") to protect and foster freedom as well as to foster property and enterprise. Americans have changed their conventional definition of what is efficient as the organization of their commercial enterprises has changed. So in the eighteenth century, efficiency meant, first and foremost, the efficiency of competition among relative equals, reflecting the economic system of the time, which rested upon many small enterprises. In the twentieth century it has come to mean the hierarchical organization of enterprise reflecting an economic system which rests upon complex bureaucratic corporations. In sum, both *Efficiency* and *Commerce* are primarily related to the concerns of *Power* and its management.

Legitimacy, on the other hand, is given meaning in the United States by the particularly American complex of values and aspirations here termed *Agrarianism*. The ideal of *Agrarianism* envisions the United States as a commonwealth of self-governing freeholders, each with a tangible stake in his community (and, hence, in American society as a whole), raised to new heights of human decency through the general diffusion of knowledge, religion, and morality. This ideal of *Agrarianism* stems from both the Puritan and Jeffersonian roots of American life and has also undergone adaptation to the changing circumstances of American history. As the embodiment of the nation's social and political mystique, it is the major source and test of *Legitimacy* in the United States. Both *Agrarianism* and *Legitimacy* are related to the problem of the attainment of *Justice* and are expressions of the continuing effort to create a more just society in the United States.

Each of the four tendencies is pulled in the direction of *Power* or *Justice* and is also modified by every other tendency. In every form it has taken, American *Agrarianism* has had a strong *commercial* aspect, beginning with the Americans' desire to make a profit from the use of the land even while valuing closeness to it for moral reasons. Unlike feudal or peasant agrarianism, it has represented the effort to create a moral commonwealth of religiously-inspired free-holders actively engaged in commerce in its various manifestations. By the same token, the values of *Agrarianism* modify *commercial efficiency* at crucial points so that maximizing profits is not the only measure of efficiency in American life even as they are themselves tailored at some points to meet the demands of *Efficiency*.

The politically defined limits of *Commerce* in America are set by the demands of *agrarian legitimacy*. Periodically, the commercial aspects of American society have run wild, only to be pulled back in line, sooner or later, on the grounds that they have been set free illegitimately (e.g. "trusts" are illegitimate even if they are efficient from a commercial point of view). This common sense of legitimacy is defined in what are essentially agrarian terms. At such points, political action is forthcoming to reshape the commercial order so as to reintegrate it in accordance with the principles of *agrarian legitimacy*. At the same time, what is commonly deemed legitimate is itself shaped by the attachment to *Commerce* as a key aspect of American civil society.

The Three Political Cultures

The national political culture is a synthesis of three major political sub-cultures that jointly inhabit the country, existing side by side or even overlapping. All three are of nationwide proportions, having spread, in the course of time, from coast to coast. At the same time each subculture is strongly tied to specific sections of the country, reflecting the streams and currents of migration that have carried people of different origins and backgrounds across the continent in more or less orderly patterns.

Considering the central characteristics that govern each subculture and their respective centers of emphasis, the three political cultures may be called *individualistic, moralistic,* and *traditionalistic*.[8] Each of the three reflects its own particular synthesis of the marketplace and the commonwealth.

The Individualistic Political Culture

The *individualistic political culture* emphasizes the conception of the democratic order as a marketplace. In its view, government is instituted for strictly utilitarian reasons, to handle those functions demanded by the people it is created to serve. A government need not have any direct concern with questions of the "good society" except insofar as it may be used to advance some common conception of the good society formulated outside the political arena just as it serves other functions. Since the individualistic political culture emphasizes the centrality of private concerns, it places a premium on limiting community intervention—whether governmental or nongovernmental—into private activities to the minimum necessary to keep the marketplace in proper working order. In general, government action is to be restricted to those areas, primarily in the economic realm, which encourage private initiative and widespread access to the market place.[9]

The character of political participation in systems dominated by the individualistic political culture reflects this outlook. The individualistic political culture holds politics to be just another means by which individuals may improve themselves socially and economically. In this sense politics is a "business" like any other that competes for talent and offers rewards to those who take it up as a career. Those individuals who choose political careers may rise by providing the governmental services demanded of them and, in return, may expect to be adequately compensated for their efforts. Interpretations of officeholders' obligations under this arrangement vary among political systems and even among individuals within a single political system. Where the norms are high, such people are expected to provide high quality government services for the general public in the best possible manner in return for the status and economic rewards considered their due. Some who choose political careers clearly commit themselves to such norms; others believe that an officeholder's primary responsibility is to serve himself and those who have supported him directly, favoring them even at the expense of the public. In some political systems, this view is accepted by the public as well as the politicians.

Political life within an individualistic political culture is based on a system of mutual obligations rooted in personal relationships. While in a simple society those relationships can be direct ones, societies with individualistic political cultures in the United States are usually too complex to maintain face to face ties. So the system of mutual obligations is harnessed through political parties that serve as "business corporations" dedicated to providing the organization necessary to maintain it. Party regularity is indispensable in the individualistic political culture because it is the means for coordinating individual enterprise in the political arena and is the one way of preventing individualism in politics from running wild. In such a system, an individual can succeed politically, not by dealing with issues in some exceptional way or by accepting some concept of good government and then striving to implement it, but by maintaining his place in the system of mutual obligations. He can do this by operating according to the norms of his particular party, to the exclusion of other political considerations. Such a political culture encourages the maintenance of a party system that is competitive, but not overly so, in the pursuit of office. Its politicians are interested in office as a means of controlling the distribution of the favors or rewards of government rather than as a means of exercising governmental power for programmatic ends.

Since the individualistic political culture eschews ideological concerns in its "businesslike" conception of politics, both politicians and citizens look upon political activity as a specialized one, essentially the province of professionals, of minimum and passing concern to laymen, and with no place for amateurs to play an active role. Furthermore, there is a strong tendency among the public to believe that politics is a dirty—if necessary—business, better left to those who are willing to soil themselves by engaging in it. In practice, then, where the individualistic political culture is dominant, there is likely to be an easy attitude toward the limits of the professionals' perquisites. Since a fair amount of corruption is expected in the normal course of things, there is relatively little popular excitement when any is found unless it is of an extraordinary character. It is as if the public is willing to pay a surcharge for services rendered and only rebels when it feels the surcharge has become too heavy. (Of course the judgments as to what is "normal" and what is "extraordinary" are themselves subjective and culturally conditioned.)

Public officials, committed to "giving the public what it wants," are normally not willing to initiate new programs or open up new areas of government activity on their own recognizance. They will do so when they perceive an overwhelming public demand for them to act, but only then. In a sense, their willingness to expand the functions of government is based on an extension of the *quid pro quo* "favor" system that serves as the central core of their political relationships, with new services the reward they give the public for placing them in office.

The individualistic political culture is ambivalent about the place of bureaucracy in the political order. In one sense, the bureaucratic method of operation flies in the face of the favor system that is central to the individualistic political process. At the same time, the virtues of organizational efficiency appear substantial to those seeking to master the market. In the end, bureaucratic organization is introduced within the framework of the favor system; large segments of the bureaucracy may be insulated from it through the merit system but the entire organization is pulled into the political environment at crucial points through political appointment at the upper echelons and, very frequently, the bending of the merit system to meet political demands.

The Moralistic Political Culture

To the extent that American society is built on the principles of "commerce" in the broadest sense of the term and that the marketplace provides the model for public relationships in this country, all Americans share some of the attitudes that are of first importance in the individualistic political culture. At the same time, substantial segments of the American people operate politically within the framework of two political cultures whose theoretical structures and operational consequences depart significantly from the individualistic pattern at crucial points.

The *moralistic political culture* emphasizes the commonwealth conception as the basis for democratic government. Politics, to the moralistic political culture, is considered one of the great activities of man in his search for the good society—a struggle for power, it is true, but also an effort to exercise power for the betterment of the commonwealth. Consequently, in the moralistic political culture, both the general public and the politicians conceive of politics as a public activity centered on some notion of the public good and properly devoted to the advancement of the public interest. Good government, then, is measured by the degree to which it promotes the public good and in terms of the honesty, selflessness, and commitment to the public welfare of those who govern.

In the moralistic political culture, individualism is tempered by a general commitment to utilizing communal—preferably nongovernmental, but governmental if necessary—power to intervene into the sphere of "private" activities when it is considered necessary to do so for the public good or the well-being of the community. Accordingly, issues have an important place in the moralistic style of politics, functioning to set the tone for political concern. Government is considered a positive instrument with a responsibility to promote the general welfare, though definitions of what its positive role should be may vary considerably from era to era.[10]

Since the moralistic political culture rests on the fundamental conception that politics exists primarily as a means for coming to grips with the issues and public concerns of civil society, it also embraces the notion that politics is ideally a matter of concern for every citizen, not just for those who are professionally committed to political careers. Indeed, it is the duty of every citizen to participate in the political affairs of his commonwealth.

Consequently, there is a general insistence that government service is public service, which places moral obligations upon those who participate in government that are more demanding than the moral obligations of the marketplace. There is an equally general rejection of the notion that the field of politics is a legitimate realm for private economic enrichment. A politician may indeed benefit economically because of his political career but he is not expected to profit from political activity and in fact is held suspect if he does.

Since the concept of serving the community is the core of the political relationship, politicians are expected to adhere to it even at the expense of individual loyalties and political friendships. Consequently, party regularity is not of prime importance. The political party is considered a useful political device but is not valued for its own sake. Regular party ties can be abandoned with relative impunity for third parties, special local parties, or nonpartisan systems if such changes are believed helpful in gaining larger political goals. Men can even shift from party to party without sanctions if the change is justified by political belief. In the moralistic political culture, rejection of firm party ties is not to be viewed as a rejection of politics as such. On the contrary, because politics is considered potentially good and healthy within the context of that culture, it is possible to have highly political nonpartisan systems. Certainly nonpartisanship is not instituted to eliminate politics but to improve it by widening access to public office for those unwilling or unable to gain office through the regular party structure.[11]

In practice, where the moralistic political culture is dominant today, there is considerably more amateur participation in politics. There is also much less of what Americans consider corruption in government and less tolerance of those actions that are considered corrupt, so politics does not have the taint it so often bears in the individualistic environment.

By virtue of its fundamental outlook, the moralistic political culture creates a greater commitment to active government intervention into the economic and social life of the community. At the same time, the strong commitment to communitarianism characteristic of that political culture tends to channel the interest in government intervention into highly localistic paths so that a willingness to encourage local government intervention to set public standards does not necessarily reflect a concomitant willingness to allow outside governments equal opportunity to intervene. Not infrequently, public officials will themselves seek to initiate new government activities in an effort to come to grips with problems as yet unperceived by a majority of the citizenry.

The moralistic political culture's major difficulty in adjusting bureaucracy to the political order is tied to the potential conflict between communitarian principles and the necessity for large-scale organization to increase bureaucratic efficiency, a problem that could affect the attitudes of moralistic culture states toward federal activity of certain kinds. Otherwise, the notion of a politically neutral administrative system creates no problem within the moralistic value system and even offers many advantages. Where merit systems are instituted, they tend to be rigidly maintained.

The Traditionalistic Political Culture

The *traditionalistic political culture* is rooted in an ambivalent attitude toward the marketplace coupled with a paternalistic and elitist conception of the commonwealth. It reflects an older, precommercial attitude that accepts a substantially hierarchical society as part of the ordered nature of things, authorizing and expecting those at the top of the social structure to take a special and dominant role in government. Like its moralistic counterpart, the traditionalistic political culture accepts government as an actor with a positive role in the community, but it tries to limit that role to securing the continued maintenance of the existing social order. To do so, it functions to confine real political power to a relatively small and self-perpetuating group drawn from an established elite who often inherit their "right" to govern through family ties or social position. Accordingly, social and family ties are paramount in a traditionalistic political culture, even more than personal ties are important in the individualistic where, after all is said and done, a person's first responsibility is to himself. At the same time, those who do not have a definite role to play in politics are not expected to be even minimally active as citizens. In many cases, they are not even expected to vote. Like the individualistic political culture, those active in politics are expected to benefit personally from their activity though not necessarily by direct pecuniary gain.

Political parties are of minimal importance in traditionalistic political cultures because they encourage a degree of openness that goes against the fundamental grain of an elite-oriented political order. Their major utility is to recruit people to fill the formal offices of government not desired by the established powerholders. Political competition in a traditionalistic political culture is usually conducted through factional alignments, an extension of the personal politics characteristic of the system; hence political systems within the culture tend to have loose one-party systems if they have political parties at all.

Practically speaking, the traditionalistic political culture is found only in a society that retains some of the organic characteristics of the preindustrial social order. "Good government" in that political culture involves the maintenance and encouragement of traditional patterns and, if necessary, their adjustment to changing conditions with the least possible upset. Where the traditionalistic political culture is dominant in the United States today, unless political leaders are pressed strongly from the outside they play conservative and custodial rather than initiatory roles.

Whereas the individualistic and moralistic political cultures may or may not encourage the development of bureaucratic systems of organization on the grounds of "rationality" and "efficiency" in government, depending on their particular situations, traditionalistic political cultures tend to be instinctively antibureaucratic because bureaucracy by its very nature interferes with the fine web of informal interpersonal relationships that lie at the root of the political system and have been developed by following traditional patterns over the years. Where bureaucracy is introduced, it is generally confined to ministerial functions under the aegis of the established powerholders.

The characteristics of the three political cultures are summarized in Table 2.1.

Returning to the matrix of value concepts that undergirds the overall American culture, we can see the political subcultural variations manifesting themselves in two ways:

1. in the differences in the shades of meaning attached to each of the four tendencies, e.g., the differences between the communitarian agrarianism of the moralistic New England town, the individualistic agrarianism of the middle states, and the plantation agrarianism of the traditionalistic South.
2. in the degree of emphasis placed on each of the four tendencies, e.g., the greater emphasis on commerce and commercial efficiency in the individualistic middle states, the particular conception of aristocratic (read oligarchic) agrarian legitimacy based on caste in the traditionalistic South, and the special kind of populist agrarian efficiency of the moralistic Northwest.

More generally, we see that the individualistic political culture draws most heavily from the value orientations of commerce, the moralistic political culture from those of agrarianism, and the traditionalistic culture emphasizes those of legitimacy (as its representatives understand the concept). Each of these different emphases weights the matrix as a whole in a different direction even while preserving all its elements intact thereby reflecting *sub* cultural rather than cultural differences. Hence we are reminded that, while the differences among the three sub-cultures are measurably real, they are not as extreme as they would be if they were reflections of different *cultures*.

The "Geology" of Political Culture

The three political subcultures arose out of very real sociocultural differences found among the peoples who came to America over the years, differences that date back to the very beginnings of settlement in this country and even back to the Old World. Because the various ethnic and religious groups that came to these shores tended to congregate in their own settlements and because, as they or their descendants moved westward, they continued to settle together, the political patterns they bore with them are today distributed geographically. Indeed, it is the geographic distribution of political cultures as modified by local conditions that has laid the foundations for American sectionalism.

Table 2.1 Characteristics of the Three Political Cultures

Concepts	Individualistic	Moralistic	Traditionalistic
Government			
How viewed	As a *marketplace* [Means to respond efficiently to demands]	As a *commonwealth* [Means to achieve the "good community" through positive action]	As a means of maintaining the *existing order*
Appropriate spheres of activity	Largely economic [Encourages private initiative and access to the marketplace] Economic development favored	Any area that will enhance the community although non-governmental action preferred Social as well as economic regulation considered legitimate	Those that maintain traditional patterns
New programs	Will not initiate unless demanded by public opinion	Will initiate without public pressure if believed to be in public interest	Will initiate if program serves the interest of the governing elite
Bureaucracy			
How viewed	Ambivalently [Undesirable because it limits favors and patronage, but good because it enhances efficiency]	Positively [Brings desirable political neutrality]	Negatively [Depersonalizes government]
Kind of merit system favored	Loosely implemented	Strong	None [Should be controlled by political elite]

Politics

Patterns of Belief

How viewed	Dirty [Left to those who soil themselves engaging in it]	Healthy [Every citizen's responsibility]	A privilege [Only those with legitimate claim to office should participate]

Patterns of Participation

Who should participate	Professionals	Everyone	The appropriate elite
Role of parties	Act as business organizations [Dole out favors and responsibility]	Vehicles to attain goals believed to be in the public interest [Third parties popular]	Vehicle of recruitment of people to offices not desired by established power-holders
Party cohesiveness	Strong	Subordinate to principles and issues	Highly personal [Based on family and social ties]

Patterns of Competition

How viewed	Between parties; not over issues	Over issues	Between elite-dominated factions within a dominant party
Orientation	Toward winning office for tangible rewards	Toward winning office for greater opportunity to implement policies and programs	Dependent on political values of the elite

Sectional concentrations of distinctive cultural groups have helped create the social interests that tie contiguous states to one another even in the face of marked differences in the standard measures of similarity. The southern states have a common character that unites them despite the great material differences between, say, Virginia and Mississippi or Florida and Arkansas. Similarly, New England embraces both Maine and Massachusetts, Connecticut and Vermont in a distinctive way. These sectional concentrations can be traced for every part of the country, and their effects can be noted in the character of the interests shared by the states in each section.

It is not easy to portray the overall pattern of political cultures. Not only must the element of geography be considered, but also a kind of human or cultural "geology" that adds another dimension to the problem. In the course of time, different streams of migration have passed over the American landscape in response to the various frontiers of national development (see below). Those streams, in themselves relatively clear-cut, have left residues of population in various places to become the equivalent of geological strata. As these populations settled in the same location, sometimes side by side, sometimes overlapping, and frequently on top of one another, they created hardened cultural mixtures that must be sorted out for analytical purposes, city by city and county by county from the Atlantic to the Pacific.[12]

Quite clearly, the various sequences of migration in each locale have determined the particular layering of its cultural geology. At the same time, even as the strata were being deposited over generations and centuries, externally generated events, such as depressions, wars, and internal cultural conflicts, caused upheavals that altered the relative positions of the various groups in the community. Beyond that, the passage of time and the impact of new events have eroded some cultural patterns, intensified others, and modified still others, to make each local situation even more complex. The simple mapping of such patterns has yet to be done for more than a handful of states and communities, and while the gross data that can be used to outline the grand patterns as a whole are available in various forms, they have been only partially correlated. However, utilizing the available data, it is possible to sketch with reasonable clarity the nationwide geography of political culture.

Political Culture and the Continuing Frontier

The geography of political culture is directly related to the continuing American frontier. Since the first settlements on these shores, American society has been a frontier society, geared to the progressive extension of man's control over his environment and the utilization of the social and economic benefits gained from widening that control, i.e., pushing the frontier line back. The very dynamism of American society is a product of this commitment to the conquest of the ever-advancing frontier, a commitment that is virtually self-generating since, like a chain reaction, the conquest of one frontier has led to the opening of another.[13] It is this frontier situation that has created the major social and economic changes that have, in turn, forced periodic adjustments in the nation's political institutions, changes of particular importance to the role and functioning of federalism and to the character and particular concerns of intergovernmental relations.

Since the first settlers arrived in 1607, the American frontier has passed through three stages. First came the *rural-land* frontier—the classic American frontier described by the historians—lasting roughly from the seventeenth through the nineteenth centuries. It was characterized by the westward movement of a basically rural population interested in settling and exploiting the land and by the development of a socioeconomic system based on agricultural and extractive pursuits in both its urban and rural components.

Early in the nineteenth century, the rural-land frontier gave birth to the *urban-industrial* frontier, which began in the Northeast and spread westward, in the course of which it transformed the nation into an industrial society settled in cities and dedicated to the spread of new technology as the primary source of the nation's economic and social forms. The dominant characteristic of this frontier was the transformation of cities from service centers or workshops for the rural areas into independent centers of opportunity, producers of new wealth, and social innovators possessing internally generated reasons for existence and growth. At first overlapping the rural-land frontier, the urban-industrial frontier became dominant by the last third of the century.

By the mid-twentieth century, it had given birth, in turn, to the *metropolitan-technological* frontier, which is characterized by the radical reordering of an industrial society through rapidly changing technologies and a settlement pattern that encourages the diffusion of an urbanized population within large metropolitan regions. These radically new technologies, ranging from atomic energy and automation to synthetics and cybernetics, and the accompanying suburbanization of the population influenced further changes in the nation's social and economic forms in accord with their new demands. Like the first two frontier stages, the metropolitan-technological frontier has also moved from east to west since the 1920's, becoming nationally dominant after World War II.

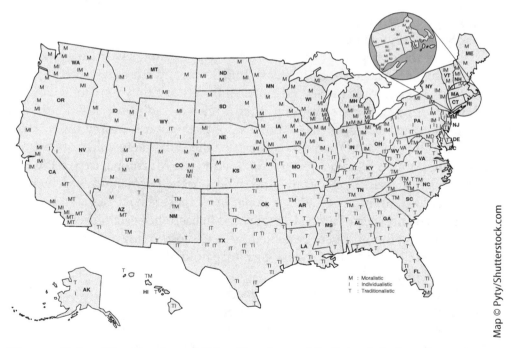

Map © Pyty/Shutterstock.com

Figure 2.2   **The Regional Distribution of Political Cultures within the States**

NOTE: Two letters juxtaposed indicates either a synthesis of two subcultures, or the existence of two separate subcultural communities in the same area, with the first dominant and the second secondary.

Each successive frontier stage has opened new vistas and new avenues of opportunity for the American people by developing new economic activities, creating new settlement patterns, and mastering new social problems growing out of the collision of old patterns and new demands. Consequently, each frontier has generated new political concerns revolving around the accommodation of the challenges and opportunities within the civil society.[14]

The basic patterns of political culture were set during the period of the rural-land frontier by three great streams of American migration that began on the east coast and moved westward after the colonial period. Each stream moved, in the persons of the westward migrants, from east to west along more or less fixed paths, following lines of least resistance which generally led them due west from the immediately previous area of settlement.

Across the northern part of the United States thrusting westward and slightly southwestward is an area settled initially by the Puritans of New England and their Yankee descendants. The Puritans came to these shores intending to establish the best possible earthly version of the holy common-wealth. Their religious outlook was imbued with a high level of political concern, in the spirit of the ancient Israelites whose ideal commonwealth they wished to reproduce. From the first, they estab-lished a moralistic political culture.

After five generations of pioneering in New England, where they established several versions of their commonwealth in the several New England states, the Puritans had developed a set of deeply rooted cultural patterns that had become, for all intents and purposes, indigenous to their part of the New World. Then, moving westward into New York State, the Yankees began their great cross-country migration. Across New York, northern Pennsylvania, and the upper third of Ohio, the Yankee stream moved into the states of the upper Great Lakes and Mississippi Valley. There they established a greater New England in Michigan, Wisconsin, Minnesota, and Iowa, and they attempted to do the same in settling northern Illinois. Beginning in the mid-nineteenth century, they were joined by Scandinavians and other northern Europeans who, stemming from a related tradition (particularly in its religious orientation), reenforced the basic patterns of Yankee political culture, sealing them into the political systems of those states. Pressing westward, Yankees settled the Willamette Valley of Oregon and eastern Washington, and were the first "Anglos" to settle California. As Mormons, they settled Utah; then as Abolitionists they settled Kansas. They became the leaders of the permanent settlements in Colorado and Montana and even moved into northern Arizona. In all these states, they were joined or followed by the same Scandinavian-northern European group and in each they established the moralistic politi-cal culture to the extent that their influence enabled them to do so. Within those states and the smaller ones colonized from them, the moralistic political culture flourishes today.

Groups of quite different ethnic and religious backgrounds, primarily from non-Puritan England and the interior Germanic states, settled the middle parts of the nation, beginning with the Middle Atlantic states of New York, New Jersey, Pennsylvania, Delaware, and Maryland. The majority of these highly diverse groups, which, in the course of living together on the Atlantic Coast for three to five generations, established the basic patterns of American pluralism, were united by one common bond in particular—the search for individual opportunity in the New World. Unlike the Puritans who sought communal as well as individualistic goals in their migrations, the pursuit of private ends predominated among the settlers of the middle states. Though efforts were made to establish mor-ally purposeful communities, particularly in Pennsylvania, the very purpose of those communities was to develop pluralistic societies dedicated to individual freedom to pursue private goals, to the point of making religion a private matter, an unheard-of step at the time. The political culture of the middle states reflected this distinctive emphasis on private pursuits from the first and, by the end of the colonial period, a whole system of politics designed to accommodate itself to such a culture had been developed with distinctive state by state variations, modified by moralistic traits only in Pennsylvania and by traditionalistic ones in Maryland and Delaware.

These groups also moved westward, across Pennsylvania into the central parts of Ohio, Indiana, and Illinois, then on into Missouri. There, reenforced by immigrants from western Europe and the lower Germanic states who shared the same attitudes, they developed extensions of their pluralistic patterns. Since those states were also settled by representatives of the other two political cultures, giving no single culture clear predominance, pluralism became the only viable alternative. So the individualistic political culture became dominant at the state level in the course of time while the other two retained pockets of influence in the northern and southern sections of each state.

After crossing the Mississippi, this middle current jumped across the continent to northern California with the gold rush (an activity highly attractive to individualistic types). Its groups subsequently helped to populate the territory inbetween. The areas of Nebraska and South Dakota bordering the Missouri River attracted settlers from Illinois and Missouri; the Union Pacific Railroad populated central Nebraska and Wyoming; and Nevada was settled from the California gold fields. Today there is a band of states (or sections of states) following the path described above, in which the individualistic political culture is dominant.

The people who settled the southern states were seeking individual opportunity in ways similar to those of their brethren to the immediate north. But, while the latter sought their opportunities in commercial pursuits, either in business or in a commercially oriented agriculture, those who settled

M — I — T

Map © Pyty/Shutterstock.com

Figure 2.3   Generalized Map of Migration of Cultural Streams across the United States

the South sought opportunity in a plantation-centered agricultural system based on slavery and essentially anticommercial in orientation. This system, as an extension of the landed gentry agrarianism of the Old World, provided a natural environment for the development of an American-style traditionalistic political culture in which the new landed gentry progressively assumed ever greater roles in the political process at the expense of the small landholders, while a major segment of the population, the slaves, were totally excluded from any political role whatsoever. Elitism within this culture reached its apogee in Virginia and South Carolina where generation after generation the leading settlers consciously worked at the creation of an "aristocracy." In North Carolina and Georgia a measure of equalitarianism was introduced by the arrival of significant numbers of Scotch-Irish migrants whose traditional culture was strongly tempered by moralistic components.

This peculiarly southern agrarian system and its traditionalistic political culture were carried westward by the southern stream. Virginia's people dominated in the settlement of Kentucky; North Carolina's influence was heavy in Tennessee; and settlers from all four states covered the southern parts of Ohio and Illinois as well as most of Indiana and Missouri. South Carolinians and Georgians, with a mixture of other settlers, moved westward into Alabama and Mississippi. Louisiana presented a unique situation in that it contained a concentration of non-Anglo-Saxons rare in the South, but its French settlers shared the same *political* culture as the other southerners, regardless of their other cultural differences. Ultimately, the southern political culture was spread through Texas, where it was diluted on that state's western fringes by individualistic type European immigrants, and Oklahoma, where a similar dilution took place in the north; into southeastern Kansas, where it clashed directly with the Yankee political culture; then across New Mexico to settle better than half of Arizona and overlap the Yankee stream in southern and central California.

The only major departures from the east-west pattern of cultural diffusion during the settlement of the land frontier came when the emigrants encountered the country's great mountain systems. The mountains served to diffuse cultural patterns because they were barriers to easy east-west movement. Thus, in the east, the Appalachian chain deflected the moralistic Scotch-Irish southward from Pennsylvania into the mountain areas of Virginia, the Carolinas, and Georgia where they were isolated for generations. There, they created special cultural pockets dominated by their traditional culture. Where they settled in the piedmont regions of those states, they developed a synthesis of traditionalistic and moralistic elements that had varying degrees of influence on the political cultures of their states.

In the west, the Rocky Mountains served to block the neat westward flow of the cultural streams and divert people from all three into their valleys from north to south in search of fortunes in mining and specialized agricultural pursuits. There the more individualistic types from all three subcultures diffused from Montana to Arizona, creating cultural pockets in all the mountain states of the west that in some cases—Wyoming, for example—altered the normal regional patterns of political culture.

The development of the urban-industrial frontier coincided with the arrival of other immigrant groups that concentrated in the burgeoning cities of the industrializing states. These groups, primarily from Ireland, Italy, central and eastern Europe, and the Balkans, also moved from east to west but settled in urban pockets adding new cultural strata to communities scattered throughout the country. Most of these settlers, though bound at first by traditional cultural patterns, soon adopted more individualistic attitudes and goals that brought them into the individualistic political culture. Since most of them settled in cities, their cultural impact was less universal in scope but more concentrated in force. In some states (such as Massachusetts) they disrupted established cultural patterns to create new ones, in others (such as New York) they simply reenforced the existing dominant individualistic pluralism, and in still others (such as Illinois) they served to tip the balance between competing cultural groups.

The Contemporary Scene: Cultural Diffusion and The Metropolitan Frontier

Though the essential patterns of the three political cultures were set when the continent was first populated, the opening of the metropolitan-technological frontier has kept them rather fluid in several ways. For one thing, migrations have continued. With the advent of the new frontier, Americans abandoned sedentary patterns widespread after 1910 and began to move again. Though their overall thrust is westward, these migrations from farm to city to suburb and from section to section no longer follow a simple east to west pattern. The first kind of migration—from farm to city, from town to metropolis, or from city to suburb—usually takes place within the same section of the country, if not the same state, and hardly alters the local patterns of political culture even as it may lead to substantial internal changes in the political culture itself. Iowans moving off their farms to Des Moines or Philadelphians moving from the central city to the suburban counties may simply reenforce existing patterns of culture. The second kind of migration may lead to the alteration of the cultural geology of particular areas—e.g., southerners moving to Detroit bring a traditionalistic political culture into a moralistic environment. In some cases, this movement cannot be identified as group migration, but in others the continuity of older modes of cultural diffusion and change is marked.[15]

California is a case in point. Its political culture remains in flux because of the continuous intensity of migration into the state, even though by the turn of the century, fairly well-defined cultural lines had been established within it. In a reversal of the national pattern, southern California had become the center of the moralistic political culture because the Yankees and their midwestern descendants predominated there. Northern California, on the other hand, had attracted the middle state migrants and had become the locus of the individualistic political culture, while central California was beginning to attract many southerners to give it strong traces of the traditionalistic political culture. The sharp cultural division between north and south (the central area was still too weak to be of importance) had already helped intensify the well-known conflict between the two sections of the state that came strongly to the fore in the Progressive era.[16]

Until recently, at least, the great migrations of the twentieth century have generally reenforced the original patterns of culture in California. Midwesterners from moralistic culture states continued to seek the Los Angeles area, and individualistic culture types, particularly from the east, flocked to the San Francisco Bay area. Each group has generally blended in well with the original political culture of its area of choice. Since Depression days, however, one substantial change has taken place. The increased migration of southerners into all parts of the state, with greatest intensity in the south and progressively less intensity moving northward, has added a strong strain of the traditionalistic political culture (or its particular individualistic manifestation that comes when its people leave their traditionalistic environment) in areas where that strain was weak or nonexistent. What has happened in those cases is the development of a conflict between the two political cultures as a consequence of the contrast between them. By and large, the radical right of southern California consists of former southerners in revolt against what are, to them, unacceptable patterns of political and social life created by the dominant nonsoutherners.

While continued migration has helped keep culture patterns fluid, at the same time, the values of the various political cultures have undergone internal change. Moral demands have generally stiffened. For example, what is today considered "conflict of interest" in the moralistic political culture was considered perfectly proper in the days of Daniel Webster who, although an authentic Yankee, could take an annual retainer from a leading Boston bank while serving in the United States Senate, without any qualms. In another context, the individualistic political culture, originally the home of the "rugged individualist," has taken on something of a collectivist tinge in the twentieth century as many of those within it have come to believe that "big government" offers opportunities for individuals that are unobtainable in any other way. Thus its representatives are often found at the forefront of the drive for greater government intervention into the economy. Meanwhile, the traditionalistic political culture has tended to adopt individualistic elements as its traditional social bases have been eroded. With its older elites no longer in positions of power because of economic and social changes, many of its traditionalistic attitudes have been transformed into bigotries designed to maintain the old racial caste system or unchallenged efforts to maintain the political status quo, by men who seek personal profit from the changes.

There is also a certain amount of assimilation from one culture to another based on changes in individual interests and attitudes. Under certain circumstances, cultural values change because of changing social status. There is some evidence that, as some people move upward into the middle- to upper-middle-class range, they may adopt at least some of the values of the moralistic political culture—which has always been a middle-class phenomenon—particularly if those values are the more acceptable ones in their communities. In true frontier fashion, this change often occurs in conjunction with a change of residence, such as migration to the suburbs. Thus it may be that as parts of Illinois are transformed into suburban areas and settled by people from individualistic cultural areas, they also acquire cultural patterns more common to the moralistic political culture. This is reflected in the rise of a new style Republican party that has gained a measure of power by opposing, on moralistic grounds, the old style "machine" politics of the Democrats and the GOP old guard, both of which symbolize the individualistic political culture in its least attractive form.

Finally, syntheses of different political cultures appear to be emerging in many states and localities where two or more subcultures have come to rest within the same political system and have found some common ground of communication. In Massachusetts, for example, where the conflict of political cultures between the moralistic Yankees and the individualistic Irish was extraordinarily intense (see below), the present generation has witnessed a kind of rapprochement in which many of the descendants of the Yankees have adopted the political techniques of the Irish, while many of the descendants of the Irish have adopted the sense of the goals and purposes of politics of the Yankees. The Kennedys serve to illustrate this point. John F. Kennedy was at one and the same time a quintessential Yankee and the leader of an "Irish mafia." Senator Edmund Muskie of Maine, of Polish descent, is another such example. Only by being the galvanized Yankee that he is could he have been the first Democrat to break the grip of the Republican party on that state. The Yankees and the Irish, such formidable antagonists in generations past, could begin to meet on common ground because they shared many common values from their respective general cultures, not the least of which was a common "puritanism."

In sum, political culture, like all culture, is dynamic. Changes occur internally within particular cultural groups, movement occurs from group to group, cultures "borrow" from one another, and both cultural erosion and cultural syntheses take place over time. All these forces for change are present

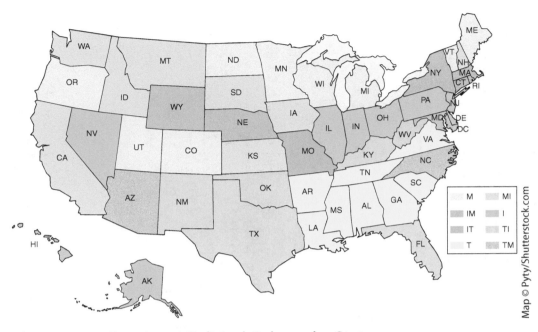

Figure 2.4   Dominant Political Culture, by State

on the American scene where they function to transform the results of cultural diffusion through migrations into cohesive state and local cultural patterns, themselves dynamic syntheses of cultural movement and change.

The Political Cultures of the States

The amalgam of the political subcultures in the several states is varied, because representatives of each are found within every state to varying degrees. In fact, unique aggregations of cultural patterns are clearly discernible in every state. These cultural patterns give each state its particular character and help determine the tone of its fundamental relationship, as a state, to the nation. Figure 2.4 presents the particular pattern of political culture in each state while Table 2.2 presents the configuration of states on a nationwide scale. In general, the states of the greater South are dominated by the traditionalistic political culture; the states stretching across the middle sections of the United States in a southwesterly direction are dominated by the individualistic political culture; and the states of the far North, Northwest, and Pacific Coast are dominated by the moralistic political culture.

Seventeen states are predominantly or overwhelmingly influenced by the moralistic political culture, sixteen are similarly influenced by the traditionalistic political culture, and seventeen by the individualistic political culture. These figures, which appear to give the moralistic political culture the edge and place the individualistic in a clear minority position, must be weighed against the relative populations of the states, shown in Table 2.3. The states dominated by the individualistic political culture, though fewer in number, have by far the greatest share of the nation's population. While the aggregate population of the traditionalistic states is growing in absolute numbers, their relative share of the nation's population is declining. Moreover, because several of them are undergoing subtle changes in the direction of the individualistic political culture, the role of the traditionalistic subculture nationally is further diminished. In terms of population, the relative strength of the moralistic

Table 2.2 State Political Cultures: The National Configuration

Section	M	MI	IM	I	IT	TI	T	TM
New England	Vt., Me.	N.H.	Conn., Mass., R.I.					
Middle Atlantic			N.Y.	Del., Penna., N.J., Md.				
Near West	Mich., Wis.		Ohio[a], Ill.[a]	Ind.				
Northwest	Minn., N.D., Colo.	Iowa, Kan., Mont., S.D., Neb., Wyo.						
Far West	Utah, Ore.	Idaho, Calif., Wash.		Nev.				
Southwest					Mo.	Tex., Okla., N.M.		Ariz.
Upper South						W.Va., Ky.	Va., Tenn.	N.C.
Lower South						Fla., Ala., Ga., Ark., La.	S.C., Miss.	
Pacific				Alas.	Haw.			

[a]Illinois and Ohio have strong traces of M in their northern counties and T in their southern counties.

KEY: M: Moralistic dominant.
MI: Moralistic dominant, strong Individualistic strain.
IM: Individualistic dominant, strong Moralistic strain.
I: Individualistic dominant.
IT: Individualistic dominant, strong Traditionalistic strain.
TI: Traditionalistic dominant, strong Individualistic strain.
T: Traditionalistic dominant.
TM: Traditionalistic dominant, strong Moralistic strain.

NOTE: The eight columns in the table should be viewed as segments on a forced continuum that actually has elements of circularity. The specific placing of the individual states should be viewed cautiously, considering the limits of the data.

Table 2.3	Populations of the Cultural Groupings, by State, 1940–70[a]				
Political Culture[b]	**Number of States**	**Total Populations (in Millions)**			
		1940	**1950**	**1960**	**1970**
M/MI	17	30,998	38,113	47,751	51,413
1M	6	13,479	23,936	27,149	29,678
I	9	3 4,491	38,748	45,969	51,183
IT	2	3,785	3,955	4,320	5,447
T/TM/TI	16	39.947	45,167	52,915	58,436

[a] Cultural grouping as of 1970; Alaska and Hawaii included in 1960 and 1970.
[b] For purposes of over all analysis, it is possible to combine the eight points on the continuum in Figure 18 into five categories.

states is increasing. The figures do not tell, however, whether the population increase in those states is reenforcing the established political subculture or injecting new elements foreign to it. Neither can the figures reveal to what extent the moralistic political subculture is gaining strength in the individualistic states as a result of social and cultural change.

Political Culture, the Frontier, and Sectionalism

The sectional pattern in the nationwide distribution of the political cultures is clearly visible in the maps and figures presented here. This is only one of the ways in which manifestations of sectionalism—the expression of social, economic, and especially political differences along geographic lines—are part and parcel of American political life. The more or less permanent political ties that link groups of contiguous states together as sections reflect the ways in which local conditions and differences in political culture modify the impact of the frontier. This overall sectional pattern reflects the interaction of the three basic factors. The original sections were produced by the variations in the impact of the rural-land frontier on different geographic segments of the country. They, in turn, have been modified by the pressures generated by the first and subsequent frontier stages. As a result, the sections are not homogeneous socioeconomic units sharing a common character across state lines but complex entities that combine highly diverse states and communities with common political interests that generally complement one another socially and economically.[17]

Sectionalism is not the same as regionalism. The latter is essentially a phenomenon—often transient—that brings adjacent state, substate or interstate areas together because of immediate and specific common interests. The portions of the nine states from Georgia to Pennsylvania that are located within the Appalachian Mountains represent one kind of region. The Mississippi Valley is another. Ties between the political entities in such regions are expediential only, a product of their common interest in overcoming very specific problems.

Sectionalism involves arrangements of much greater permanence which, as essentially political phenomena, link whole states and persist despite the emergence of immediate conflicts or divergences among its component states from time to time. For example, New England is a section bound by the tightest of social and historical ties even though the differences between the states of lower New England (Massachusetts, Rhode Island, Connecticut), which have been fully absorbed into the metropolitan-technological frontier, and those of upper New England (Maine, New Hampshire, Vermont), which are still in the process of being absorbed and retain much of their older character, are often more noticeable to the casual observer. There are, indeed, periodic conflicts between the various regions in New England. Nevertheless, the six states consciously seek to cooperate with one another in numerous ways, joining together to deal with common problems of transportation, communications, education, economic development, and law enforcement in recognition of the bonds of both history and necessity. By the end of the 1960's, their cooperative efforts had been sufficiently institutionalized to create what is essentially a six-state confederation within the larger American Union. It is through such acts of political will that sectionalism best manifests itself.

Most sections have continuing intrasectional conflicts of long duration that persist within the context of their overall sectional unity in response to national concerns. For example, the intrasectional conflict between the states of the Far West over water resources, though a perennial issue, does not detract from their long-term community of interest in matters of commerce and education. More important for our purposes, certain common sectional bonds give the states of each section a special relationship to national politics, particularly in connection with those specific political issues that are of sectional importance, such as the race issue in the South, the problems of the megalopolis in the Northeast, and the problems of agriculture and agribusiness in the Northwest. One problem in understanding the influence of sectionalism on politics is the proper identification of those specific issues from among many apparent ones. During the heyday of the Populist movement, western and southern Populists made common cause against what they believed to be northeastern exploitation, despite the great cultural and even doctrinal differences separating them. When the Populist movement failed, the temporary intersectional alliance came to an end for lack of binding common interests. Today certain students of American reform have failed to distinguish between the two kinds of populism simply because they were aligned at one point in time.[18]

Regionalism can often be a function of sectionalism. Indeed, each section can contain several regions just as some regions cross into several sections. The interest of the northeastern states in gaining federal aid for urban rapid transit facilities is a temporary interest generated by an immediate regional problem fostered by the existence of a continuous urbanized belt from Maine to Virginia, often called the megalopolis, that has generated common problems in those states.[19] At the same time, it is a manifestation of larger sectional communications concerns that have existed in various forms since the colonial period.

Most attempts to discuss politics in regional or sectional terms are based on the regional scheme devised by the United States Bureau of the Census. While that scheme has its value, it is not necessarily the best, particularly for political analysis. For one thing, it ignores the regional patterns set by the three political subcultures. For another, it ignores the larger pattern of settlement in the country that is based on the linear thrusts of the frontier, usually westward. Here we will propose a different sectional scheme, as shown in Figure 2.5.

The nation's sectional alignments are rooted in the three great historical, cultural, and economic spheres into which the country is divided: the greater Northeast, the greater South, and the greater West. The three spheres can be outlined with nearly perfect accuracy by the three semicircles indicated in Figure 2.5. Following state lines, the greater Northeast includes all those states north of the Ohio and Potomac Rivers and east of Lake Michigan. The greater South includes the states below that line but east of the Mississippi plus Missouri, Arkansas, Louisiana, Oklahoma, and Texas. All the rest of the states compose the greater West.[20] Within that framework, there are eight sections constructed

Figure 2.5   Spheres, Sections, and Urbanized Areas (1960) of the United States

around two essential characteristics: (1) All reflect the linear thrust of the frontier, generally opening to the west but, in a larger sense, opening from the heavily settled sectional heartland to its open hinterland. Thus, the Northwest opens from the Minneapolis–St. Paul area generally westward into Montana, New England opens from Boston generally northward, and the Far West—the one exception to the westward rule—from California generally eastward to the Rockies (which was the way that section was originally settled). (2) Each has sufficient internal diversity to reflect the social and economic complexity of the nation as a whole while also sharing sufficiently homogeneous political and cultural patterns to offer a unique variation of the national pattern.

Part of the response of each state to national politics and policies is related to the state's position in its section or sphere. Such responses are conditioned on whether a given state is a sectional leader, like Illinois, permanently subordinate, like South Dakota, or perpetually in opposition to the sectional leader, like Ohio; whether it possesses an "empire city," like Atlanta, that dominates the section, or is tributary to such a metropolis in another state; or whether the people have a greater stake in sectional or state concerns, generally or in regard to specific issues.

The movement of the center of population westward since 1790 closely reflects the shifting limits of the three great spheres and their relationship to the three political subcultures. The line of movement as indicated in Figure 2.6 follows almost precisely along the line of division between the greater Northeast and the greater South while the center point itself marks the general beginning of the greater West as that sphere has taken shape over time. Since the West is initially a product of the land frontier, its boundaries shifted substantially as long as pioneering on that frontier continued in a meaningful way. In the twentieth century, that shift has slowed down considerably and the eastern limits of the greater West have hardened. Roughly speaking, the individualistic political culture

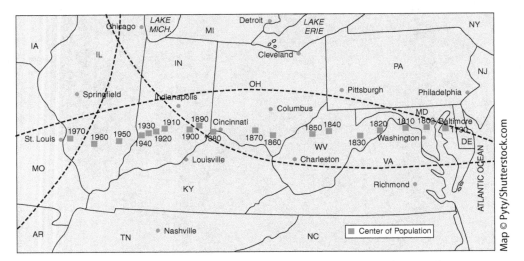

Figure 2.6   Center of Population for Coterminus United States, 1790–1970

proceeds westward along the northern edge of the center of population line reaching approximately 150 miles north of that line where it begins to shade off into the moralistic culture area. South of the line, it begins to shade off into the traditionalistic culture area almost immediately. West of the center of population, the spread of the three cultures is generally more diffused.

Political Culture: Some Caveats

By now the reader has no doubt formed his own value judgments as to the relative worth of the three political subcultures. For this reason a particular warning against hasty judgments must be added here. Each of the three political subcultures contributes something important to the configuration of the American political system and each contains certain characteristics that are inherently dangerous to the survival of that system.

The moralistic political culture, for example, is the primary source of the continuing American quest for the good society. At the same time, there is a tendency toward fanaticism and narrow-mindedness noticeable among some of its representatives. The individualistic political culture is the most tolerant of out-and-out political corruption, yet it has also provided the framework for the integration of diverse groups into the mainstream of American life. When representatives of the moralistic political culture, in their striving for a better social order, try to limit individual freedom, they usually come up against representatives of the individualistic political culture, to whom individual freedom is the cornerstone of their pluralistic order, though not for any noble reasons. Reversed, of course, the moralistic political culture acts as a restraint against the tendencies of the individualistic political culture to tolerate license in the name of liberty.

The traditionalistic political culture contributes to the search for continuity in a society whose major characteristic is change, yet in the name of continuity, its representatives try to deny blacks (or Indians, or Hispanic-Americans) their civil rights. When in proper working order, the traditionalistic culture has produced a unique group of first-rate national leaders from among its elites, but without a first-rate elite to draw upon, traditionalistic culture political systems degenerate into oligarchies of the lowest level. Comparisons like these should induce a cautiousness in evaluation of a subject that, by its very nature, evokes evaluation.

It is equally important to use caution in identifying individuals and groups as belonging to one cultural type or another on the basis of their public political behavior at a given moment in time. While immediate political responses to the issues of the day may in themselves reveal the political culture of the respondents, they do not necessarily do so. Usually, deeper analysis of what is behind those responses is needed. In other words, the names of the political cultures are not substitutes for the terms "conservative" and "liberal" and should not be taken as such.

End Notes

1. The ideas presented in this and the following chapter should be considered in the nature of hypotheses rooted in an effort to organize the complex phenomena that shape American civilization and its politics so as to enhance our understanding of both. As the elements in an overarching hypothesis, the three factors can best be understood through a combination of qualitative analysis and quantitative measurement. When the first edition of this volume was published in 1966, relatively little quantitative data was available since there had yet to be sufficient research into the character and influence of the three factors either on a national basis or in specific states. Since then, there has been a rapid growth of interest in the hypotheses presented here and at least some very solid research has been completed bearing on them, including Samuel C. Patterson, *The Political Cultures of the American States* (Iowa City: University of Iowa, 1966); Ira Sharkansky, *Regionalism in American Politics* (Indianapolis and New York: Bobbs-Merrill, 1969); Ira Sharkansky, *Spending in the American States* (Chicago: Rand McNally, 1968); and Ira Sharkansky, "The Utility of Elazar's Political Culture," *Polity*, 2, no. 1 (Fall 1969); 66–83. The Center for the Study of Federalism has been responsible for the following relevant additions to the literature: André Moore, *Political Culture in Pennsylvania: An Empirical Analysis* (Philadelphia: Center for the Study of Federalism, 1970); Daniel J. Elazar and Joseph Zikmund II, *Culture and Political Culture*, and Daniel J. Elazar, *American Political Culture and Its Subcultures, Working Kits numbers 1 and 2 of the Study of American Political Culture* (Philadelphia: Center for the Study of Federalism, 1969). Also available from the Center are R. Michael Stevens, *Occupation Legislator: The Influence of Political Culture on Pennsylvania Legislators* (Philadelphia: Center for the Study of Federalism, 1970); and *American Political Culture: A Bibliography of Source Materials* (Philadelphia: Center for the Study of Federalism, 1970). Finally, the author's *Cities of the Prairie* (New York: Basic Books, 1970) is now available with a more comprehensive statement of his theory. See also Richard Dawson and James Robinson, "Interparty Competition, Economic Variables, and Welfare Politics in the American States," *Journal of Politics*, 25 (May 1963): 265–89; Thomas R. Dye, *Politics, Economics and the Public: Policy Outcomes in the American States* (Chicago: Rand McNally, 1966); Richard I. Hofferbert, "Ecological Development and Policy Change in the American States," *Mid-West Journal of Political Science*, 10 (November 1966): 464–85; Herbert Jacob and Kenneth N. Vines, *Politics in the American States* (Boston: Little, Brown, 1965); Richard R. Dohm, Reform from *Within: The Development of the City Administrator Form of Government in Small Missouri Cities* (Columbia, Mo.: University of Missouri, School of Business and Public Administration, University Extension Division, 1970); and Richard R. Dohm, "Political Culture of Missouri," in *Providing Public Services in Missouri: Issues and Alternatives* (Columbia, Mo.: University of Missouri, University Extension Division,

1971). The data used here represent the substance of the author's research as delineated in another connection in footnote nine of Chapter One. Space limitations make it necessary to concentrate on only a few aspects of these factors to indicate something of their character and influence.

2. Governmental Affairs Institute, *A Survey Report on the Impact of Federal Grants-in-Aid on the Structure and Functions of State and Local Governments, submitted to the Commission on Intergovernmental Relations* (Washington, D.C.: Government Printing Office, 1956). The statements in this and the following paragraphs are based in large part on the findings in the twenty-five states covered in that report.

3. For a study of this problem in one state, see *The Office of Governor* (Urbana: Institute of Government and Public Affairs, University of Illinois, 1963). This has been confirmed by the subsequent work of the Advisory Commission on Intergovernmental Relations and the various groups seeking to strengthen state government. See, also, Joseph A. Schlesinger, "The Politics of the Executive," in Jacob and Vines, *Politics in the American States.*

4. The merit system example has the additional advantage of revealing some of the complexities encountered in this kind of analysis. While the overt state by state differences are relatively clear-cut, significant nuances of complexity just below the surface make the role of the three overarching factors more pronounced. Thus, willingness to embrace merit systems is not to be equated with opposition to patronage systems, per se. For example, the same state can actually maintain both if its public does not associate patronage with political corruption but rather with Jacksonian ideas of democratic access to government offices. In some states, the concept "political employee" immediately conjures up the image of the less than honest party hack or of a shiftless relative of an elected office-holder. In those states, the introduction of "nonpolitical" merit standards is placed in juxtaposition to the patronage system and is considered a revolutionary change in that it supposedly separates "politics" from "administration." In some states, however, the patronage appointee is not considered dishonest or somehow deficient a priori, and political appointment is recognized as a source of good and responsive officeholders. In those states merit systems are often introduced in response to a temporary lapse from the accepted public standards of public employment by the political organization in power that has led to a public reaction against the method of appointment or, perhaps even more often, they are advanced as a means to raise professional standards in certain branches of the state service where professionalism is considered desirable. For still other variations in the subsurface meaning of civil service reform, see Chapter Five.

5. Gross state by state variations in political behavior and program support in several important fields are chronicled within a comparative framework in *Dye, Politics, Economics and the Public* and Jacob and Vines, *Politics in the American States.* Jack Walker has carefully studied patterns of innovation in the various states. See his "The Diffusion of Innovations Among the American States," *APSR*, 63 (September 1969): 880–89.

6. For a more complete definition of political culture, see Gabriel A. Almond, "Comparative Political Systems," *The Journal of Politics*, 18 (1956): 391–409. Political culture is a part of general culture but is separable from it for analytical purposes. In fact, there can be apparently great differences between a general culture and its political cultural segment.

   Specific elements of political culture frequently have their origins in historical events or situations which cause great and long-lasting changes among those who share the experiences they generate. These changes are then transmitted—and often intensified—through the process of acculturation to the descendants of the original group, including both "blood" and "galvanized" (those adopted into the group) descendants. Perhaps because of the close relationship between political culture and historical phenomena, historians have done more to trace the ingredients that combine to create the patterns of political culture in western societies than have other social scientists. Though they have not done so to investigate political culture as such, they have provided the raw materials for such an investigation through their studies of other phenomena, such as migration patterns, political alliances and antagonisms, the historical roots of continuing social behavior, and the like. This chapter draws heavily on their work in both acknowledged and unacknowledged ways. See, for example, Gabriel A. Almond and G. Bingham Powell, Jr., *Comparative Politics: A Developmental Approach* (Boston: Little, Brown, 1966); Lucien W. Pye, *Aspects of Political Development* (Boston: Little, Brown, 1966); and Lucien W. Pye and Sidney Verba, eds., *Political Culture and Political Development* (Princeton, N.J.: Princeton University Press, 1965).

7. For an analysis by political scientists of the national political culture in a comparative setting, see Gabriel A. Almond and Sidney Verba, *The Civic Culture* (Princeton: Princeton University Press, 1963). Two recent treatments of the origins of the American political culture are Daniel J. Boorstin, *The Americans: The National Experience* (New York: Random House, 1965), and Seymour Martin Lipset, *The First New Nation: The United States in Historical and Comparative Perspective* (New York: Basic Books, 1963).

8. The names given the three political subcultures are meant to be descriptive, not evaluative. By the same token, the descriptions of the three that follow are intended to be models or ideal types that are not likely to be fully extant in the real world.

9. It is important to examine this description and the ones following it very carefully after first abandoning many of the preconceptions associated with such idea-words as individualistic, moralistic, marketplace, etc. In this case, for example, nineteenth-century individualistic conceptions of minimum intervention were oriented toward laissez faire with the role of government conceived to be that of a policeman with powers to act in certain limited fields. In the twentieth century, the notion of what constitutes minimum intervention has been drastically expanded to include such things as government regulation of utilities, unemployment compensation, and massive subventions to maintain a stable and growing economy—all this within the framework of the same political culture. The demands of manufacturers for high tariffs in 1865 and the demands of labor unions for workmen's compensation in 1965 may well be based on the same theoretical justification that they are aids to the maintenance of a working marketplace. Culture is not static. It must be viewed dynamically and defined so as to include cultural change in its very nature.

10. As in the case of the individualistic political culture, the change from nineteenth- to twentieth-century conceptions of what government's positive role should be has been great, i.e., support for Prohibition has given way to support for wage and hour regulation. At the same time, care must be taken to distinguish between a predisposition toward communal activism and desire for federal government activity. For example, many moralistic types oppose federal aid for urban renewal without in any way opposing community responsibility for urban redevelopment. The distinction they make (implicitly at least) is between what they consider legitimate community responsibility and what they believe to be central government encroachment, or between "communalism" which they value and "collectivism" which they abhor. Thus, on some public issues we find certain moralistic types taking highly conservative positions despite their positive attitudes toward public activity generally. Moralistic types may also prefer government intervention in the social realm—i.e., censorship or screening of books and movies—to similar

government intervention in the economy, holding that the former is necessary for the public good and the latter, harmful.

11. In this context, it should be noted that regular party systems are sometimes abandoned in local communities dominated by the individualistic political culture to institute nonpartisan electoral systems in an effort to make local governments more "businesslike" and to take local administration "out of politics." Such anti-political efforts are generally products of business-dominated reform movements and reflect the view that politics is necessarily "dirty" and illegitimate. In this context, see Edward C. Banfield, ed., *Urban Government* (New York: Free Press of Glencoe, 1961), Sections III and IV, and Elazar, *Cities of the Prairie*, Part Three.

12. A more detailed and elaborate discussion than can be given here of the origins and spread of the three subcultures is found in Elazar, *Cities of the Prairie*. Since the patterns of the political subcultures are tied closely to the patterns of the general subcultures in the United States, it is possible to gain some impression of the spread of the former from data prepared to illustrate the spread of the latter. One of the best sources for that data, though somewhat dated, is Charles O. Paullin's *Atlas of the Historical Geography of the United States* (Washington and New York: Carnegie Institution and American Geographical Society, 1932). The correlations between religious affiliation and political culture are clear and striking. Edwin S. Gausted's *Historical Atlas of Religion in America* (New York: Harper, 1962) includes maps showing the spread of religious denominations as of 1950, which are also very useful in following the patterns of political culture.

13. The frontier process emerging from the meeting of civilization and raw nature is a dynamic one; men approach the untamed area with a view to bringing it under their control because it appears to offer indefinite possibilities for expansion as well as a chance to begin again from the beginning, to implement goals that appear difficult or impossible to implement in the civilized areas about them. A frontier situation possesses the following elements: (1) the exploration of that which was previously unexplored and the development of that which was previously undeveloped; (2) a psychological orientation toward exploration, development, growth, opportunity, and change—often typified in the "boom" spirit; (3) an economy that is growing in scope and changing in character; (4) manifold opportunities for exploration and pioneering, coupled with a strong element of risk; (5) widespread freedom for people to engage in frontierlike activities and generally to have free access to the developing sector; (6) substantial movements of population in search of opportunity or improved living conditions; (7) an emergent or "unfinished" society that is continually responding to the advancing frontier by changing its social and settlement patterns; and (8) the creation of new opportunities on many levels of society as a consequence of pushing back the frontier. The basic statement of the frontier theory is still that of Frederick Jackson Turner and can best be found in his *The Frontier in American History* (New York: Holt, 1920). For an introduction to other aspects of frontier theory, see Nelson Klose, *A Concise Study Guide to the American Frontier* (Lincoln: University of Nebraska Press, 1964). The best recent restatement of the theory is that of Ray Allen Billington in *America's Frontier Heritage* (New York: Holt, Rinehart and Winston, 1967).

14. The history and significance of the American land frontier has been set forth in great detail by Turner and his students. See, for example, Turner, *The Frontier in American History*, and Ray Allen Billington, *Westward Expansion: A History of the American Frontier* (New York: Macmillan, 1949). Much less has been written about the urban-industrial frontier. Two good studies are John Kouwenhoven, *Made in America*, rev. ed. (Garden City, N.Y.: Anchor Books, 1962) on the role of the new technology of the midnineteenth century and Anselm Strauss, *The Image of the American*

City (Glencoe, Ill.: Free Press, 1961) on the urbanization aspects of the urban-industrial frontier. Walt W. Rostow's *The Stages of Economic Growth* (New York: Cambridge University Press, 1960) provides a theory of economic growth that strongly supports the hypothesis presented here. The frontier aspects of the contemporary metropolitanization process have hardly been treated at all. The best discussion available is that of Samuel Lubell, *The Future of American Politics* (New York: Harper, 1952). See also, Daniel J. Elazar, *Some Social Problems in the Northeastern Illinois Metropolitan Region* (Urbana: University of Illinois, 1961) and *Cities of the Prairie*.

15. One important study of the effects of these new migrations on American politics is Lubell, *The Future of American Politics*, pp. 60–67, 75–78. See also Kevin Phillips, *The Emerging Republican Majority* (New Rochelle, N.Y.: Arlington House, 1969).

16. See George E. Mowry, *The California Progressives* (Berkeley: University of California Press, 1951).

17. The classic work on sectionalism is that of Frederick Jackson Turner, particularly the collection of his essays published as *The Significance of Sections in American History* (New York: Holt, 1932). More recent works of importance include Merrill Jensen, ed., *Regionalism in America* (Madison: University of Wisconsin Press, 1951) and Harvey S. Perloff, Edgar S. Dunn, Jr., Eric E. Lampard, and Richard F. Muth, *Regions, Resources, and Economic Growth* (Baltimore: Johns Hopkins Press, 1960).

18. Richard Hofstader is one of the most distinguished students of American reform who succumbs to that kind of overgeneralization; see, for example, his *The Age of Reform* (New York: Knopf, 1955). See also Eric F. Goldman, *Rendezvous with Destiny* (New York: Knopf, 1952) for the history of the Populist alliance and its dissolution.

19. Jean Gottmann, *Megalopolis: The Urbanized Eastern Seaboard of the United States* (New York: Twentieth Century Fund, 1961).

20. Perloff et al., *Regions, Resources, and Economic Growth*, makes an excellent case for this scheme of spheres as the basis for the country's economic regions. See also Strauss, *Image of the American City*, for a presentation of sociological evidence demonstrating the validity of this scheme.

It should be noted that between the points of intersection of the semicircles lie three areas—the Ohio Valley, the western South, and the western Great Lakes—which are transition zones between the spheres. Sharing the characteristics of two or more spheres, they have especially complex patterns of culture and politics. See Elazar, *Cities of the Prairie*.

CHAPTER 3
PARTICIPATION, ELECTIONS, AND REPRESENTATION

BUSH V. GORE

SUPREME COURT OF THE UNITED STATES

531 U.S. 98 (2000)

Majority Per Curiam Opinion:

On December 8, 2000, the Supreme Court of Florida ordered that the Circuit Court of Leon County tabulate by hand 9,000 ballots in Miami-Dade County. It also ordered the inclusion in the certified vote totals of 215 votes identified in Palm Beach County and 168 votes identified in Miami-Dade County for Vice President Albert Gore, Jr., and Senator Joseph Lieberman, Democratic Candidates for President and Vice President. The Supreme Court noted that petitioner, Governor George W. Bush asserted that the net gain for Vice President Gore in Palm Beach County was 176 votes, and directed the Circuit Court to resolve that dispute on remand. . . . The court further held that relief would require manual recounts in all Florida counties where so-called "undervotes" had not been subject to manual tabulation. The court ordered all manual recounts to begin at once. Governor Bush and Richard Cheney, Republican Candidates for the Presidency and Vice Presidency, filed an emergency application for a stay of this mandate. . . .

On November 8, 2000, the day following the Presidential election, the Florida Division of Elections reported that petitioner, Governor Bush, had received 2,909,135 votes, and respondent, Vice President Gore, had received 2,907,351 votes, a margin of 1,784 for Governor Bush. Because Governor Bush's margin of victory was less than "one-half of a percent . . . of the votes cast," an automatic machine recount was conducted . . ., the results of which showed Governor Bush still winning the race but by a diminished margin. Vice President Gore then sought manual recounts in Volusia, Palm Beach, Broward, and Miami-Dade Counties, pursuant to Florida's election protest provisions. A dispute arose concerning the deadline for local county canvassing boards to submit their returns to the Secretary of State (Secretary). The Secretary declined to waive the November 14 deadline imposed by statute. The Florida Supreme Court, however, set the deadline at November 26. We granted certiorari and vacated the Florida Supreme Court's decision, finding considerable uncertainty as to the grounds on which it was based.

On November 26, the Florida Elections Canvassing Commission certified the results of the election and declared Governor Bush the winner of Florida's 25 electoral votes. On November 27, Vice President Gore, pursuant to Florida's contest provisions, filed a complaint in Leon County Circuit Court contesting the certification.

The petition presents the following questions: whether the Florida Supreme Court established new standards for resolving Presidential election contests, thereby violating Art. II, § 1, cl. 2, of the United States Constitution and failing to comply with 3 U.S.C. § 5, and whether the use of standardless manual recounts violates the Equal Protection and Due Process Clauses. With respect to the equal protection question, we find a violation of the Equal Protection Clause.

[. . .]

Much of the controversy seems to revolve around ballot cards designed to be perforated by a stylus but which, either through error or deliberate omission, have not been perforated with sufficient precision for a machine to count them. In some cases a piece of the card—a chad—is hanging, say by two corners. In other cases there is no separation at all, just an indentation.

The Florida Supreme Court has ordered that the intent of the voter be discerned from such ballots. For purposes of resolving the equal protection challenge, it is not necessary to decide whether the Florida Supreme Court had the authority under the legislative scheme for resolving election disputes to define what a legal vote is and to mandate a manual recount implementing that definition. The recount mechanisms implemented in response to the decisions of the Florida Supreme Court do not satisfy the minimum requirement for non-arbitrary treatment of voters necessary to secure the fundamental right. Florida's basic command for the count of legally cast votes is to consider the "intent of the voter. . . ." This is unobjectionable as an abstract proposition and a starting principle. The problem inheres in the absence of specific standards to ensure its equal application. The formulation of uniform rules to determine intent based on these recurring circumstances is practicable and, we conclude, necessary.

The law does not refrain from searching for the intent of the actor in a multitude of circumstances; and in some cases the general command to ascertain intent is not susceptible to much further refinement. In this instance, however, the question is not whether to believe a witness but how to interpret the marks or holes or scratches on an inanimate object, a piece of cardboard or paper which, it is said, might not have registered as a vote during the machine count. The factfinder confronts a thing, not a person. The search for intent can be confined by specific rules designed to ensure uniform treatment.

The want of those rules here has led to unequal evaluation of ballots in various respects. . . . As seems to have been acknowledged at oral argument, the standards for accepting or rejecting contested ballots might vary not only from county to county but indeed within a single county from one recount team to another.

[. . .]

Upon due consideration of the difficulties identified to this point, it is obvious that the recount cannot be conducted in compliance with the requirements of equal protection and due process without substantial additional work. It would require not only the adoption (after opportunity for argument) of adequate statewide standards for determining what is a legal vote, and practicable procedures to implement them, but also orderly judicial review of any disputed matters that might arise. In addition, the Secretary of State has advised that the recount of only a portion of the ballots requires that the vote tabulation equipment be used to screen out undervotes, a function for which the machines were not designed. If a recount of overvotes were also required, perhaps even a second screening would be necessary. Use of the equipment for this purpose, and any new software developed for it, would have to be evaluated for accuracy by the Secretary of State. . .

The Supreme Court of Florida has said that the legislature intended the State's electors to "participate fully in the federal electoral process," as provided in 3 U.S.C. § 5. . . .That statute, in turn, requires that any controversy or contest that is designed to lead to a conclusive selection of electors be completed by December 12. That date is upon us, and there is no recount procedure in place under the State Supreme Court's order that comports with minimal constitutional standards. Because it is evident that any recount seeking to meet the December 12 date will be unconstitutional for the reasons we have discussed, we reverse the judgment of the Supreme Court of Florida ordering a recount to proceed.

JUSTICE **STEVENS**, with whom JUSTICE GINSBURG AND JUSTICE BREYER join, dissenting.

The Constitution assigns to the States the primary responsibility for determining the manner of selecting the Presidential electors. See Art. II, § 1, cl. 2. When questions arise about the meaning of state laws, including election laws, it is our settled practice to accept the opinions of the highest courts of the States as providing the final answers. On rare occasions, however, either federal statutes or the Federal Constitution may require federal judicial intervention in state elections. This is not such an occasion.

The federal questions that ultimately emerged in this case are not substantial. Article II provides that "each *State* shall appoint, in such Manner as the Legislature *thereof* may direct, a Number of Electors." *Ibid.* (emphasis added). It does not create state legislatures out of whole cloth, but rather takes them as they come—as creatures born of, and constrained by, their state constitutions.

[. . .]

Admittedly, the use of differing substandards for determining voter intent in different counties employing similar voting systems may raise serious concerns. Those concerns are alleviated—if not eliminated—by the fact that a single impartial magistrate will ultimately adjudicate all objections arising from the recount process. Of course, as a general matter, "the interpretation of constitutional principles must not be too literal. We must remember that the machinery of government would not work if it were not allowed a little play in its joints. . . ." If it were otherwise, Florida's decision to leave to each county the determination of what balloting system to employ—despite enormous differences in accuracy—might run afoul of equal protection. So, too, might the similar decisions of the vast majority of state legislatures to delegate to local authorities certain decisions with respect to voting systems and ballot design.

Even assuming that aspects of the remedial scheme might ultimately be found to violate the Equal Protection Clause, I could not subscribe to the majority's disposition of the case. As the majority explicitly holds, once a state legislature determines to select electors through a popular vote, the right to have one's vote counted is of constitutional stature. As the majority further acknowledges, Florida law holds that all ballots that reveal the intent of the voter constitute valid votes. Recognizing these principles, the majority nonetheless orders the termination of the contest proceeding before all such votes have been tabulated. Under their own reasoning the appropriate course of action would be to remand to allow more specific procedures for implementing the legislature's uniform general standard to be established.

In the interest of finality, however, the majority effectively orders the disenfranchisement of an unknown number of voters whose ballots reveal their intent—and are therefore legal votes under state law—but were for some reason rejected by ballot-counting machines.

[...]

What must underlie petitioners' entire federal assault on the Florida election procedures is an unstated lack of confidence in the impartiality and capacity of the state judges who would make the critical decisions if the vote count were to proceed. Otherwise, their position is wholly without merit. The endorsement of that position by the majority of this Court can only lend credence to the most cynical appraisal of the work of judges throughout the land. It is confidence in the men and women who administer the judicial system that is the true backbone of the rule of law. Time will one day heal the wound to that confidence that will be inflicted by today's decision. One thing, however, is certain. Although we may never know with complete certainty the identity of the winner of this year's Presidential election the identity of the loser is perfectly clear. It is the Nation's confidence in the judge as an impartial guardian of the rule of law.

I respectfully dissent.

[...]

JUSTICE **GINSBURG,** with whom JUSTICE STEVENS joins, and with whom JUSTICE SOUTER and JUSTICE BREYER join as to Part I, dissenting.

I

[...]

The extraordinary setting of this case has obscured the ordinary principle that dictates its proper resolution: Federal courts defer to state high courts' interpretations of their state's own law. This principle reflects the core of federalism, on which all agree. "The Framers split the atom of sovereignty. It was the genius of their idea that our citizens would have two political capacities, one state and one federal, each protected from incursion by the other." *Saenz* v. *Roe*, 526 U.S. 489, 504, n. 17. . . . THE CHIEF JUSTICE's solicitude for the Florida Legislature comes at the expense of the more fundamental solicitude we owe to the legislature's sovereign. U.S. Const., Art. II, § 1, cl. 2 ("Each *State* shall appoint, in such Manner as the Legislature *thereof* may direct," the electors for President and Vice President) (emphasis added). . . . Were the other members of this Court as mindful as they generally are of our system of dual sovereignty, they would affirm the judgment of the Florida Supreme Court.

I dissent.

THE LEAGUE OF DANGEROUS MAPMAKERS

Who's most to blame for our divisive politics? How about the gerrymanderers quietly deciding where your vote goes. Inside the dark art and modern science of making democracy a lot less democratic.

ROBERT DRAPER

Every 10 years, after U.S. census workers have fanned out across the nation, a snowy-haired gentleman by the name of Tom Hofeller takes up anew his quest to destroy Democrats. He packs his bag and his laptop with its special Maptitude software, kisses his wife of 46 years, pats his West Highland white terrier, Kara, and departs his home in Alexandria, Virginia, for a United States that he will help carve into a jigsaw of disunity.

Where Hofeller travels depends to some degree on the migratory patterns of his fellow Americans over the previous decade. As the census shows, some states will have swelled in population, while others will have dwindled. The states that gained the most people are entitled, under the Constitution, to additional representation in the form of new congressional districts, which (since the law allows only 435 such districts) are wrenched from the states that lost the most people. After the 2010 census, eight states (all in the South and the West) gained congressional districts, which were stripped from 10 others (in the Midwest and the East Coast, as well as Katrina-ravaged Louisiana).

The creation of a new congressional district, or the loss of an old one, affects every district around it, necessitating new maps. Even states not adding or losing congressional representatives need new district maps that reflect the population shifts within their borders, so that residents are equally represented no matter where they live. This ritual carving and paring of the United States into 435 sovereign units, known as redistricting, was intended by the Framers solely to keep democracy's electoral scales balanced. Instead, redistricting today has become the most insidious practice in American politics—a way, as the opportunistic machinations following the 2010 census make evident, for our elected leaders to entrench themselves in 435 impregnable garrisons from which they can maintain political power while avoiding demographic realities.

For the past four decades, it is what Tom Hofeller has done for a living.

Hofeller maintains an office at the Republican National Committee on Capitol Hill, though he is now the RNC's paid consultant rather than, as in years past, its official redistricting director. At 69, he is a professorial if somewhat impish fellow (in his early days, a California House speaker dubbed him "the kid with the shit-eating grin") who is more than content not to be a household name. His after-hours life includes singing tenor in his church choir and reading multitudes of books that seldom have anything to do with politics. Hofeller's earliest clients included Democrats, and today he describes himself as a moderate Republican. The adjective is irrelevant, however. His chosen field is, according to Georgia Congressman and House Republican redistricting vice chair Lynn Westmoreland, "the nastiest form of politics that there is": Tom Hofeller's objective is to design wombs for his team and tombs for the other guys.

And so his cyclical travels take him mainly to states where the Republicans are likely to be drawing the new maps. (In most states, an appointed committee consisting of legislators from the majority party produces the map, which is then brought to the legislative body for a vote. Other states relegate the duties to an appointed commission.) At meetings, Hofeller gives a PowerPoint presentation titled "What I've Learned About Redistricting—The Hard Way!" Like its author, the presentation is both learned and a bit hokey, with admonitions like "Expect the unexpected" and "Don't get 'cute.' Remember, this IS legislation!" He warns legislators to resist the urge to overindulge, to snatch up every desirable precinct within reach, when drawing their own districts.

But Hofeller's helpful tips give way to the sinister warnings of a gimlet-eyed, semi-clandestine political operative: "Make sure your security is real." "Make sure your computer is in a PRIVATE location." "'Emails are the tool of the devil.' Use personal contact or a safe phone!" "Don't reveal more than necessary." "BEWARE of non-partisan, or bi-partisan, staff bearing gifts. They probably are not your friends."

Be discreet. Plan ahead. Follow the law. Don't overreach. Tom Hofeller relishes the blood sport of redistricting, but there is a responsible way—as Hofeller himself demonstrated this past cycle in the artful (if baldly partisan) redrawing of North Carolina's maps—and also a reckless way. So that his message will penetrate, he tells audiences horror stories about states that ignored his warnings and went with maps that either were tossed out by the federal courts or created more political problems than they solved.

Already Hofeller has picked out which cautionary tale he will relay during the next decennial tour. The new horror story, he's decided, will be Texas, which stood, this past cycle, as a powerful example of how reckless a redistricting process can become. That mangled effort also provides a stark contrast to the maps Hofeller helped create in North Carolina—drawings that demonstrate how in the blood sport of redistricting, the most cravenly political results are won with calculating prudence.

As the election returns rolled in on the evening of November 2, 2010, Hofeller had already started gearing up for the next round of redistricting. "I'm sitting and watching, less interested than many in the congressional races," he recalled. "I'm the one saying 'Okay, so we won Congress. The question is, are we going to keep it?' And then what I see is that we gained 700 state legislative seats. The night just kept getting better and better. Things happened in some states"—in terms of controlling whole legislative bodies—"that we never expected. Alabama! North Carolina!"

It seemed like Reconstruction all over again for the GOP. Because the Republican tsunami coincided with the 2010 census, Tom Hofeller's party was suddenly able to redraw many of the 435 congressional maps to its own partisan advantage. Without asking for guidance from Hofeller or other veterans of the trade, delirious party officials predicted that after all the connivances were set in motion, the GOP would be able to reward itself with an additional 15 safe House seats before a single vote was cast in the 2012 elections.

It hasn't quite turned out that way. Partly this is because Democrats understood the stakes and went to extraordinary lengths to blunt the assault. In California, the Democrats (according to e-mails obtained by ProPublica) successfully swayed a newly formed independent citizens' redistricting commission, through an intricately coordinated guerrilla operation that will likely accrue them six or seven new seats. In Republican-controlled Florida, Nancy Pelosi—in relentless pursuit of the House speakership she lost after the 2010 midterms—helped fund the successful "Fair Districts" referendum to ban partisan redistricting. The measure seems to have persuaded Florida map-drawers to exhibit some self-restraint, and thus a number of surefire Republican seats were wiped from the boards. Of course, Pelosi has not suggested that the Fair Districts concept be applied to states where her party wields legislative control, such as Maryland and Illinois, where the Democrats further cut into the GOP's gains by drawing nakedly partisan maps that simply vaporized Republican-held districts.

Tom Hofeller certainly did his part to maximize the returns on the GOP's 2010 electoral bounty. Hired by North Carolina's top GOP legislators just after the midterms to advise in the drawing of their state's new maps, the political cartographer spent many hours on the phone with the state legislature's redistricting chairmen. (Hofeller is careful to avoid leaving an e-mail trail. As his PowerPoint presentation cautions, "A journey to legal HELL starts with but a single misstatement! . . . Remember recent e-mail disasters!!!") While talking, Hofeller would expertly manipulate his computer's Maptitude software, a lightning-fast graphics system that processes neighborhood population data, including racial composition, so that a user can draw and redraw hypothetical district lines.

By July 2011, Hofeller had helped produce what a Democratic operative ruefully terms "exceptionally smart" maps—ones that, assuming they survive a lingering court challenge, may very well install a 10–3 GOP stronghold in place of the present 7–6 Democratic congressional majority.

Hofeller already knew North Carolina, the focal point of several landmark redistricting cases in which he'd testified, well. The Tar Heel State has a history of election discrimination and is therefore one of the jurisdictions covered by Section 5 of the Voting Rights Act, which requires that electoral maps be approved by either a federal court or the Justice Department. (Like all other states, North Carolina is also covered by Section 2, which forbids discriminatory practices more broadly.) Hofeller and the other Republican mapmakers therefore took particular care not to "retrogress" the racial makeup of the districts represented by the African-American Democrats G. K. Butterfield and Mel Watt—since doing so would have meant running afoul of the Voting Rights Act.

Instead, he reserved his chief mischief for the remaining districts. Hofeller and his cohort hoarded several of Raleigh's white precincts and moved them into the 2nd District, which had been held by Democrats for 108 of the previous 110 years, until a former intensive-care nurse named Renee Ellmers rode the Tea Party wave to an upset victory in 2010. The new drawings would give the neophyte Ellmers a safe Republican district to last at least at decade. Recognizing that North Carolina's many Democratic voters had to be put somewhere, the mapmakers shoveled as many as possible into the Democratic districts of Watt and of David Price, a former Duke professor who represented the liberal bastion of Chapel Hill. Most of those Democrats, however, were stripped from the districts of the moderate Democratic incumbents Mike McIntyre, Larry Kissell, and Brad Miller. In the Democrat Heath Shuler's 11th District, the mapmakers simply gouged out the progressive core, Asheville, and affixed it to the 10th, the state's most Republican district over the previous 60 years. The new maps have made quite an impact. Shuler and Miller have announced that they will not seek another term. McIntyre (whose house has now been drawn out of his own district) and Kissell are widely viewed as among the most imperiled Democrats facing reelection in November.

Progressive groups immediately filed suit challenging the North Carolina maps, contending that the state deliberately diluted minority voting power. Hofeller happens to be an old hand at redistricting litigation, and the maps will probably survive into the next decade. (Meanwhile, in a dazzling show of circular logic, Phil Berger, the top Republican state senator, recently refused to allow consideration of a redistricting-reform bill that he had supported back when his party was in the minority, citing the fact that North Carolina is "engaged in litigation on that issue.")

Still, legal battles have been the other major factor in diminishing the Republican Party's success. Given that blacks and Latinos tend to vote overwhelmingly Democratic, Republicans have often taken pains to maximize their control of the districts in a way that does not violate the terms of the Voting Rights Act. But the new census results have presented the GOP with a particularly confounding puzzle—one that lies at the center of this cycle's redistricting controversies. On the one hand, the biggest gains in U.S. population over the past decade have been in two Republican-controlled states: Florida, which thereby received two new congressional districts, and Texas, which was granted a whopping four.

But on the other hand, most of each state's new residents are African Americans and (especially) Hispanics. In Texas, the population has swelled by 4.3 million over the past decade. Of those new residents, 2.8 million are Hispanic and more than half a million are African American. While those groups grew at a rate of 42 percent and 22 percent, respectively, the growth in white Texans was a meager 4.2 percent. In other words: without the minority growth, Texas—now officially a majority-minority state—would not have received a single new district. The possibility that a GOP map-drawer would use all those historically Democratic-leaning transplants as a means of gaining Republican seats might strike a redistricting naïf as undemocratic.

And yet that's exactly what the Texas redistricting bosses did last year. Shrugging off the warnings of Tom Hofeller and other Washington Republicans, the Texans produced lavishly brazen maps that resulted in a net gain of four districts for Republicans and none for minority populations. The entirely predictable consequence is that the Texas maps have spent more than a year bouncing between three federal courts, including the Supreme Court. The legal uncertainty has had national ramifications. It meant, for example, postponing the Texas primary from March 6 until May 29, which cost Texas its role as a prominent player in the Super Tuesday presidential sweepstakes—a very lucky break for the eventual nominee, Mitt Romney, who likely would have lost the state to Newt Gingrich or Rick Santorum.

But the chaos produced by the overreach in Texas isn't anomalous. Rather, it is very much in keeping with the new winner-take-all culture of redistricting, an endeavor that has somehow managed to grow in both sophistication and crassness, like an ageless strain of cancer that inhabits a host body for so long that the two seem inseparable, even as the former quietly destroys the latter from the inside out.

How ingrained is the practice of politically motivated redistricting in America? So ingrained that it existed even before Congress did. Late in 1788, just after Virginia voted to ratify the Constitution and thereby join the Union, Patrick Henry persuaded his state's legislature to fashion the nascent 5th Congressional District in such a way as to force Henry's political enemy James Madison, of Montpelier, to run against the formidable James Monroe, of Highland. Madison prevailed and later went on to become America's principal author of the Bill of Rights as well as its fourth president. Serving as his second vice president was Elbridge Gerry, who as the governor of Massachusetts in 1812 had presided over a redrawing of the state map so blatant in its partisan manipulations that the curiously tailored shape of one Boston-area district resembled a salamander. The term *gerrymander* has been used ever since to describe the contorting of districts beyond all reason save political gain.

Though the constitutionally intended purpose of redistricting is to maintain proper apportionment of elected representatives, several states, for much of the 20th century, didn't bother to adjust their district boundaries at all. The result, in Texas for instance, was that a powerful rural legislator like House Speaker Sam Rayburn could represent some 200,000 voters, while in the adjacent Dallas district, Bruce Alger represented roughly 900,000. In 1962, the Supreme Court ruled that such malapportionment violated the Fourteenth Amendment's guarantee of equal protection under the law. One of the dissenters, Justice Felix Frankfurter, warned against judges' entering a "political thicket." The high court subsequently ignored him. In the 1980s, the Court took umbrage at the redistricting orchestrated by Georgia Democrats and their leader, state Representative Joe Mack Wilson, who flatly declared, "I don't want to draw nigger districts." A decade later, the Court argued that efforts to *boost* minority representation could also go too far, citing Mel Watt's North Carolina district, a wormy creature of such narrowness that, so it was said, a person driving down Interstate 85 with doors open on both sides could kill people in two districts. Justice Sandra Day O'Connor tsk-tsked that "appearances do matter," and the Supreme Court decreed in 1996 that even districts drawn so as to maximize minority representation should retain "compactness, contiguity and respect for political subdivisions."

O'Connor's admonition notwithstanding, as works of art, redistricting maps continue to evoke a crazed but symbolically rich dreamscape of yearnings, sentimentality, vendettas, and hyper-realism in American political life. Districts weave this way and that to include a Congress member's childhood school, a mother-in-law's residence, a wealthy donor's office, or, out of spite, an adversary's pet project. When touring Republican strongholds, Tom Hofeller enjoys showing audiences the contours of Georgia's 13th District, as proposed after the 2010 census, which he likens to "flat-cat roadkill." (The map that was ultimately approved is shaped more like a squirrel that hasn't yet been hit by a car.) This redistricting cycle's focus of wonderment, in Hofeller's view, is Maryland's splatter-art 3rd District, which reminds him of an "amoeba convention." He tends not to mention the gimpy-legged facsimile that is his own rendition of North Carolina's 4th District.

The byzantine trade of redistricting was long dominated by brainy eccentrics like Hofeller and his Democratic counterparts Mark Gersh and Michael Berman. But that began to change in the 1990s, when the availability of mapping software (such as Maptitude, RedAppl, and autoBound) and block-by-block census data for the whole country opened up the field to a waiting world of political geeks. The democratization of redistricting—made manifest last year in Virginia, which held a student competition, complete with cash prizes, to draw the best maps—is a lovely thing, perhaps. But as one redistricting veteran told me, "There's an old saying: Give a child a hammer, and the world becomes a nail. Give the chairman of a state redistricting committee a powerful enough computer and block-level census data, so that he suddenly discovers he can draw really weird and aggressive districts—and he will."

This amateur-hour dynamic presaged the Texas redistricting fiasco. My native state has a long heritage of bellicose gerrymandering, which began with pronouncedly racist maps drawn by Democrats more than half a century ago and continued with Tom DeLay's knee-capping of Democratic incumbents in his notorious mid-census redistricting in 2003. But no one ever accused the DeLay machine of being out of its depth. In 2011, by contrast, the individual principally responsible for drawing the state's congressional district maps, Ryan Downton, was a lawyer and co-owner of a medical-imaging firm. The seemingly random hiring of a relative novice like Downton (who was defeated in May 2012 as a Republican candidate for the state legislature) was in keeping with a willful ignorance embraced by the state legislature's two appointed redistricting chiefs, neither of whom had the slightest experience in this arcane field. (Downton says he was hired because of his litigation expertise, since so many redistricting cases end up in court.) As the veteran Texas Democratic redistricting strategist Matt Angle told me, "People who actually have an understanding of the Voting Rights Act—like Hofeller, who's 10 times more competent than the people who drew these maps—they wouldn't have been part of this."

According to one of the Texas Republicans intimately involved in the map-drawing project, "Tom [Hofeller] and [Republican National Committee counsel] Dale Oldham created an adversarial relationship with the leadership here in Texas. Incredibly brilliant people who tend to think they're right, and if you don't agree with them, they don't put much effort towards convincing you. And that rubbed raw with the leadership here in Texas."

Whether through personality conflicts or out of hubris, the Texas Republicans decided to do things their own way, with no guidance from Hofeller or other Washingtonians. When I asked Lynn Westmoreland, the House redistricting vice chair, to describe his role in the state's redistricting process, he replied in a weary voice, "Well, the Texas legislature basically told me, 'We're Texas, and we're gonna handle our maps.' You know, I'm just saying that when you have a population increase of 4 million, and the majority of that is minority, you'd better take that into consideration."

These statistical realities left the Republican-controlled state legislature and Governor Rick Perry with three choices when it came to redistricting. They could bow to the demographics, draw three or four new "minority-opportunity districts"—in which Latino and/or African American voters would have the opportunity to elect the candidate of their choice—and then set themselves to the task, as Governor George W. Bush once did, of appealing to the state's fastest-growing population. Or they could opt for the middle ground and create one or two such districts. Or, says Gerry Hebert, a lawyer who has handled numerous election and redistricting cases for Democrats, "they could use the redistricting process to cling to what power they have and hang on for as long as they can."

Earlier this year, I had a breakfast of waffles and fried chicken wings at the Poly Grill, a Fort Worth diner in the heart of a formerly Anglo east-side neighborhood named Polytechnic Heights, which, as a testament to the region's fluid demographics, is now thoroughly black and Hispanic. With me was Marc Veasey, a 41-year-old African-American Democrat and lifelong Fort Worth resident. Veasey is the community's representative in the state legislature and would like to be its U.S. congressman. Specifically, Veasey has been expecting one of Texas' four new districts to be placed here, because of the explosive population growth of blacks and Latinos in the area.

Many House Republicans, like the Texan and House Judiciary Committee Chairman Lamar Smith, reportedly agreed with Veasey that a new minority—opportunity district belonged here—though for different reasons. Failing to create such a district would mean that each of the half dozen—plus

Republican members of Congress in the Metroplex would have to absorb increasing numbers of minority voters. Several once-safe GOP districts might thereby become swing districts by the end of the decade. Better, as Smith and others saw it, to preserve the existing seats by funneling the minority population into a new district.

But the Texas map-drawers refused to create such a district in the area. Over breakfast, Veasey explained to me what that lack of minority representation meant. Presently, Polytechnic Heights—one of many minority enclaves in the Metroplex that DeLay's redistricters spread across five Republican districts, thereby "cracking" a potent voting bloc—falls in the district of Michael Burgess, a white Republican who last year told a local Tea Party group that he favors impeaching President Obama. "[Burgess] goes around saying 'I represent more African Americans than any other Republican in the entire U.S. Congress. Look at me, look at my outreach,'" Veasey said. "There's no way African Americans would ever have any influence in this district at all. His votes prove it. His rhetoric proves it."

In February, after court testimony in San Antonio and Washington, D.C., Veasey and his fellow Democrats prevailed in a suit charging the state of Texas with producing maps that discriminated against blacks and Hispanics. A three-judge panel ordered that the new 33rd District be drawn into Veasey's stomping grounds—and Veasey promptly entered the race. He won the primary, and in November he'll likely capture what will presumably be a safe Democratic seat.

While the San Antonio court awarded the 33rd District to the Democrats, it also left largely intact the state's drastic redrawing of the 27th District, a territory that includes Corpus Christi, the home of Congressman Blake Farenthold. In the 2010 election, despite being an Anglo Republican who does not speak Spanish in a district that's 74 percent Hispanic, Farenthold upset the longtime Democratic incumbent, Solomon Ortiz, by a margin of about 800 votes. "I won, which disproves the fact that all Hispanics vote Democrat," Farenthold told me. "I go back to my premise that most Hispanics, especially in south Texas, if given a test on the issues that would place you as Democrat or Republican, would fall into the Republican category."

In fact, Farenthold's opponent, Ortiz, received 86.6 percent of the Latino votes cast. But Hispanic turnout in the 27th was abysmal that year. The Tea Party—backed Farenthold garnered more than 80 percent of the non-Latino vote, which put him over the top.

Over freshly shucked oysters at a Corpus Christi restaurant one afternoon, I relayed to Farenthold the testimony of the state GOP's map-drawers: basically, they all acknowledged that Farenthold would have had a hard time being reelected in 2012 if they hadn't drawn him a friendlier map. District 27, which they obligingly constructed for him last year, sheds the border city of Brownsville, climbs up the coast and swallows portions of Ron Paul's existing district, then abruptly hooks westward into the deeply conservative Bastrop County. The new configuration resembles a Glock pistol held at a 45-degree angle. If Farenthold was so sure he had a Hispanic following, I asked him, then why hadn't he insisted on keeping his district as it was?

Farenthold, whom I find to be one of the more charmingly plainspoken members of Congress, laughed. "Listen," he said of the new map, "I'll take a 60-plus [percent] Republican district over a swing district any day. Duh!"

Given Congress's low standing, I wondered aloud to Farenthold whether allowing incumbents like him to escape the wrath of his constituents by installing him in a safer district wasn't thwarting democracy.

"I'm willing to run on my record in any district I live in," the freshman maintained. He pointed out that "at least 50 percent" of his new district would be composed of his present constituents. He added, "On a metaphysical level, sure, there's gonna be some politics in it. But elections have consequences. You elect a Republican legislature, you'll get more Republican-drawn districts. It works both ways."

I asked Farenthold if being in the new district would in any way change how he conducted himself. "The district I'm in now is a swing district," he said. "This [new] district is a much stronger Republican district. You say the same thing, but you use different words. Immigration would be an issue—you're probably not going to change your mind on your core immigration issues, but you'll be a little softer about how you talk about it in a swing district than in a harder-core Republican district."

During his last few years in the House, John Tanner of Tennessee pursued a lonely quest to interest his colleagues in a redistricting-reform bill. Tanner was a co-founder of the fiscally conservative Blue Dog Democrats, who were all but wiped out in 2010, the year Tanner himself decided to head for the sidelines. He had introduced his bill first in 2005, when the Republicans controlled the House, then in 2007 and again in 2009, when Democrats were in charge and Nancy Pelosi was the speaker. "She and Steny [Hoyer, then the majority leader,] said, 'That's a good idea, we'll take a look at it,'" he recalled with a smirk. "But the hard left and the hard right don't want it."

Tanner says that redistricting's impact has evolved over time, from simply creating safe seats for incumbents to creating rigid conservative and liberal districts, wherein the primary contests are a race to the extremes and the general elections are preordained. "When the [final] election [outcome] is [determined] in the party primary—which now it is, in all but less than 100 of the 435 seats—then a member comes [to Washington] politically crippled," the retired congressman told me. "Look, everyone knows we have a structural deficit, and the only way out of it is to raise revenues and cut entitlements. No one who's reasonable thinks otherwise. But what happens? The Democrats look over their left shoulder, and if someone suggests cutting a single clerk out of the Department of Agriculture, they go crazy. Republicans look over their right shoulder, and if someone proposes raising taxes on Donald Trump's income by $10, they say it'll be the end of the world. So these poor members come to Washington paralyzed, unable to do what they all know must be done to keep the country from going adrift, for fear that they'll get primaried.

"It's imposed a parliamentary model on a representative system," Tanner went on. "It makes sense for Democrats to vote one way and Republicans to vote another in a parliamentary system. It's irrational in a representative form of government. So what that's done is two things. First, it's made it virtually impossible to compromise. And second, as we've seen in this past decade, it's damn near abolished the ability and responsibility of Congress to hold the executive branch of the same party accountable. The Bush years, we were appropriating $100 billion at a time for the Iraq War with no hearings, for fear that [those would] embarrass the administration. Hell yeah, that's due to redistricting! The Republicans in Congress and the Bush administration became part of the same team. We're totally abdicating our responsibility of checks and balances.

"Tanner's bill (which fellow Blue Dogs Heath Shuler and Jim Cooper reintroduced last year, to similar non-effect) would have established national standards for redistricting and shifted the map-drawing duties from state legislatures to bi-partisan commissions. Such commissions already exist in a handful of states, while Iowa relies on nonpartisan map-drawers whose end product is then voted on by the state legislature. Tom Hofeller points to the California citizens' commission as evidence that politics will inevitably find its way back into the process. "There's no such thing as nonpartisan," he told me.

Perhaps unsurprisingly, Hofeller insists that the dire consequences of his vocation are overblown. "We've had gerrymandering all along, so there's no proof that that's the cause of all the polarization," he told me. "I'm here to tell you that there are two other major factors that are much, much more prevalent than redistricting. One is the 24-hours-a-day, 7-days-a-week news media, where you only get noticed if you're extreme. And the other is McCain-Feingold, which pushed a great deal of money to the extremes." In limiting the size of financial contributions to national parties, the campaign finance-reform law encouraged donors to funnel their cash to opaque outside groups. (See James Bennet's cover story on this subject.)

"That's part of the problem," Tanner conceded when I asked him about the super-PAC ads flooding the airwaves. "But you can trace how the members got here back to gerrymandering. I don't give a damn how much money you spend. These guys are gonna be responsive to the people that elected them, to avoid a party primary. And so they come here to represent their political party, not their district or their country. That attitude has infected the Senate, too. Look at Orrin Hatch," he said, referring to the veteran Utah senator who fought off a primary challenge from an ultraconservative. "Now you'd think he was an original member of the Tea Party. It makes you sick to see him grovel."

Some redistricting experts argue that Americans have polarized themselves, by gravitating toward homogenous communities, a demographic trend observed in Bill Bishop and Robert Cushing's 2008 book, *The Big Sort*. But, says one Texas Republican map-drawer, "redistricting has amplified the Big Sort by creating safe Republican and safe Democratic districts. Look at Texas. If you count [Blake Farenthold's] 27th as the result of a fluke election, the [racially polarized West Texas] 23rd is the only swing district in the state." In this sense, the only difference that the new maps will make is that instead of one swing district out of 32, there will now be one out of 36. As to what this portends, former Texas Congressman Martin Frost, a Democrat, told me, "I won't mention anyone by name, but I know certain Republicans in the Texas delegation who would be inclined to be more moderate, if they didn't have to fear a primary challenge."

One Texas Republican who dipped his toe in the moderate waters, by voting for last summer's debt-ceiling deal, was Congressman Michael Burgess. Tea Partiers lambasted him to his face, saying, "You caved." An analysis by *National Journal* found that politicians like Burgess were the exception—that most House members who voted to raise the debt ceiling were from swing districts, while "the further a member's district is from the political center, the more likely it is that he or she opposed the compromise."

We know what happened after that whole debacle: the Dow Jones plummeted, Standard & Poor's downgraded America's credit rating, and Congress's approval rating sank to an unprecedented low of 9 percent. That intensity of public disgust has hardly abated, and it is felt across the political spectrum:

according to an NBC/*Wall Street Journal* poll released this past January, at least 56 percent of all liberals, moderates, and conservatives would like to see everyone in the legislative branch fired this November.

If this is so, then perhaps Tom Hofeller is right. Perhaps redistricting reform is unnecessary. Perhaps instead the system is self-correcting: the extremists whom the map-drawers have helped to create will be judged as obstructionists unworthy of their safe seats and, by means of electoral laxative, flushed out of the body politic. Thus cleansed, America can then slowly return to what James Madison called "this propensity of mankind to fall into mutual animosities." When that happens, we know who will be there to draw the battle lines.

NO, GERRYMANDERING IS NOT DESTROYING DEMOCRACY

Cook Political Report suggests there are fewer competitive races than at any time in recent history. Which prompted Gawker to rail against gerrymandering. It's not quite that simple. The problem may be with the voters as much as the elected officials.

PHILIP BUMP

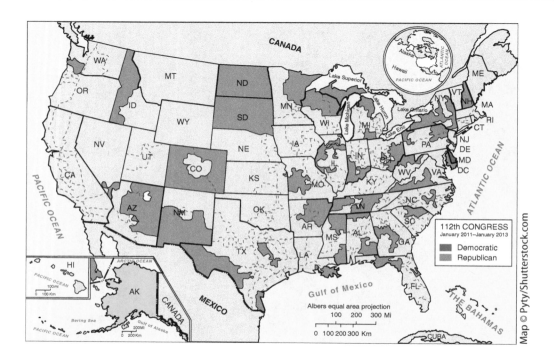

Map © Pyty/Shutterstock.com

As deeply unpopular as Congress is, most members of the House of Representatives who stood for re-election last year won their races—some 91 percent of the 390 people who wanted to return to the body. The *Wall Street Journal*, by way of the non-partisan Cook Political Report, suggested Monday that there are fewer competitive House seats than at any time in recent history. Which prompted Gawker's Hamilton Nolan to rail against gerrymandering, lamenting that "the shit that we tolerate in this country boggles the mind." As is often the case, however, it's not quite that simple. The problem may lie with the voters as much as the elected officials.

Yes, elected officials—and, moreover, political parties—seek to have congressional districts drawn in a way that minimizes the number of contested races every two years. It's in both parties' self-interest to do so, if not the voters': fewer competitive races mean less fundraising and staff needs. And Cook, which provides regularly-updated analysis of the competitiveness of each House race sees fewer competitive races in 2014 than a decade ago. The *Journal*:

Of 435 districts in the Republican-controlled House, the nonpartisan Cook Political Report rates only 90 as competitive, meaning those seats have a partisan rating that falls within five points of the national average. The rating measures how each district votes relative to how the country as a whole voted in the most recent presidential election.

The number of competitive districts as at its lowest since Cook first started the partisanship rating in the 1998 election cycle. That year, it rated 164 seats—more than one-third of the House—as "swing" seats that could back either party.

That was a high for the time period, mind you. As a *Journal* graphic indicates, by 2002, that figure was 111. By 2012, it had only dropped to 99.

It's worth noting that these are just projections. Last year, Cook ranked only 29 races as "toss-ups," by the time the election rolled around. Of those 29, just over half actually were toss-ups, races that were settled within a margin of five percentage points. (We'll note that this percentage marker isn't how Cook evaluates a race's closeness. It evaluates a range of data for its analysis.) Thirty races total— nearly twice as many as those rated "toss-ups"—ended up in that range.

(What's particularly interesting, though, is that Democrats did *much* better in those toss-up races than did Republicans. Of the 29 seats that Cook labelled as toss-ups, Democrats won 20, by an average margin of 5.69 percent. Republicans won nine, by an average margin of 4.9 percent.)

For the sake of comparison, we looked at how the House elections broke down in 1960. That year, there were more close races—45 in total. But there were also a staggering number of members of Congress who ran unopposed. Seventy-two—about 17 percent of Congress—saw no opposition at all. Last year? Two did. The average margin of victory in 2012 was just over 30 percent. In 1960, it was 23.8 percent—if you exclude the candidates that ran unopposed. If you grant them 100 percent of the vote—they did run unopposed, after all—the 1960 margin shoots up to 36.4 percent.

The point being: Even before five decades of gerrymandered congressional districts, congressional races weren't as close as Cook might suggest.

In addition to gerrymandered districts, the *Journal* cites a rationale for the declining number of close races.

> Another factor in the declining number of competitive districts is that voters are dividing themselves geographically more than they did 10 or 20 years ago, political observers say. Americans are now more likely to live in communities where their neighbors share their political views. That steady, decades-long shift produces more-partisan congressional seats.

That is mirrored by a study completed after last year's election, by Eric McGhee of The Monkey Cage. After the election, a common complaint among Democrats, echoing Nolan's, was that Democrats won a majority of votes but a minority of seats. Which is true: 48.7 percent of the national House vote was Democratic, versus 47.6 for Republicans.

So McGhee modeled the 2012 race using the previous Congress' districts. (Redistricting generally occurs after each Census, so 2012 used new boundaries nationally.)

Democrats do gain more seats under this simulation—seven more total—but fall far short of matching their predicted vote share. The point should be clear: even under the most generous assumptions, redistricting explains less than half the gap between vote share and seat share this election cycle.

McGhee suggested that Democrats fare worse in part because of geography. "Democrats also do worse because they are more concentrated in urban areas," he wrote. "They 'waste' votes on huge margins there, when the party could put many of those votes to better use in marginal seats." In other words, Democrats move to cities and overwhelmingly vote for Democrats. If Democrats want to re-take the House, they should move to Wyoming.

Nolan raises another idea: take political parties out of the redistricting process.

> [H]ave districts drawn by a nonpartisan committee, whose goal is to make them as com-pact and straightforward as possible and to have them comprise existing communities, so that a single representative can, theoretically, represent a single set of community interests. Alternately, have them drawn by a fucking computer program that knows how to draw rectangles.

California passed a resolution a few years ago that allowed them to do exactly that. The bipartisan California Citizens Redistricting Commission developed the state's new Congressional boundaries, a fucking computer program being deemed less preferable. And the result? Four of the state's 53 congressional seats were in the five percentage-point range. The average margin of victory was about 28 points—slightly below the national average.

STATE POLITICS AND PRESIDENTIAL VOTING, 1988–2000

JAMES G. GIMPEL AND JASON E. SCHUKNECHT

We started with the noncontroversial idea that states differ from one another in their political identities and that these differences are the result of the federal structure of American government (chap. 1). Presidential elections and the domination of two national parties have gone a long way toward watering down the effects of federal structure on political diversity across states and localities. The political institutions that force everyone to live with the same two major parties impose order on what might otherwise be political chaos. The focus of campaign media coverage through nightly network news shows is not customized to individual locales. But serious presidential candidates realize that a one-size-fits-all strategy does not work, preferring to tailor their message according to the prevailing winds at local campaign stops. . ..

Accounting for the myriad ways in which states and localities differ is a more complicated task. Local political orientations will vary mainly for compositional but also for contextual reasons (as discussed in chap. 1). Composition refers to the fact that constituencies are simply different from one locale to the next: in one state African Americans are a consequential voting bloc, in another they are not. Contextual explanations can vary according to the aspects of place location that are emphasized, but in recent years scholars have understood context mainly in terms of local communication and socialization patterns that disrupt or otherwise alter the usually smooth linkage between compositional traits and political attitudes and behavior.

For example, two blue-collar workers in the same industry—one from suburban Pittsburgh, the other from suburban Nashville—may wind up voting differently. The Pennsylvania worker's economic interest guides his vote, and the psychological connection between occupation and vote is upheld by a social setting that never questions this long-standing identification—the vote choice may never be open to discussion, and it is certainly never challenged. The Tennessee worker, though, traffics among those who think differently about politics and confronts regular challenges to the notion that workers in his industry should vote the way they do in Pennsylvania. . .. The result: in Tennessee, occupation (the compositional trait) fails to account for much of a voter's political attitudes or behavior, while in Pennsylvania it does. In Tennessee, we need an additional variable to explain voting that may not be necessary in Pennsylvania, namely, some measure of the voter's social setting (the context). In Pennsylvania, though, the voter's composition and setting are identical, and the context variable explains no more than what we captured by including the voter's occupation. This does not mean that context effects are absent in the Pennsylvania voter's neighborhood, but that they play a silent and congruent role (a collinear one, in statistics parlance), rather than an incongruent and vocal one.

In this and subsequent chapters, we present information showing that states share some important similarities but are also remarkably variable in the way their electorates divide when presented with the same candidates. While regions within states are sometimes easily identifiable, in many cases the political distinctiveness of substate sections disappears once we control for the compositional characteristics that make these regions unique. Not every region has a discernible impact on political attitudes independent of its basic population composition. . ... In addition, the foundations for political regionalism differ from state to state. What makes Chicago stand out from the rest of Illinois is not necessarily the same thing that makes Houston a unique political setting within Texas. What this means is that regionalism within states is not easily reducible to one or two population characteristics that are common to all states—a fact that greatly complicates the task of electioneering.

In the next few pages, we set several states side by side in an examination of presidential voting between 1988 and 2000. Comparing states' presidential votes makes sense because each state is confronting the same candidate choices, whereas in congressional and gubernatorial elections, different alternatives are present in each state. If state electorates choose differently when confronted by candidates running for national office, then they are likely to differ even more when they turn to consider their local candidates. By *choose differently* we mean that electorates are dissimilar in the extent to which basic political traits and characteristics of populations cue the vote. These political variables typically include items pollsters care a lot about and political scientists have identified as influences on decision making. Various theories of voting have suggested that among the predictors of candidate support are party identification and political ideology, along with traits that are associated with group identities, such as race, income, sex, age, and religious affiliation. . ...

Although we do not have comparable survey data on all twelve of the states we cover in chapters 3 through 14, we do present models of presidential vote choice for seven of them in the 1988–96 elections and all twelve in the 2000 presidential race. The appendix at the end of this chapter presents complete results for these models. Our data source is the Voter Research and Surveys and Voter News Service network-sponsored exit polls conducted on election day of each year. These polls are conducted only among voters as they leave the polling booth at randomly selected locations within each state. Because the VRS/VNS surveys are very short polls, containing few questions, we are unable to use them to estimate the impact of every theoretically relevant influence on presidential voting, but we have made our model as complex as the data allow.

Another drawback of these exit polls is that measures are not as elaborate as in university-sponsored surveys such as the *American National Election Studies*. Partisan identification, for instance, is measured on a simple 3-point scale that exaggerates the presence of independent voters in the electorate and does not capture the variable strength of voters' partisan commitments. A more complex 7-point scale would more accurately gauge the extent to which partisanship predicts vote choice (Green and Schickler 1993). Still, the 3-point scale is not far off the mark. In comparing its performance to the more reliable 7-point scale, Green and Schickler found that the simpler scale was a slightly weaker predictor of vote choice ($r = .653$, compared with $r = .670$ for the 7-point scale) (524). Researchers inevitably make compromises in empirical inquiries based on data availability. The main advantage of the exit polls is that they represent states, whereas national polls do not. We traded a survey that drew on a sample representing state electorates, but had slightly more error-prone instrumentation, for alternatives that had optimal instrumentation but could say nothing about state electorates.

Our model of vote choice is summarized in Figure 3.1. We estimate the influence of a number of key variables on the presidential vote to determine whether differences across states are real or trivial. Generally speaking we draw the following hypotheses from the extensive voting behavior literature: Democratic support will be (1) higher among self-identified Democrats than among self-identified Republicans; (2) higher among liberals than among moderates and conservatives; (3) higher among blacks and Latinos than among non-Hispanic white voters; (4) higher among women than men; and (5) higher among low-income voters than among the wealthy. From previous research, we would also have good reasons for suspecting that (6) elderly voters will be more likely to support Democrats than younger voters and (7) Democratic support will be greater among Jewish voters than among Catholics and Protestants.

Voting in the 1988–1996 Presidential Elections

We have insisted that we are likely to find important differences across states in the extent to which the preceding hypotheses hold. What are these? The most obvious prediction would be about the generally conservative tone of the electorate in states such as Texas, Florida, and Georgia. In these states, we expect to find less Democratic support among self-identified conservatives and Republican voters than we might in other states. Consistent with the findings of national polls, it is also reasonable to expect less Democratic support among women, lower-income voters, and Jews. In states such as New York and Maryland, with strong politically liberal traditions, we might find the least support for Republicans among women, Jews, the poor, blacks, and Latinos, groups typically given to Democratic voting

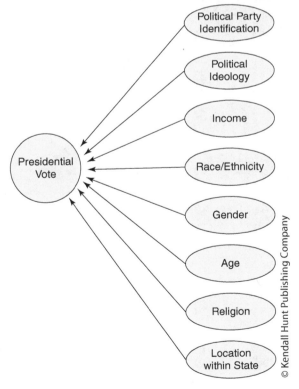

Figure 3.1 A model of the presidential vote

according to national election studies. In states with moderate political traditions, such as Illinois and Michigan, we might expect the traditional hypotheses based on national polls to hold up well.

Results from our tests of these long-standing hypotheses about voting behavior appear in Table 3.1. The cell entries in this table show the percentage of each group listed on the far left column that supported the Democratic candidate in the 1988–96 presidential elections controlling for all of the other variables listed in the table. The difference in support between each group listed (e.g., Republican identifiers vs. Other identifiers) is also presented to gauge the total effect each indicator had on increasing the percentage of support for the Democrat. For example, we can see from the table that in California, about 46 percent of non-Democrats voted for Democratic presidential candidates, and 71 percent of Democrats voted for Democratic presidential candidates. The difference is 25 points, indicating the magnitude by which Democrats favor Democratic presidential candidates compared with non-Democrats. The percentage of Democratic identifiers declaring that they voted for Democratic presidential candidates does vary, ranging from a high of 72 percent in Michigan to a low of 60 percent in Georgia and Florida. In fact, Democratic loyalty to Democratic candidates is lowest in the three Southern states shown: Georgia, Texas, and Florida (Table 3.1).

Republican support for Democratic presidential candidates also varies widely from state to state. The results in Table 3.1 show that over 40 percent of New York and California Republicans voted

Table 3.1 Estimated Percentage of Each Group Voting Democratic, 1988–96, by State							
Variable and State	**CA**	**FL**	**GA**	**IL**	**MI**	**NY**	**TX**
Non-Democrat	46	38	35	43	37	45	33
Democrat	71	60	60	68	72	70	64
Difference	25	22	25	25	35	25	31
Non-Republican	65	55	52	61	58	61	52
Republican	41	31	29	32	33	41	30
Difference	24	24	23	29	25	20	22
Liberal	71	64	58	67	62	70	59
Conservative	43	35	36	40	40	41	37
Difference	28	29	22	27	22	29	22
Poor	59	53	47	54	53	55	50
Wealthy	55	40	43	51	46	55	41
Difference	4	13	4	3	7	0	9
Nonblack	55	44	39	50	49	53	43
Black	72	71	71	75	64	74	66
Difference	17	27	32	25	15	21	23
Non-Hispanic	56	47	45	52	50	55	45
Hispanic	61	49	60	69	47	65	54
Difference	5	2	15	17	3	10	9
Men	55	44	45	50	46	49	42
Women	58	49	45	53	52	57	47
Difference	3	5	0	3	6	8	5

Variable and State	CA	FL	GA	IL	MI	NY	TX
Age 18–29	56	41	43	51	48	50	44
Over age 60	58	51	47	53	52	58	47
Difference	2	10	4	2	4	8	3
Non-Catholic	58	48	45	53	51	58	46
Catholic	55	46	42	52	49	51	46
Difference	3	2	3	1	2	7	0
Non-Jewish	57	46	45	52	50	54	46
Jewish	65	62	57	66	63	60	52
Difference	9	16	12	14	13	6	6
Non-Protestant	58	49	46	53	50	56	47
Protestant	53	45	44	52	51	50	44
Difference	5	4	2	1	1	6	3
Outside region A[a]	58	47	45	52	49	53	46
Inside region A	54	51	47	53	64	58	47
Difference	4	4	2	1	15	5	1
Outside region B[a]	57	47	44	53	48	53	46
Inside region B	58	47	48	52	55	68	47
Difference	1	0	4	1	7	5	1
Outside region C[a]	56	48	44	52	49	54	45
Inside region C	61	46	47	53	54	60	50
Difference	5	2	3	1	5	6	5
Outside region D[a]	57	47	–	–	49	55	45
Inside region D	56	48			55	53	47
Difference	1	1			6	2	2
Election year 1988	59	48	45	53	52	55	48
Election year 1992	50	46	45	52	47	54	42
Difference	9	2	0	1	5	1	6
Election year 1988	57	46	44	52	50	54	45
Election year 1996	57	52	47	53	51	57	48
Difference	0	6	3	1	1	3	3

SOURCE: ICPSR, Voter Research and Surveys and Voter News Service, *Election Day Exit Polls* 1988, 1992, 1996.

NOTE: Cell entries show the estimated percentage of each group voting Democratic in the pooled 1988–96 presidential elections and the difference in Democratic support between the groups listed in each row computed from multivariate probit models (table A2.1) with the remaining independent variables held constant at their sample means. Differences reported are absolute values.

[a]Regions are coded as follows:
CA: A = Southern California; B = Los Angeles city; C = Bay Area; D = Central CA.
FL: A = Miami; B = South Florida; C = North Florida; D = Tampa.
GA: A = Central; B = Atlanta; C = North.
IL: A = Chicago; B = Chicago suburbs; C = South.
MI: A = Detroit; B = Oakland County and Detroit suburbs; C = University Belt; D = Southwest MI.
NY: A = Long Island; B = New York City; C = Upstate Urban; D = Rural NY.
TX: A = East TX; B = Dallas; C = Houston; D = South.

for the Democratic candidate, compared with only 29 percent of Georgia Republicans. Ideological polarization—the difference between liberal and conservative support for Democratic candidates—ranged from a high of 29 points (Florida) to a low of 22 (Texas, Georgia, and Michigan). Those identifying themselves as conservatives were most likely to vote for Democrats in New York and California and least likely to vote for Democrats in the three Southern states.

Testing for differences in the political preferences of rich and poor people is important because it shows where economic cleavages may exist independent of political party identification, ideology, and related variables such as race. Our results show that class cleavages are present in some states and absent in others. The biggest difference between wealthy and poor voters was in Florida. The difference between wealthy and poor voters in New York and Illinois, on the other hand, was negligible. Wealthy and poor voters both gave majorities of their support to Democratic candidates in California, New York, and Illinois.

Race-based voting is evaluated by examining the differences between black and nonblack voters, and Hispanic and non-Hispanic voters (Table 3.1). Extremely high percentages of black voters support Democratic candidates, but there was surprising variation too. Black voters were least supportive of Bill Clinton and Michael Dukakis in Texas and most supportive of these Democrats in Illinois and New York. Hispanic voters were least supportive of the Democrats in Florida and Michigan and most supportive of Democrats in California, Illinois, and New York. Democratic support among Illinois Hispanics (at 69 percent) was much higher than among Florida Hispanics (at 49 percent).

The gender gap refers to the difference in support for a candidate or policy position that exists between men and women. When we consider the gap in support for Democratic presidential candidates in 1988 through 1996, we see that the differences are not vast—ranging from 0 to 8 points. The gap was widest in New York, but there was no gender gap in Georgia, and it was negligible in Illinois, once we controlled for other variables that influenced vote choice.

Age differences are important because they signal intergenerational change. In the table we compare the oldest age cohort (those over age 60) to the youngest (those between 18 and 29). Ten points separated the oldest from the youngest age cohorts in Florida, with the elderly being far more supportive of Democratic candidates. A similar generation gap existed in New York. In none of these states did we find the older voters to be more Republican than the younger voters, although in several states, such as California, Illinois, Texas, and Michigan, the difference between the two was too small to be statistically different from zero.

In the past, religion has been an influential predictor of political behavior. The importance of religious cleavages in the American electorate has faded. Catholics were once far more Democratic than they are now, at the beginning of the new century, and Protestants far more Republican. The generalization that Jews have been found to be more liberal and Democratic than non-Jews probably still held through the 2000 election. In fact we found that Jews are more Democratic than non-Jews, but there was considerable geographic variation in the extent to which Jews were loyal to Democratic candidates. The Jewish vote was solidly Democratic in California, Illinois, Michigan, and New York, as compared to only an estimated 52 percent in Texas and 57 percent in Georgia. Moreover, in New York, the gap between Jewish and non-Jewish support for Democrats was only 6 points, suggesting weaker cleavage along this dimension than exists in many other states.

By the 1980s, Catholics were no longer to be counted among the Democratic faithful in every state. Catholics were slightly less likely than non-Catholics to vote Democratic in all of the states but Texas (Table 3.1). The gap in support between Catholics and non-Catholics was highest in New York. Those declaring themselves to be generic Protestants were somewhat less likely to vote Democratic than non-Protestants, but the difference was not great given the heterogeneity of Protestant denominations and belief systems. The widest gap was in New York, where Protestants were 6 points less likely to vote Democratic than those not so affiliated.

As a final addition to our models, we included the impact of substate regions on citizens' vote choices. The substate regions defined in the VRS/VNS exit polls do not always correspond to the true economic and political regions within each state, nor do they correspond to our coming discussions of political geography in chapters 3 through 14. It is likely that context is most relevant at a more precise level of aggregation than the expansive regions given to us in these polls. . ... But we can examine whether any of these regions made a difference to vote choice, once the main individual-level ingredients of voting models have been included. Is it possible that there are contextual effects once partisanship, ideology, race, income, gender, and age have been addressed?

For the most part, Table 3.1 reveals that these regional effects on Democratic voting in the 1988–96 elections are small, but for a very important reason relating to the compositional explanation for geographic differences. Regions, counties, and neighborhoods take on their character largely because of the social, economic, and political characteristics of the people that reside within them. Often there is no distinctive source of regionalism that can be isolated as a source of conflict apart from other attributes of voters. . ... In our regression model, we have taken account of the survey respondents' most important political characteristics explicitly. In other words, the region of residence describes very little about the voter's politically relevant identity that is not already captured by their race, partisanship, political ideology, income, and religion. The inclusion of these other variables left very little for region or context to explain (King 1996).

Nevertheless, there are exceptions in several states, including Michigan, California, and New York, where there are apparent contextual effects associated with living in Detroit, the San Francisco Bay area, and New York City. A few other broad geographic areas appeared to impose a distinct contextual imprint, including Long Island, the Detroit suburbs, southwestern Michigan, Atlanta, Houston, and southern California. Places with no distinct regional identity in these presidential elections included south and east Texas, all of Florida except Miami, southern Illinois, the Chicago suburbs, and New York's upstate urban and rural areas. Clearly these places may be politically unique from other substate regions, but the reason for this was captured by other traits. Once these variables were accounted for, the distinctiveness of the region faded. Interestingly, Chicago also did not stand out from the rest of Illinois in its support for Democratic presidential candidates, once race, partisanship, and related variables were included in the model. Apparently, Los Angeles's politically unique character was captured by other political variables, as it did not stand out in relief against the rest of California in our multivariate analysis.

Voting in the 2000 Presidential Election

The Voter News Service election day exit polls in the 2000 election used different regional categories in Illinois, Georgia, and Michigan than were used in the previous three elections. Table 3.2 presents results similar to those of Table 3.1, only for Democratic voting in the 2000 election for all twelve states. Region codes for several other states not included in Table 3.1 were also altered for the 2000 poll. Across these states, there are about a dozen regions that stand out as having an independent impact on vote choice even after the most obvious individual-level causes of voting have been taken into account. We find, for example, that several large cities voted decisively for Albert Gore for reasons other than just the partisanship, ideology, race, income, and related traits of their constituents (see Table 3.2). These included Denver, Chicago, Detroit, Minneapolis, and Portland. Houston area voters were about 10 percent more likely to vote for George W. Bush than those from other parts of Texas. And south Texas, north Florida, and central California all stand out as political regions where contextual effects may be creating a distinctive politics. As in Table 3.1, the effects of region are not usually very large, but some are as big as 9 or 10 percent, typically exceeding the effects of age and gender, and equaling the effect of income.

There are two ways of looking at these intriguing results. First, if we were to insist on the compositional route to explanation, it is possible that if we specified additional individual attributes, the uniqueness of the regions we have just mentioned would disappear. Perhaps if we were to control for the respondents' occupation or employment status (variables that were not included on the VNS survey), region would have no separate impact. But a second possibility is that at least some of these broadly defined regions do exhibit a real context effect on political behavior, independent of voter characteristics. Perhaps this is where we must develop explanations rooted in unique local institutional arrangements (church, school, labor unions, kinshipties) that disrupt lines of communication that would otherwise bring the region into conformity with other places. Or these local arrangements may create unusual networks of communication that make the area distinct. Alternatively, this may be the place where "political culture" explanations come into play. To us, though, the superior alternative to political culture explanations is to investigate the collection of socialization experiences unique to individual locales, examining why certain places create political biases that are not explained simply by compositional characteristics.

Similarities and Differences across States

As we compare the data in tables 3.1 and 3.2 across states, we find that not all of the differences were statistically significant, but the larger ones are. Let us now take note of some of the more obvious differences across settings for some of the same population subgroups. Florida and Georgia are very similar in their political behavior, but Michigan and Florida are worlds apart. Illinois and Texas differ considerably, while California and New York share some electoral characteristics.

Hispanics in Texas and Florida were far less likely to vote for Democrats than Hispanics in Illinois, New York, or California. Why is this the case? The answer probably relates to the ancestry and nationality of the Latino population—that is, an unspecified compositional variable. Cubans are drawn to the Republican party in Florida, and so too are many of the native-born Hispanics in Texas. Illinois and New York, by contrast, have a larger Puerto Rican population, and these voters have long-standing ties to the Democratic party. In California, the Hispanic population is predominantly Mexican and more supportive of issue positions consonant with the Democratic party platform, such as college admissions quotas and spending on public assistance. . . . Alternatively, Hispanics in Texas may not think of themselves as a cohesive group sharing a collective sense of political grievance, whereas Latinos in California and Illinois do. . ... From the contextual standpoint, some of these political and policy differences may be traceable to the fact that Latinos in California and Illinois

Table 3.2 Estimated Percentage of Each Group Voting Democratic, November 2000, by State

Variable and State	CA	CO	CT	FL	GA	IL	MD	MI	MN	NY	OR	TX
Non-Democrat	40	35	47	43	42	46	47	45	37	47	35	40
Democrat	73	65	70	67	64	74	73	71	60	76	66	60
Difference	33	30	23	24	22	28	26	26	23	29	31	20
Non-Republican	62	57	63	62	60	63	65	63	57	65	56	55
Republican	37	19	31	33	34	37	44	35	17	44	26	32
Difference	25	38	32	29	26	26	21	28	60	21	30	23
Liberal	65	54	70	63	64	69	72	69	60	69	58	58
Conservative	44	39	37	43	42	41	47	41	31	47	36	43
Difference	21	15	33	20	22	25	25	28	29	22	22	15
Poor	56	45	60	55	52	51	58	52	46	56	44	54
Wealthy	53	50	52	50	52	61	61	56	48	61	49	45
Difference	3	5	8	5	0	10	3	4	2	5	5	9
Nonblack	53	47	54	49	44	55	53	53	46	57	46	39
Black	67	57	73	76	71	73	78	67	57	74	66	78
Difference	14	10	19	27	67	18	25	14	11	17	20	39
Non-Hispanic	53	46	54	53	52	52	60	54	47	58	60	57
Hispanic	59	51	64	51	50	57	67	53	45	68	46	48
Difference	6	5	10	2	2	5	7	1	2	10	14	9
Men	52	45	51	52	52	54	58	52	47	56	43	48
Women	57	49	58	53	52	59	61	57	47	61	49	52
Difference	5	4	7	1	0	5	3	5	0	5	6	4
Age 18–29	51	47	56	53	52	56	56	55	45	57	44	49
Over age 60	57	46	54	52	52	57	64	53	49	60	8	52
Difference	6	1	2	1	0	1	8	2	4	3	4	3
Non-Catholic	54	45	53	53	52	57	59	54	48	58	47	50
Catholic	56	52	57	52	54	56	61	54	45	59	45	50
Difference	2	7	4	1	2	1	2	0	3	1	2	0
Non-Jewish	54	47	54	52	52	56	59	54	46	57	46	50
Jewish	66	40	68	75	70	70	72	75	64	71	59	56
Difference	12	7	14	23	18	14	13	21	18	14	13	6
Non-Protestant	55	47	54	53	52	58	59	54	46	59	47	51
Protestant	53	49	57	51	53	53	62	55	47	57	46	49
Difference	2	2	3	2	1	5	3	1	1	2	1	2
Outside region A[a]	56	43	54	52	52	55	59	53	44	58	44	50
Inside region A	52	54	57	53	53	64	69	63	51	60	54	52
Difference	4	11	3	1	1	9	10	10	7	2	10	2
Outside region B[a]	54	44	52	53	52	55	59	54	46	58	46	50
Inside region B	56	54	59	50	54	61	61	57	48	62	46	53
Difference	2	10	7	3	2	6	2	3	2	4	0	3

(Continued)

Table 3.2 Estimated Percentage of Each Group Voting Democratic, November 2000, by State (Continued)												
Outside region Cᵃ	54	47	53	55	53	58	59	52	46	59	47	49
Inside region C	56	47	60	47	49	51	62	60	49	58	44	59
Difference	2	0	7	8	4	7	3	8	3	1	3	10
Outside region Dᵃ	56			53		58		54		59		47
Inside region D	49	–	–	51	–	52	–	56	–	56	–	55
Difference	7			2		6		2		3		8

SOURCE: ICPSR, Voter News Service, *Election Day Exit Polls* 2000.

NOTE: Cell entries show the estimated percentage of each group voting Democratic in the 2000 presidential election and the difference in Democratic support between the groups listed in each row computed from multivariate probit models (table A2.2) with the remaining independent variables held constant at their sample means.

ᵃRegions are coded as follows:
CA: A = Southern California; B = Los Angeles city; C = Bay Area; D = Central CA.
CO: A = Denver/Boulder; B = Jefferson and Arapahoe County Suburbs; C = Mountains.
CT: A = Large Cities; B = CT Valley; C = NY Suburbs.
FL: A = Miami; B = South Florida; C = North Florida; D = Tampa.
GA: A = Central; B = Atlanta; C = North.
IL: A = Chicago; B = Cook County; C = Collar; D = South.
MD: A = Baltimore city; B = Baltimore suburbs; C = Washington suburbs.
MI: A = Detroit; B = Oakland County and Detroit suburbs; C = University Belt; D = Southwest MI.
MN: A = Minneapolis; B = Metro area; C = Rural Democrats.
NY: A = Long Island; B = New York City; C = Upstate Urban; D = Rural NY.
OR: A = Portland; B = Coast; C = Southern OR.
TX: A = East TX; B = Dallas; C = Houston; D = South.

are an overwhelmingly urban constituency, principally concentrated in each state's largest cities in highly segregated neighborhoods, whereas the Hispanic population in Texas is more evenly dispersed in smaller cities and rural areas where it comes into more regular contact with Anglo Texans.

In the 2000 presidential race, ideological polarization between liberals and conservatives was greater in Connecticut, Illinois, Michigan, and Minnesota than it was in Georgia, Colorado, or Texas (see Table 3.2). This variability suggests that ideology does not do the same work in all states. Contextual and compositional explanations may account for these differences. Ideological polarization reflects the diversity of the populations in these states. . .. The extent of ideological extremism is caused by the mobilization of competing biases within communities. Bias is mobilized, in part, by interest groups, and interest group activity is more intense in more diverse states than in more homogeneous ones. . .. Among the states where interest groups are the most prevalent are California and Florida.

Rival and competing interests will also be highly mobilized in states that are key political battlegrounds in presidential elections. California, Florida, and Illinois are among the most populous, and together they cast over 100 electoral votes. Campaign politics is carried out with unusual intensity in these states given their status as prizes in the presidential sweepstakes. The intensity of campaign politics contributes directly to the ideological polarization of their electorates on election day. Georgia is an important state casting 13 electoral votes, but it isn't nearly as important as these others. The presidential contenders cannot ignore it entirely, but it is usually not a major target, either.

Race and ideology differed considerably across states in the manner in which they acted to cue votes on election day, but partisanship did as well. Morris Fiorina has pointed out that partisanship changes over time, according to conditions such as international tension, the domestic economic situation, and personal unemployment, as well as in response to the candidates who are running (1981). It is equally plausible that partisanship will vary from place to place, and across groups that claim to be affiliated with each party. . ... In Georgia, an estimated 29 percent of Republicans voted for Democratic candidates in the 1988–96 presidential elections, compared with an estimated 41 percent in California and New York (see Table 3.1). (A closer inspection reveals that it was Bill Clinton who won so many GOP votes in California, not Michael Dukakis.) These differences are too large to be written off as random errors of survey research. That so many California Republicans voted for Bill Clinton, but many fewer Georgians did, speaks to the way in which the Republican identifiers in these two states evaluated the choices before them. Partisans of the California GOP obviously saw far more in Bill Clinton than those so identifying in Georgia.

Findings like these lead inexorably to the important but often neglected question of what determines one's partisanship and whether the content of the party labels is different in one location than in another. Partisanship may be stable over time, but variable across space. Discussions of what determines partisanship have focused on affect—voters' likes and dislikes about parties and party candidates, as well as their issue positions and responses to major events. . ... The source of many of these affective preferences is preadult socialization—what voters learn about political party positions as children at home and in school. What people like and dislike about the parties will almost certainly vary with the social context in which they are raised. Georgians may be attracted to the Republicans because they have learned to be attentive to where the parties stand on issues such as gun control, abortion, and school prayer. Californians who call themselves Republicans might do so chiefly because they have learned to be attentive to partisan positions on free trade and national defense, and to appreciate where the typical GOP candidate stands on these matters. Partisans' loyalty to their party on election day will depend on the issue positions that candidates make central to their campaigns and how those positions square with what the voters have learned to care about.

The Electoral Foundations of the Two Major Parties

We do not have the detailed polling data necessary to exhaustively evaluate these propositions about the variable meaning of party identification across settings, but previous work has shown that the constituency groups underlying each party vary in size and influence across states . . ... These differences help us to understand how Democrats like Bill Clinton and Albert Gore might be more attractive to Republicans in California than in Georgia.

If the coalitions underlying support for a candidate vary across states, then it is probably reasonable to hypothesize that the electoral coalitions underlying the local parties also vary to a nontrivial degree. States known for being one-party Democratic strongholds are probably that way because they have larger proportions of traditional Democratic constituencies than states that are more competitive or Republican.

To highlight some compositional differences of momentous importance, we have identified the proportion of Republicans identifying themselves as ideologically conservative Protestants in each of the twelve states in the 2000 elections (see Figure 3.2). While it is surely true that the Republican party has become the political home of Christian traditionalists and the Democratic party the home of religious liberals and secularists. . . our evidence suggests that this generalization holds for some states far better than for others. In Georgia and Oregon, for instance, more than one-third of all

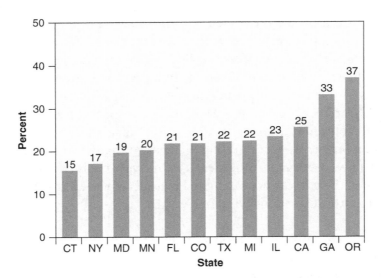

Figure 3.2   Proportion of Republicans identifying themselves as conservative Protestants, November 2000, by state.

(Data from Voter News Service, *Election Day Exit Polls*.)

self-identified Republicans also classified themselves as Protestant and conservative. In Connecticut and New York, these voters are a much smaller share of the GOP pie (Figure 3.2). A Republican candidate campaigning for nomination in Oregon will be required to appease a larger bloc of traditionalist Christian voters than the candidate in Connecticut.

We also examined the size of the middle-class population identifying with the Democratic party on the supposition that Democratic politics is more likely to be informed by the economic values of middle-class voters in some states, and less so in others (see Figure 3.3). The comparisons are striking. In Colorado, 59.3 percent of self-identified Democrats were earning between $30,000 and $75,000 in 2000, compared with only 40.2 percent of Illinois Democrats (Figure 3.3). In Georgia, Oregon, and Colorado, the Democratic party is firmly anchored in the middle class. In Illinois, Texas, California, and Michigan, a much larger percentage of the Democratic electorate sits on the lower rungs of the economic ladder. These comparisons are of consequence because Democratic candidates are far more likely to support Republican-sponsored tax cuts valued by middle-income voters in the places where their base is predominantly middle class than in areas where a sizable plurality of their constituency is dependent upon social welfare assistance.

In racial terms, the parties had starkly contrasting electoral bases at the beginning of the new century. For more than forty years Republicans have not had a racially diverse electoral base in any of these states, but especially not in Minnesota where they were 97 percent white (Democrats in Minnesota are almost equally white). The Texas Democratic party was the most racially diverse. Maryland and Georgia Democrats were close behind. In the final two decades of the twentieth century, black voters were a significant constituency within the Maryland, Texas, Illinois, and Florida Democratic parties, but were a relatively small proportion of the Democratic rank and file in Minnesota and Colorado. Hispanic voters were a significant Democratic bloc in Texas, Colorado, Florida, and California, but had almost no presence in Georgia, Maryland, Michigan, or Minnesota.

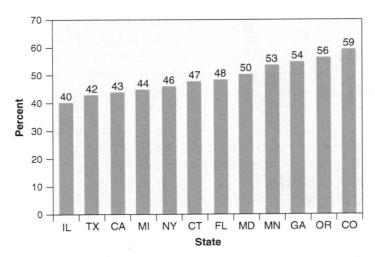

Figure 3.3   Proportion of Democrats in middle-income brackets (between $30,000 and $75,000), November 2000, by state.

(Data from Voter News Service, *Election Day Exist Polls*.)

These contrasting electoral bases *within* each party clearly indicate the need for careful scrutiny of individual states as a precursor to the formation of a comprehensive campaign plan. A campaign designed to appeal to Minnesota's predominantly white Democrats would almost certainly go awry in Maryland, where 40 percent of Democratic identifiers are black. These polls are only suggestive of what more detailed studies might reveal about differences in the social, economic, religious, and ideological bases of the two major parties as one moves from state to state. In examining other differences, we found that in some states, the most wealthy voters constituted about the same proportion of the electoral base for both parties, suggesting an absence of economic biases in the local political system. According to recent polls from New York state, about one out of every seven Democrats earned more than $100,000 per year, compared with only one out of every nine Republicans. The notion that the Republicans are the party of the rich and the Democrats are not is simply wrong in some states and in some elections.

Republican and Democratic Issue Priorities: The 2000 Election

We have suggested that parties may look very different from one state to another simply because of the size of particular constituencies—the compositional explanation carries a lot of weight. Both compositional and contextual influences play a role in defining the issues that are salient in particular locales. Republicans in California spent a great deal of time through the 1990s addressing the immigration issue. Not a word could be heard about immigration matters from the Maryland Republican party. The peculiar issue sensitivities of local party electorates place a premium on detailed studies of individual states. No candidate can afford to campaign nationwide without having some information about the receptivity of voters to alternative messages.

We sought for ways of testing just how different local issue agendas can be through use of the VNS exit polls from November 2000. These polls asked respondents about the issue that was most important for them in the presidential election. The voters surveyed were given seven choices reflecting major campaign issues that year: (1) world affairs; (2) medicare and prescription drug coverage; (3) health care more generally; (4) the economy and jobs; (5) taxes; (6) education; and (7) the social security system. Given the generality of these themes, and the truncated choice presented to respondents, we may not find as much variation as we would if the question were open-ended, but examining the variation within parties across states may still be instructive.

The tabulations are presented for each state in Table 3.3. Taxes ranked highest among Republicans across all states in 1996, but was clearly not the most important theme in 2000. The theme ranked *consistently* highest across all states was "the economy and jobs," although "world affairs" was also ranked highly. Even so, these items were more of a concern among the GOP voters in some states than in others. Oregon and Texas Republicans were more concerned about education than those in the other ten states. In Maryland and New York, Republicans highlighted world affairs above all other priorities. The differences were great enough that, armed with this information, a GOP candidate would be well advised to spend more time talking about foreign policy in certain states, but not others.

Democrats clearly had different issue priorities than Republicans, judging from Table 3.3, with a consistently higher percentage ranking the economy and jobs their number one issue. Predictably, for Democrats in Florida, social security ranked quite high. In Minnesota, Democrats gave the nod to education as their second priority behind the economy. Education was not as important to Democrats in Maryland (13.9 percent) and Texas (15.0 percent) as it was in Colorado (21.2 percent) and Oregon (28.7 percent).

One may be led to ask whether the differences shown in Table 3.3 are sufficiently important that a presidential candidate would be led to change his message and approach as he traveled from state to state. Our answer is that although a few major issues consistently dominate the voters' minds across most states, variations in the intensity of feeling about these issues will be hard to ignore. Florida voters will be more concerned about a candidate's position on medicare, the cost of prescription drugs, and the solvency of social security than those elsewhere. Going into Florida without a well-considered message on aging-related issues would be a mistake. If a Democratic candidate has a strong record on education, the places to discuss that record are Colorado, Minnesota, New York, and Oregon, states where Democratic voters perceived education to be an important issue.

A candidate who ignores key issues in a place where voters care greatly about them is risking the loss of those voters to an opponent. Hence, Bill Clinton and Al Gore won Republican and Independent voters in California, New York, and Florida by having a more convincing message than their opponents on social security and health care. Independent voters in Oregon and Illinois gave their votes to Gore if they were most concerned about education and the economy in 2000. It would appear that in most states, the education issue did not work to George W. Bush's advantage among those who listed it as their top concern.

Conclusions

This chapter provided a side-by-side comparison of electorates as they behaved in the 1988–96 and 2000 presidential elections. Even though there were key similarities across states, there were significant cross-state differences in the degree to which certain groups of voters supported the Democratic candidate for president. We have also emphasized that the contribution of a number of demographic groups to each party's electoral base not only differed across parties, but also across states within the

Table 3.3 Issues That Mattered Most, November 2000, by State

Issue	CA	CO	CT	FL	GA	IL	MD	MI	MN	NY	OR	TX
Republicans												
World affairs	20.4	18.5	19.2	15.9	15.8	16.0	28.6	18.5	13.7	22.5	13.3	13.8
Medicare/prescriptions	4.5	6.5	11.1	6.3	5.0	10.9	5.0	13.2	7.2	6.1	6.0	6.9
Health care	8.4	4.8	13.8	12.6	5.8	9.3	6.7	7.0	9.6	10.0	12.0	5.2
Economy and jobs	21.7	26.8	23.0	20.9	29.5	24.5	20.2	21.6	22.1	20.3	15.7	17.2
Taxes	16.2	15.5	11.5	16.3	23.0	12.5	13.4	16.0	19.3	11.3	12.0	22.4
Education	17.2	19.6	13.4	17.2	8.6	16.0	18.5	14.6	17.7	16.4	28.9	22.4
Social security	11.7	8.3	8.0	10.9	12.2	10.9	7.6	9.1	10.4	13.5	12.0	12.1
Democrats												
World affairs	11.6	11.0	12.9	12.2	12.4	10.5	10.5	12.2	12.5	15.9	6.9	11.4
Medicare/prescriptions	8.5	5.5	10.8	12.8	12.4	11.5	11.5	7.5	9.4	10.2	14.4	14.3
Health care	10.2	12.3	13.6	8.2	8.9	14.9	14.9	10.1	13.1	10.0	8.6	8.6
Economy and jobs	25.2	31.4	27.1	28.9	33.3	28.9	28.9	36.8	24.0	26.4	23.6	17.1
Taxes	5.5	6.4	5.8	5.0	6.2	7.1	7.1	3.4	6.4	4.3	3.4	9.3
Education	18.7	21.2	16.9	16.2	14.0	13.9	13.9	16.3	20.7	20.8	28.7	15.0
Social security	20.3	12.3	12.9	16.6	12.9	13.2	13.2	13.7	14.0	12.4	14.4	24.3

SOURCE: Voter News Service, *Election Day Exit Polls*, 2000, weighted data.

NOTE: Cell entries in the first section of the table reflect the percentage of all Republican respondents who mentioned this item as the issue that mattered most for them. Cell entries in the second section of the table reflect the percentage of all Democratic respondents who mentioned this item as the issue that mattered most for them.

same party. Because demographic groups such as blacks, Hispanics, Jews, and the poor have distinct ways of thinking about politics and view campaigns differently, the relative contribution of these groups to a party's support base guides the issue positions and policy priorities of party candidates and officeholders. We have also shown that state electorates had differing issue agendas in these presidential elections. Although national campaigns typically wind up hammering on just a few simple themes, the degree to which voters respond to these themes does vary from place to place. The message candidates get out will determine the loyalty of their own partisans, as well as the extent to which they can attract crossover voters.

Finally, we have seen that regionalism within many states, as defined in the VNS exit polls, disappears when you control for important compositional elements of the electorate: party identification, race, political ideology, religion, and other demographic variables. Notably, the voting locales where regionalism persisted are often those in or adjacent to large central cities such as Minneapolis, Detroit, Baltimore, Portland, and Denver. Although these regional effects in urban areas are small, they are potentially quite significant, adding between 5 and 8 percentage points to a presidential candidate's margin in most cases. In admitting that these regional effects may point to patterns of communication that have distinguished these areas from others sharing the same population characteristics, we open ourselves to the criticism that not all of the compositional variables have been included that could account for the apparent uniqueness of the places that stand out. Perhaps our measures of party identification and ideology, for example, are too crude in that they do not measure the multiple meanings or dimensions of the concepts they represent. We know, for example, that to be an economic liberal is not the same thing as being a social liberal. What may make large cities distinct from other areas is that they are especially high in social liberalism, but are highly similar on a scale of economic liberalism. . ... Our simplistic measure of ideology does not distinguish these two.

It is also the case that sectionalism can either persist or disappear if the substate regions are defined differently than they were in the VNS exit polls. In the end, however, we would argue that it does no harm to the study of political geography to suggest that regional effects are often traceable to the collection of political and demographic traits of populations clustered in certain places. In this spirit, Gary King (1996) argues that the goal of political geographic research should be to make regional effects disappear—presumably by specifying the appropriate compositional variables. If anything, our findings take the mystery out of the study of electoral geography and regionalism, clearing a place for geographic research within political science and other disciplines without relying upon hazy notions such as "political culture."

References

Green, Donald and Eric Schickler. 1993. "A Multiple Method Approach to the Measurement of Party Identification." *Public Opinion Quarterly* 57: 503–535.

King, Gary. 1996. "Why Context Should Not Count." *Political Geography* 15: 159–164.

REDISTRICTING IN 2020

THOMAS L. BRUNELL AND ADRIENNE GATHMAN
University of Texas at Dallas

After every decennial census each state is required to redraw electoral boundaries for all state legislative districts and congressional districts. The primary purpose of this process is to equalize the population across these districts within each state. However, there are other factors at work, most notably partisan politics. As a student of American politics, we want to give you an introduction into what to watch for as the new round of redistricting approaches.

The results of the 2020 Census will be finalized in early 2021 and the data will be distributed to each state. Prior to the next elections in 2022 the states have to redraw all the boundaries for legislative and congressional districts. The process of redistricting is taken care of at the state government level. Most states redraw the lines by passing a state law, wherein the legislature passes the bill and the governor must sign it. However, the process does vary from state to state, most notably in those states, like California and Arizona, in which a commission draws the lines rather than the state legislature (National Conference of State Legislatures 2018b).

Since the partisan composition of each state government will affect the maps that get drawn, the first major battle in the redistricting process will be legislative and gubernatorial elections in the year 2020. Those contests will help shape the partisan landscape at the state level, which in turn, affects the type of map one might expect. If a state has unified government—where one party controls both chambers of the state legislature and the governor's office, then these are the states we could expect to draw the maps that favor their own party. If the state government has divided partisan control—where the power in the state legislature is shared by both parties, then it is far more difficult to create maps that favor one party or the other since each party can veto the legislation to create the new lines.

There are guidelines or principles that guide the redistricting process, which is to say there are limitations to what kinds of districts get drawn. First and foremost, the districts within a state are required to have more or less the same number of people. Prior to some landmark cases in the 1960's some states had districts that were dozens and even hundreds of times more populated in one part of the state relative to other parts. The Supreme Court ruled in a series of landmark cases that voting power in a state shouldn't be dependent upon where one lives. Thus, the one person—one vote requirement was instituted (National Conference of State Legislatures 2018a).

Secondly, the districts have to be contiguous, which means that the district has to be one single polygon, and you cannot have half the district in the north part of the state and the other half in the southern region with no connecting geography. Essentially, one must be able to travel from any point in the district to any other point. This could be accomplished by a single road, or by a ferry route or a bridge if water runs through the district (Levitt 2010).

Third, districts are supposed to be compact. Compactness has to do with the shape of the district itself. A rectangle is compact, where a district that looks like a bug splat on the windshield of a car is not. There is a great deal of latitude with compactness as courts are typically unwilling to force a state to redraw districts just because the shapes are ugly. While a rectangular district is not inherently better than some oddly shaped districts, often times a bunch of really ugly districts is a signal that something is going on, usually to benefit one of the political parties.

Fourth, districts are supposed to preserve communities of interest. What exactly does this mean? Several things really—districts are drawn so that communities are kept together in one or multiple districts. Often times this means that a state will try to keep counties and cities in one district. For larger cities and counties it is impossible to be in a single district because the population is too large, in these cases the lines are drawn to minimize the number of districts a single city or county is divided into. If you look at a map of the congressional boundaries in a state with an overlay of county boundary lines, it is pretty clear that counties are often used as the building blocks for districts.

Fifth, remappers can protect incumbents in the new map, though they are not required to do so. Technically anyone living in a state can run for any congressional seat, though obviously not living in a district will pose serious problems for any candidate. Thus where one resides and in which district one's house is drawn matters. The location of incumbents' homes is one of the first bits of data that gets overlayed with the census data. If two or more incumbents' houses are drawn into a single district, the expectation, and usually the reality, is that these incumbents will run against one another. Strategic pairing of incumbents is a tried and true method to get rid of high profile members from the other party. If the Democrats want to get rid of a certain Republican, they can draw a district that puts the Republican's home in the same district of a popular Democrat's home and draw the district so that the underlying partisanship favors Democrats.

Finally, the Voting Rights Act and related Supreme Court decisions play a major role in what districts end up looking like in many states. *Thornburg v. Gingles* (1986) requires, under most conditions, a state with a significant minority population (African American, Hispanic, American Indian, etc.) to draw districts in those parts of the state in which minorities live that give minority voters "an equal opportunity to elect a candidate of their choice." These districts are often called "majority minority districts" because they are drawn in such a way that a majority of the population is comprised of racial or ethnic minorities.

Another permanent feature of the redistricting process is litigation. Indeed there were still a handful of states in the midst of litigation well into 2018, which is at the end of the redistricting cycle. At this time we are still waiting for the U.S. Supreme Court to hand down what could be a blockbuster decision in *Gill v. Whitford* regarding partisan gerrymandering. An additional partisan gerrymandering case, *Benisek v. Lamone*, will be heard by the Supreme Court in March 2018, and as the decisions are expected during the summer of 2018, other cases including *Rucho v. Common Cause, Rucho v. League of Women Voters of North Carolina*, and *Diamond v. Torres*, among others, are stagnant as they wait. As such, the maps still in contention are likely to remain in place for the 2018 election and the constitutionality of partisan gerrymandering remains mostly uncertain and undefined (Li, Wolf, and Farmer 2018).

Partisan Gerrymandering

What is partisan gerrymandering, and why are courts still debating the constitutionality of it and the resulting maps 8-years after the most recent census? Gerrymandering's most basic definition is redistricting in a manner to favor or benefit one group, which leads to disproportionately increasing their political power (Levitt 2010). No matter how lines are drawn, whether by commission or the legislature, the districts will always have some political impact as populations and political beliefs must be shifted to different districts to accommodate the traditional redistricting principles. Gerrymandering takes it a step further in its impact, as it is the intentional shifting of political power to benefit one group over another, rather than a simple byproduct of the redistricting requirements. Partisan gerrymandering, therefore, is redistricting in a manner that benefits one political party and their political power, while simultaneously hindering the opposing party's power.

Partisan gerrymandering is not a new concept. Even before the ratification of the Constitution, political leaders attempted to draw district lines in ways that diluted the power of certain votes while bolstering the power of others. This was often done by packing more people into one district than another, as the one person, one vote standard was not a legally required concept until the 1960s. The term gerrymander itself was coined in response to the lines approved by Massachusetts Governor Elbridge Gerry in 1812, as they were meant to guarantee overwhelming success for the Democratic-Republicans in the upcoming elections. One of the districts was said to look like a beast, which was christened the "Gerry-mander" by the press (Levitt 2010). While the practice of gerrymandering has evolved over time with new interests and groups being satisfied, or dissatisfied, the term given to the practice has not changed.

As noted, partisan gerrymandering occurs when the lines are drawn to unduly benefit one political party over the other. For example, a state with 10 districts and a population that is 60% Republican and 40% Democratic would expect districts reflecting the population with 6 districts majority Republican and 4 majority Democratic, or even 5 and 5. If the districts are drawn in a way that makes it easier for one party to win a disproportionate majority of the elections and therefore increase their political power exponentially compared to the other party, this is likely a partisan gerrymander.

There are couple different ways in which a partisan gerrymander is generally accomplished. First, if cracking is employed, each of the 10 districts could be drawn in a manner where 40% of the district population is Democratic and 60% is Republican, essentially guaranteeing that all 10 seats would vote Republican. Cracking is accomplished when similar populations, in this case Democrats, are broken up to prevent them from ever constituting a majority in a district. Packing is the second major method employed by district drawers in their gerrymandering efforts. This occurs when as many people as possible are shoved into as few districts as possible. Continuing with the previous example, this could mean 2 districts with 80% Democratic populations, so the remaining 8 districts are majority Republican. In both examples, cracking and packing, the Republican Party takes the advantage at the disadvantage of the Democratic Party. While the example is a Republican gerrymander, partisan gerrymanders can be and have been led by both parties, as it all comes down to who has the power in the legislature or commission at the time the lines are to be drawn. As noted, partisan gerrymandering is not a new concept, nor is it a tool of singular party.

While neither new nor single-party dominated, partisan gerrymandering is not popular with voters according to recent public opinion polls, regardless of their party affiliation (Frankovic 2017). However, that dislike has not translated to the practice being infrequently used or consistently unconstitutional. It has, though, translated to a number of lawsuits after every census. All this litigation has determined up to this point, however, is that an unconstitutional partisan gerrymander is very difficult to establish, as the previous definitions set an extremely high bar for unconstitutionality. Prior to 2004, the standard was set in *Davis v. Bandemer* (1986) wherein a violation occurred if the voting strength of a particular group of voters was diluted, if there was excessive violation of boundaries, if there was an unjustifiable partisan advantage created, and if there was party entrenchment. This standard though was so high that no partisan gerrymander was found unconstitutional, so the practice was essentially legal for twenty years with very little recourse for citizens who felt their vote was being diluted (National Conference of State Legislatures 2018a).

In *Vieth v. Jubelirer* (2004), the Supreme Court determined the issue remained justiciable, but a clearer definition than the one provided in *Bandemer* of an unconstitutional partisan gerrymander could not be established by a majority of Supreme Court justices. As such, the law surrounding partisan gerrymandering remains vague and unclear, which is why the resolutions of the *Gill v. Whitford* and *Benisek v. Lamone* cases remain so important, especially for redistricting in 2020. A completely new set of standards to determine the constitutionality of partisan gerrymandering could be established prior to this next round of redistricting, which could completely change how districts are drawn and what they end up looking like.

Racial Gerrymandering

While partisan gerrymandering is not well defined by the courts and determining if a map is unconstitutional based on partisan drawing of the districts is extremely difficult, racial gerrymandering has at minimum been clearly defined as unconstitutional and unacceptable by the Supreme Court. Racial gerrymandering is the drawing of districts in a way that hinders the voting power of a racial or ethnic group. For a racial gerrymander to be unconstitutional, race and/or ethnicity have to have been the predominant factor in drawing the districts, which violates the Equal Protection Clause of the 14th Amendment, unless there is a narrowly tailored, compelling government reason for using race as the predominant factor. While using race as the predominant factor is unconstitutional, map drawers still have to comply with and meet the standards set forth in the Voting Rights Act of 1965. Balancing such standards with the unconstitutionality of using race or ethnicity as the predominant reason for drawing a district has not always been a smooth process.

For redistricting in 2020, the major Voting Rights Act section of concern is Section 2, which essentially states that a state cannot discriminate on the basis of race when it comes to voting. Section 2 guarantees minority voters an equal opportunity to participate politically and elect whom they want to elect. In conjunction with Section 2, the Supreme Court determined that cracking minority populations to prevent them from having a majority in a district is illegal, as it dilutes their voting power (*Thornburg v. Gingles* 1986). *Gingles* (1986) therefore set out the standards for determining when a majority-minority district must be drawn. A state must draw a majority-minority district when the minority group is sufficiently numerous and compact for a majority in a single district, when the minority group is "politically cohesive," or votes as a whole, and when the majority group votes sufficiently as a bloc to prevent minorities from electing their preferred candidate (*Gingles* 1986). If each of these is met, a majority-minority district must be drawn to allow the minority population an opportunity to elect their preferred candidate.

While *Gingles* (1986) set out a standard for drawing majority-minority districts, questions still remain as to how to draw these districts without violating the 14th Amendment by using race as the predominant factor in drawing the districts. Case law has at this point made it clear that meeting the one person, one vote standard is not a predominant explanation in district drawing, so an unconstitutional racial gerrymander can still be found even if the one person, one vote standard is met and said to predominate (*Alabama Legislative Black Caucus v. Alabama* 2015). It has also been made clear that setting a specific or target minority percentage of the population for a district or districts is a clear indication that race predominated and is therefore an unconstitutional racial gerrymander (*Cooper v. Harris* 2017). Finally, the court has left open whether other traditional redistricting principles, such as compactness and protecting incumbents are sufficient predominant explanations for districting, but it is clear that a map employing traditional criteria can still be a racial gerrymander (*Bethune-Hill v. Virginia State Bd. of Elections* 2017). Much like partisan gerrymandering, racial gerrymandering remains an area of law that faces continuous litigation. The one clear standard to avoid a racial gerrymander challenge in redistricting in 2020 is to prevent race from being a predominant factor in the drawing of the districts. The most assured way to do this is to mention race as little as possible while drawing and to especially not set a target population percentage, as that is a clear indicator of predominance and therefore unconstitutional.

Conclusion

Redistricting is a political process with outcomes that are inherently political. It doesn't matter how districts get drawn, there will be political consequences and there will be winners and losers. Suggestions for reform are usually focused on reforming the process of redistricting—taking the power out of the hands of state legislators and giving it to someone else—like a commission of some sort or another, or having a computer algorithm draw "fair" districts. Process-based reform can help make districts fairer for both parties, but it is certainly no guarantee. Results oriented reform, in which legislators are required or forbidden from doing certain things, is far more promising in terms of getting fairer maps. So if we want to end partisan gerrymandering, instead of creating a commission to draw districts, require the state legislators to draw districts so that one party is not heavily favored in the map (i.e. they are likely to win way more districts given their partisan strength than the other party).

References

Alabama Legislative Black Caucus v. Alabama. 2015. 575 U.S. _____, 135 S. Ct. 1257.

Bethune-Hill v. Virginia State Bd. Of Elections. 2017. 580 U.S. _____, 137 S. Ct. 788.

Cooper v. Harris. 2017. 581 U.S. _____, 137 S. Ct. 1455.

Davis v. Bandemer. 1986. 478 U.S. 109.

Frankovic, Kathy. 2017. "YouGov U.S.: Few Support Partisan Gerrymandering." October 4. https://today.yougov.com/news/2017/10/04/few-support-partisan-gerrymandering/ (February 3, 2018).

Levitt, Justin. 2010. A Citizen's Guide to Redistricting. New York: Brennan Center for Justice. http://www.brennancenter.org/sites/default/files/legacy/CGR%20Reprint%20Single%20Page.pdf.

Li, Michael, Thomas Wolf, and Alexis Farmer. 2018. "Brennan Center for Justice: The State of Redistricting Litigation (Late January 2018 Edition)." February 2. http://www.brennancenter.org/blog/state-redistricting-litigation (February 3, 2018).

National Conference of State Legislatures. 2018a. "Redistricting and the Supreme Court: The Most Significant Cases." January 30. http://www.ncsl.org/research/redistricting/2009-redistricting-commissions-table.aspx (February 1, 2018).

National Conference of State Legislatures. 2018b. "Redistricting Commissions: State Legislative Plans." January 25. http://www.ncsl.org/research/redistricting/2009-redistricting-commissions-table.aspx (February 1, 2018).

National Conference of State Legislatures. 2009. Redistricting Law 2010. Washington, D.C.: National Conference of State Legislatures.

Thornburg v. Gingles. 1986. 478 U.S. 30.

Vieth v. Jubelirer. 2004. 541 U.S. 267.

CHAPTER 4
DIRECT DEMOCRACY

REPRESENTATION AND DIRECT DEMOCRACY IN THE UNITED STATES[i]

CAROLINE TOLBERT
University of Iowa

DANIEL A. SMITH
University of Florida

Direct democracy is currently flourishing in the American states. The mechanisms of direct democracy, specifically the initiative, affect issues of representation in two fundamental ways. In reviewing the scholarly literature on direct democracy, we first highlight the instrumental outcomes of ballot propositions and how they directly or indirectly shape governance and public policy. We then examine the spillover or educative effects ballot measures have on the broader electoral landscape and political processes. We suggest the educative effects of the process on civic engagement, political participation, interest groups and political parties may prove to be equally, or more, important than any policy resulting from its instrumental use.

Introduction

[...]Though direct democracy has a global presence (Boyer 1992; Butler and Raney 1994; Johnston et al. 1996; Qvortrup 2002; LeDuc 2003), and often is portrayed as not only having its roots but also flourishing in Switzerland (Sullivan 1892; Kobach 1993; Zimmerman 1999; see also Lutz, this issue), its set of plebiscitary processes are practised extensively in the United States. Over 70 per cent of Americans live in a city or a state the allows the initiative, a process by which citizens or groups are able to draft new laws or amend their state constitution without the consent of their elected representatives (Matsusaka 2005). Over three-quarters of citizens living in cities in the western portion of the United States have the initiative (Price 1975; Matsusaka 2004), and 24 of the 50 American states allow the process. The initiative, and its lesser-used cousin the popular referendum, allows individuals or groups outside the legislative arena to draft legislation and qualify it for the election ballot by collecting a specified number of voter signatures. In contrast, legislative referendums are proposed laws or amendments referred by legislative bodies to voters for a popular vote. Often used by political entrepreneurs (Smith 1998), the initiative has been the most important mechanism of direct democracy in the United States largely due to its agenda-setting power. Direct democracy is also a big-ticket item. In comparison to the $700million spent on the closely contested 2004 presidential election campaign, close to $400million was spent on state-wide initiative and referendum campaigns in the same year (Friel 2004). Given how widespread the process is, and how expensive issue campaigns are, an important question is whether the process improves or compromises the representation of citizens (Magleby 1984; Cronin 1989; Linde 1994; Bowler et al. 1998; Gerber 1999; Collins 2001).

Representation and Direct Democracy in the United States, Caroline J. Tolbert and Daniel A. Smith, Representation, VOL. 42, ISSUE 1, PP 25–44, 8/22/2006. Reprinted by permission of Taylor & Francis Ltd, http://www.tandfonline.com.

Broadly speaking, direct democracy affects the question of representation in two ways. First, ballot measures have instrumental outcomes that may directly or indirectly shape governance and public policy. Second, direct democracy has spillover educative effects, which can shape both the broader electoral and political processes. After providing a brief overview of the cyclical usage in the US of direct democracy—with specific attention to the initiative process—we examine the research on both the instrumental outcomes and the educative effects of direct democracy. [. . .]

Cycles of Direct Democracy

[. . .] Over the course of the twentieth century the use of direct democracy was cyclical, as the propensity for citizens and groups to place measures on the ballot in the American states ebbed and flowed over the decades (Magleby 1984; Tolbert 2003; Waters 2001). Between 1911 and 1920, a period when many states initially adopted the mechanisms of direct democracy, citizens considered 293 initiatives on statewide ballots. By the 1960s, the number of initiatives qualifying for statewide ballots had fallen below 100. The downward trend reversed, however, following the 1978 passage of Proposition 13, California's property-tax-slashing proposition (Sears and Citrin 1982; Schrag 1998). The landslide adoption of the measure created an explosion in ballot initiative use throughout the American states (Bowler et al 1998; Smith 1998). Between 1981 and 1990, citizens across the nation considered 271 statewide initiatives; in the next decade, citizens voted on almost 400 (389 initiatives), including 93 statewide initiatives in 1996 alone (Waters 2003). [. . .]

Initiative fever continues. Nationwide in the 2004 general election, there were no fewer than 163 statewide measures on the ballots in 34 states, including 54 citizen initiatives, 107 legislative referendums and two popular referendums (Ballot Initiative Strategy Center 2004). In addition, there also were hundreds more local initiatives and referendums in all 50 states. Substantively, these ballot propositions cover a remarkable range of issues; some of the issues involved are complex, while others are relatively straightforward. Whereas some ballot propositions make national headlines, others remain obscure in terms of public or media attention. In some of the two dozen states that permit initiatives, citizens have cast votes on issues as diverse as banning gay marriage, punishing negligent doctors, limiting the taxation and spending powers of state governments, funding stem cell research, election reform (non-partisan redistricting, mail ballots, campaign finance reform and same-day voter registration, to name a few), environmental protections, increasing the minimum wage and ending social welfare benefits for illegal aliens. Over the past century ballot initiatives have touched on some of the most important political issues from women's suffrage, the direction election of US senators and prohibition to, more recently, term limits for elected officials, tax limitations and ending affirmative action. Virtually no subject is off limits. [. . .]

Representation and the Instrumental Effects of Direct Democracy

With a few notable exceptions, most research on direct democracy in the American states has examined how the initiative affects public policy. In assessing the impact of the initiative on policy, scholars have focused on the use of the process to achieve policy outcomes both directly and indirectly, whether government policy is more responsive in initiative states, voter competence and the preferences of voters when making such policy decisions and whether or not direct democracy negatively affects the rights of minority groups. [. . .]

Policy Representation

The literature shows that ballot propositions affect public policy and that states that have the initiative and those with frequent use of the process have different policies than non-initiative states. Initiative states are more likely to have lower taxation and government spending over the second half of the last century (Matsusaka 1995, 2004; but see Marschall and Ruhil 2005 for a critique). [. . .] States with the initiative process are much more likely to adopt policies that constrain how legislators govern: they have higher adoption rates of term limits, supermajority requirements for tax increases and tax and expenditure limits (Bowler and Donovan 1995; Tolbert 1998; New 2001). Initiative states are also more likely to adopt election reforms, such as campaign finance restrictions (Pippen et al. 2002; Tolbert 2003; Donovan and Bowler 2004; cf Donovan and Snipp 1994 on term limits), abortion and parental notification requirements (Gerber 1996; Arceneaux 2002; Burden 2005) and official English laws (Hero and Tolbert 1996). The implementation of these laws, however, is not always a given (Gerber et al. 2001; Gerber et al. 2004). While opinion polls indicate that large majorities of Americans in the 1990s favoured term limits for elected officials at the state and national level (80 per cent), with one exception (Louisiana) only lawmakers from initiative states are term-limited.

Thus a critical question is whether policy that results from popular votes is more representative of voter preferences. [. . .] The most robust evidence in support of the policy representation of direct democracy is Matsusaka's (2004) book, which shows that fiscal policies are systematically associated with the presence of the initiative among the 50 states and US cities over the past century. During the contemporary period (1970–2000) the initiative reduced overall spending (expenditures) by both state and local governments, decentralising expenditures and shifting spending away from state and towards local government. Simultaneously, initiative states increased their reliance on user fees and charges for services and away from broad-based taxes, a finding supported by Bowler and Donovan (2004a). Public opinion data from this period show that a majority of citizens supported each of three policy changes associated with the initiative process. However, given the findings, we might assume that direct democracy results in fiscally conservative policies. During the first half of the century, Matsusaka (2004) somewhat surprisingly finds the opposite to be true. Initiative states from 1902 to 1942 spent more than non-initiative states. Weighing in on a long-standing debate, his research provides evidence that government policies are more responsive to public opinion in states that allow citizens to make laws without the consent of their elective officials.

[. . .]

But does the process benefit citizen preferences over concentrated economic interests? Gerber's (1999) comprehensive study of the role of interest groups suggests citizen groups are the true beneficiaries of the process. She examines campaign contributions made to groups supporting and opposing 161 ballot measures in eight states between 1988 and 1992, including California. Gerber hypothesises that economic interest groups, because they generally lack non-financial resources (such as the ability to mobilise personnel), are expected to be limited in their use of ballot propositions to make policy. In contrast, citizen groups are more likely to promote ballot propositions if they are able to raise sufficient monetary resources. [. . .] When economic interest groups spend in favour of their own initiative, they rarely win, but they are effective at defeating policies proposed by citizen groups. Gerber concludes that economic groups are at a disadvantage in initiative contests because they lack broad popular support.

Gerber's (1999) findings are corroborated by an earlier study that looked at the 53 ballot initiative contests in California from 1986 to 1996 and found that the passage rate for propositions benefiting narrow economic interests (and opposed by narrow groups) was only 14 per cent, compared to almost 60 per cent for initiatives sponsored and opposed by broad-based citizen groups (Donovan et al. 1998). In sum, high expenditures in support of an initiative do not lead to an increased probability of passage, a finding that suggests other factors (such as the framing of ballot questions, campaign rhetoric, media, coverage and the substance of the measure) might be at play (Guber 2001; Smith and Herrington 2000; Branton 2003; Nicholson 2003; Smith 2004).

Multiple studies have established that initiatives are most likely to pass when they are supported by citizen groups (Gerber 1999) and when the policy 'allocates broad, nondivisible benefits to large, diffuse constituency' (Bowler and Donovan 2004b, 142; Donovan et al.1998).

Yet money remains very important in initiative campaigns—paid petition signature drives, televisions ads, extensive legal battles (McCuan et al.1998; Donovan et al. 2001)—and some political entrepreneurs are able to employ populist rhetoric (Smith 1998; Craig et al. 2001) to obscure the financial support received from corporate entities (Broder 2000; Ellis 2002; Garrett and Smith 2005).

Though scholars continue to debate whether the primary function of the initiative—that it allows the popular will to check the power of state governments and elected officials by enabling citizens to enact public policy—is effective, policy representation is far from the only research on the instrumental effects of the initiative.

Voter Competence and Preferences

Are voters able to make decisions consistent with their own preferences? If voters are confused by the long and complex legal language of ballot propositions, it would seem unlikely the process could improvecitizenrepresentation(Magleby1984).Though the process of direct democracy entails binary (yes/no) choices on sometimes complex policy questions with long-term consequences (Chambers 2001), voters are generally understood to be able to use limited information to make competent choices on ballot measures (Lupia 1994; Gerber and Lupia 1995, 1999; Bowler and Donovan 1998; Lewkowicz 2006). The literature reveals that voters are able to take shortcuts and use simple cues (endorsements or opposition) from interest groups, the media and elected officials to cast an informed vote on ballot measures (Bowler and Donovan 1998; Lupia 1994). For example, research shows that television ads paid for by 'yes' or 'no' campaigns on a ballot proposition often provide cues, such as the names of sponsors or opponents or the names of prominent groups, as well as newspapers and politicians who have taken positions on the measure (Bowler and Donovan 2002a). Some research finds opposition cues may be more effective in drawing votes away from a proposition than supporting cues (Lewkowicz 2006). Because voter cues often flow from partisan elites (Karp 1998) and organised interests (Smith 2001b), the result is that individual partisanship is the most important predictor of voting behaviour in initiative elections in the American states and over time (Hasen 2000; Smith and Tolbert 2001; Branton2003).This use of cue-taking can help explain the pattern of ideological consistency in votes observed across a range of initiatives on the state ballot (Banducci 1998). In short, voters are not often fooled in direct democracy elections, and if uncertain about the effects of a policy tend to vote 'no' to preserve the status quo (Bowler and Donovan 1994). The policies that result from the process reflect what the majority of citizens want, as bizarre as they sometimes can be (Tolbert 2001).

Minority Rights

One of the fundamental questions concerning the practice of direct democracy deals with the consequences the process has on minority representation, and the fear articulated by Madison ([1788]1961) in Federalist #10 of 'majority tyranny' under a pure democracy. Axiomatically, of course, direct democracy is a majoritarian system of representation. 'As a majoritarian institution,' Donovan et al. (2000, 173) reason, 'direct democracy requires majorities of voters to support a particular policy and, by definition, minority groups are disadvantaged.' As Chambers (2001) notes, direct democracy undermines iterative deliberation because it 'introduce[s] an extreme form of majoritarianism that is inappropriate for deep constitutional questions' and 'often present[s] the voter with the image of inflexibility (debate cannot alter the framing of the question) and irreversibility (constitutional proposals are entrenched).' Some go farther and claim that 'because it enables the voters' racial beliefs and fears to be recorded and tabulated in their pure form, the referendum has been a most effective facilitator of that bias, discrimination, and prejudice which has marred American democracy from its earliest day' (Bell 1977). But this classic argument advanced by Bell—that the initiative process, when contrasted with state legislatures, systematically disadvantages racial and ethnic minorities—has found little empirical support (Cronin 1989; Donovan and Bowler 1998a; Hajnal et al. 2002).

The effect of direct democracy on minority rights remains contested. Although debate over the question of minority rights has been a staple among those investigating the process in the American states for over 100 years (Cree 1892; Sullivan 1892; Beard and Schultz 1912; Munro 1912; Wilcox 1912; Barnett 1915; Crouch 1950), there is no consensus among scholars as to whether minority rights are compromised in actual ballot outcomes. Some scholars suggest the availability of the initiative process, combined with high racial and ethnic diversity in some American states, has fuelled a white backlash (Schrag 1998; Tolbert and Hero 2001; Alvarez and Butterfield 2000) or 'new populism' where ballot initiatives are used to circumvent state legislatures where minority groups (Latinos, Asians and African Americans) have representation (Cain 1992; Hero 1998). Others have found empirically that the initiative may result in harmful consequences for racial, ethnic, sexual and language minorities (Haider-Markel and Meier 1996; Tolbert and Hero 1996, 2001; Gamble 1997; Chavez 1998; Schrag 1998; Haider-Markel 1999, 2001; Cain and Miller 2001) and voters have effectively used the process to undo protections and social policy benefits for minorities passed by state legislatures (Cain 1992; Hero 1998). Still others argue that indirectly the process of direct democracy itself may foster the suppression of minority rights by affecting public opinions of already marginalised minority groups (Donovan et al. 2000; Wenzel et al. 1998).

[...]

A comprehensive study of California ballot initiatives examined outcomes across the array of issues addressed through direct democracy in California over the period 1980–98 (47 propositions) using 15 pooled Los Angeles Times polls. It found that racial and ethnic minorities—and Latinos, in particular—lost regularly on a number of racially targeted propositions (Hajnal et al. 2002).

[...]

Others suggest it is not direct democracy per se that make minorities vulnerable, but a social context of high racial diversity (Tolbert and Hero 2001; Branton 2004). One sage of California politics suggests that the state's increased use of direct democracy in the last three decades coincides with dramatic changes in the state's racial/ethnic composition, writing that 'neopopulism has its roots in the state's changing demographics—white, affluent elderly taxpayers who vote, as against the younger, preponderantly black and Latino people who use the services but vote in much lower numbers' (Schrag 1998, 15). Since non-Hispanic whites constitute a majority of California's electorate but a minority of the general population, initiative elections may provide a mechanism for whites to exert their policy preferences over those of minority groups.

[. . .]

On the other hand, several scholars have found that only occasionally do initiatives deprive minorities of their rights (Donovan and Bowler 1997; Frey and Goette 1998; Zimmerman 1999; Gerber and Hug 2001; Hajnal et al. 2002), and when initiatives do curb minority rights, they do so incrementally and not radically. Minorities' rights and policy benefits are more vulnerable in local referendums elections than statewide or national elections, where the scope of conflict is broader (Donovan and Bowler 1998a). While there are some differences in the probability of various racial and ethnic groups winning in referendum elections overall, these differences are quite small, and Latinos, Asians, blacks and white non-Hispanics tend to vote with the majority most of the time (Hajnal et al. 2002). The reason is that racial and ethnic minorities have a whole series of issues and concerns, from economic policy to election reform, that may be addressed by direct democracy.

[. . .]

The new frontier for civil rights in American politics is gay and lesbian rights, and direct democracy has been no stranger in this battle (Button et al. 1997; Witt and McCorkel 1997). The battle over gay rights has been a common and contentious area of direct democracy, with conservative Christian activists repeatedly placing policies on the ballot to restrict the civil rights of gays and lesbians (Haider-Markel and Meier 1996; Donovan and Bowler 1997; Gamble 1997). These attempts have generally been more successful at the local level than the state level (Donovanand Bowler 1998); however, the process was used to adopt defence of marriage act (DOMA) laws in the 1990s (Haider-Markel 1999, 2001), and in the 2004 elections, 13 states had initiatives or referendums on the ballot to ban same-sex marriage (Haider-Markel and Joslyn 2005; Donovan et al. 2005). All 13 propositions passed by large margins. As Cain and Miller (2001) suggest, there is some evidence that the initiative process is sometimes prone to produce laws that disadvantage relatively powerless minorities, more than legislatures do. The scholarly debate over the consequences for minority rights in direct democracy contests is far from settled, but caution about the negative effects of the process are more warranted here than in other areas.

Representation and the Educative Effects of Direct Democracy

Only recently have political scientists begun examining the spillover effects of direct democracy— that is, directing attention not on the substantive policy outcomes that result from ballot measures, but on how ballot measures affect the electoral process itself. This understanding of the process is informed by the recent wave of literature we have termed the 'educative effects' of direct democracy (Smith and Tolbert 2004). The use of initiatives and referendums has been found to have spillover effects in that they can alter citizen attitudes and behaviour as well as the strategies of interest groups and political parties.

[. . .]

Turnout, Civic Engagement, and Political Efficacy

Progressive-era reformers envisioned direct democracy inspiring and educating the masses, in that the process could enhance civic participation (Mattson 1998; but see Hofstadter 1955). Furthermore, reformers believed that the educative effects of the process could mitigate the power of party machines and interest groups in the states (Allswang 2000). In a recent book, Smith and Tolbert (2004) measure this progressive-era wisdom against the contemporary reality of citizen lawmaking in the US and find the use of the initiative is linked to increased political participation (turnout), civic engagement, political interest and in some cases political knowledge, as well as more non-profit and citizen interest groups in the American states. They also examine the strategic use of direct democracy by political parties, finding considerable evidence that political organisations use the process not solely for instrumental ends, but to alter the electoral landscape by mobilising base supporters, driving wedges into opposing coalitions, and draining the coffers of political opponents.

Chief among the educative effects is the positive impact of direct democracy on political participation, a critical component of representation in a democracy. Research finds the presence of ballot measures increases turnout in low-profile mid-term elections (M. Smith 2001; Lacey 2005; Tolbert et al. 2001), as well as in higher-profile presidential elections (Tolbert and Smith 2005)

[. . .]

Partisan Voting and Political Parties

After decades of assuming that voting on ballot measures is immune from political party involvement (Magleby 1984), scholars have recently begun to reassess whether voting on ballot propositions is informed by partisanship. Recent studies indicate that partisanship is the most powerful predictor of voting behaviour on ballot propositions (Branton 2003). Political parties in the US are understood to be strategic actors (often clandestinely) in ballot campaigns with the aim of mobilising the partisan base and creating wedge issues in the election (Smith and Tolbert 2001; cf. Budge 1996, 2002; Smith, DeSantis, and Kassel 2006; Kousser and McCubbins 2005). Drawing on data from California proposition contests from 1994 to 2000, new research finds that partisan elite cues facilitate electoral participation (Lewkowicz 2006), as well as persuade vote choice in ballot elections.

[. . .]

Money and Interest Groups

A century ago, Populist and then Progressive reformers advanced the devices of direct democracy in the United States with the shared goals of limiting, if not eliminating, the corrosive effect of corporate money on the legislative process. The champions of direct democracy argued that by empowering ordinary citizens to participate in the making of public policy via the initiative, 'the people' would be able to circumvent state legislatures that were controlled by political bosses and entrenched special interests. Acting as electionday legislators, citizens could approve ballot measures and reclaim the right of 'government by the people' (Schmidt 1989; Goebel 2002; Piott 2003). By devolving policy-making to the people, the leading proponents of the process thought they could break the political stranglehold on state legislatures by party bosses and vested economic interests.

Far from eliminating money from the political process as the advocates of the process had hoped, money has played a central part in direct democracy in the American states for over a century (Crouch 1950; McCuan et al. 1998; Allswang 2000; Smith and Lubinski 2002). Critics of direct democracy, especially lawmakers, argue that the process has spun out of control, with ordinary citizens and economic interests, rather than elected officials, having too much power to shape legislation and tinker with state constitutions (Broder 2000; Ellis 2002; Schrag 1998). The former president of the Florida Senate, Jim King, warned ominously of the potential 'Californication' of Florida due to the rash of initiatives appearing on the 2002 and 2004 statewide ballots (Ulferts 2003).

[. . .]

Direct Democracy and Candidate Elections

Scholars, even those who study direct democracy, have been slow to recognise the impact that ballot propositions can have on candidate elections. Yet since the progressive era (Mattson 1998), observers of direct democracy have noted that ballot propositions can have indirect effects on candidate races. As a case in point, the re-election in 2004 of US President George W. Bush was possibly due to a single ballot measure (banning same-sex marriage) in the most important swing state in the election, Ohio (Donovan et al. 2005). Although the presidential candidates dedicated little time to overt discussion of the topic, same-sex marriage emerged as a galvanising issue early in the 2004 election cycle, as President Bush had previously proposed a national amendment to the US constitution banning gay marriage. Gay marriage ban referendums were on ballot of five 'battleground' states early in the presidential campaign. In all, measures banning gay marriage were placed on ballots in 13 states in 2004, with voters in 11 states presented with the question in November in conjunction with the general election. Every measure passed, receiving 70 per cent support on average. While the scholarly debate continues over the mobilising effects of gay marriage (see Abramowitz 2004; Burden 2004; Freedman 2004; Campbell and Monson 2005; Donovan et al. 2005; Hillygus and Shields 2005), there is little doubt that the ballot measure motivated some voters to the polls. Summing up the conventional wisdom of many political pundits following the election, a story in the New York Times stated that the statewide measures banning same-sex marriage 'appear to have acted like magnets for thousands of socially conservative voters in rural and suburban communities who might not otherwise have voted, even in this heated campaign' (Dao 2004).

[. . .]

Conclusion

In his book *A Government by the People*, which is the most learned history of the adoption and earliest usage of direct democracy in America, Goebel (2002, 198–9) concludes on a pessimistic note, writing that 'the historical analysis of direct democracy since its inception a century ago makes abundantly clear that the initiative and referendum have never served, and probably never will serve, as the means to strengthen democracy in America, to truly build a government by the people'. A closer reading of the recent empirical evidence amassed by social scientists suggests that Goebel's conclusion may be off the mark. While money still is crucial to ballot success, and while policies may reflect the interests of the median voters but sometimes undermine the interests of minorities, the process has positive effects that may enhance the representation and participation of citizens. As Frederick C. Howe (1915), a Progressive reformer and commissioner of immigration at the Port of

New York, told an audience at the annual meeting of the Academy of Political Science soon after the elections of 1912, direct democracy has an 'educative influence', as it can 'lead to constant discussion, to a deeper interest in government, and to a psychological conviction that a government is in effect the people themselves. And this is the greatest gain of all.' It is perhaps this silver lining of direct democracy—the educative, transformative effects of the process—that will prove to be more lasting than any policy resulting from its instrumental use.

[...]

References

ABRAMOWITZ, ALAN. 2004. Terrorism, gay marriage, and incumbency: Explaining the Republican victory in the 2004 presidential election. *The Forum* 2(4): Article 3. Available online at http://www.bepress.com/forum/vol2/iss4/art3.

ALLSWANG, JOHN. 2000. *The initiative and referendum in California, 1898–1998.* Stanford, CA: Stanford University Press.

ALVAREZ, R. MICHAEL and L. BEDOLLA. 2004. The revolution against affirmative action in California: Racism, economics, and proposition 209. *State Politics and Policy Quarterly* 4: 1–17.

ALVAREZ, R. MICHAEL and TARA BUTTERFIELD. 2000. The resurgence of nativism in California? The case of Proposition 187 and illegal immigration. *Social Science Quarterly* 81: 167–79.

ARCENEAUX, KEVIN. 2002. Direct democracy and the link between public opinion and state abortion policy. *State Politics and Policy Quarterly* 2: 372–87.

BALDASSARE, MARK. 2000. *California in the new millennium: The changing social and political landscape.* Berkeley, CA: University of California Press.

BALLOT INITIATIVE STRATEGY CENTER. 2004. Election results 2004. Available online at http://ballot.org.

BANDUCCI, SUSAN. 1998. Direct legislation: When is it used and when does it pass? In *Citizens as legislators: Direct democracy in the United States,* edited by Shaun Bowler, Todd Donovan and Caroline Tolbert. Columbus, OH: Ohio State University Press.

BARNETT, JAMES. 1915. *The operation of the initiative, referendum, and recall in Oregon.* New York: The Macmillan Company.

BATES, FRANK. 1915. Constitutional amendments and referred acts, November election 1914. *American Political Science Review* 9: 101–7.

BEARD, CHARLES and BIRL SHULTZ, eds. 1912. *Documents on the state-wide initiative, referendum and recall.* New York: The Macmillan Company.

BELL, DERRICK. 1977. The referendum: Democracy's barrier to racial equality. *Washington Law Review* 54: 1–29.

BENZ, MATTHIAS and ALOIS STUTZER. 2004. Are voters better informed when they have a larger say in politics? *Public Choice* 119: 21–59.

BOEHMKE, FREDRICK. 2002. The effect of direct democracy on the size and diversity of state interest group populations. *Journal of Politics* 64: 827–44.

_____. 2005. *The indirect effect of direct legislation: How institutions shape interest group systems.* Columbus, OH: Ohio State University Press.

BOWLER, SHAUN and TODD DONOVAN. 1994. Economic voting and ballot propositions. *American Politics Quarterly* 22: 27–40.

_____. 1995. Popular responsiveness to taxation. *Political Research Quarterly* 48: 79–100.

_____. 1998. *Demanding choices: Opinion and voting in direct democracy.* Ann Arbor, MI: University of Michigan Press.

_____. 2002a. Do voters have a cue? TV ads as a source of information in referendum voting. *European Journal of Political Research* 41: 777–93.

_____. 2002b. Democracy, institutions and attitudes about citizen influence on government. *British Journal of Political Science* 32: 371–90.

_____. 2004a. Evolution in state governance structures: Unintended consequences of state tax and expenditure limitations. *Political Research Quarterly* 57: 189–96.

_____. 2004b. The initiative process. In *Politics in the American states: A comparative analysis*, 8th edn, edited by Virginia Gray and Russell Hanson. Washington, DC: Congressional Quarterly Press, pp. 129–56.

BOWLER, SHAUN, TODD DONOVAN and CAROLINE TOLBERT, eds. 1998. *Citizens as legislators: Direct democracy in the United States.* Columbus, OH: Ohio State University Press.

BOWLER, SHAUN, STEPHEN NICHOLSON and GARY SEGURA. 2006. Earthquakes and aftershocks: Race, direct democracy, and partisan change. *American Journal of Political Science* 50(1): 146–59.

BOYER, PATRICK. 1992. *Direct democracy in Canada: The history and future of referendums.* Toronto: Dundurn Press.

BOYLE, JAMES. 1912. *The initiative and referendum: Its folly, fallacies, and failure*, 3rd ed. Columbus, OH: A.H. Smythe.

BRANTON, REGINA. 2003. Examining individual-level voting behavior on state ballot propositions. *Political Research Quarterly* 56: 367–77.

_____. 2004. Voting in initiative elections: Does the context of racial and ethnic diversity matter? *State Politics and Policy Quarterly* 4: 294–317.

BRODER, DAVID. 2000. *Democracy derailed: Initiative campaigns and the power of money.* New York: Harcourt Brace Publishers.

BUDGE, IAN. 1996. *The New challenge of direct democracy.* Cambridge: Polity Press.

_____. 2002. Political parties in direct democracy. In *Referendum democracy: Citizens, elites and deliberation in referendum campaigns*, edited by Matthew Mendelsohn and Andrew Parkin. New York: Palgrave.

BURDEN, BARRY. 2004. An alternative account of the 2004 Presidential Election. *The Forum* 2(4): Article 2. Available online at http://www.bepress.com/forum/vol2/iss4/art2.

_____. 2005. Institutions and policy representation in the States. *State Politics and Policy Quarterly* 5: 373–93.

BUTLER, DAVID and AUSTIN RANNEY, eds. 1994. *Referendums around the world: The growing use of direct democracy.* Washington, DC: AEI Press.

BUTTON, JAMES W., BARBARA A. RIENZO and KENNETH D. WALD. 1997. *Private lives, public conflicts: Battles over gay rights in American communities.* Washington, DC: Congressional Quarterly Press.

CAIN, BRUCE. 1992. Voting rights and democratic theory: Toward a color-blind society? In *Controversies in minority voting*, edited by Bernard Grofman and C. Davidson. Washington DC: Brookings Institution.

CAIN, BRUCE and KENNETH MILLER. 2001. The populist legacy: Initiatives and the undermining of representative government. In *Dangerous democracy? The battle over ballot initiatives in America*, edited by Larry Sabato, Bruce Larson and Howard Ernst. Lanham, MD: Rowman and Littlefield.

CAMOBRECO, JOHN. 1998. Preferences, fiscal policies, and the initiative process. *Journal of Politics* 60: 819–29.

CAMPBELL, ANNE. 2001. In the eye of the beholder: The single subject rule for ballot initiatives. In *The Battle Over Citizen Lawmaking*, edited by M. Dane Waters. Durham, NC: Carolina Academic Press.

CAMPBELL, DAVID and J. QUINN MONSON. 2005. The case of Bush's re-election: Did gay marriage do it? Paper presented at Midwest Political Science Association, Chicago, IL, April 7–10.

CHAMBERS, SIMONE. 2001. Constitutional referendums and democratic deliberation. In *Referendum Democracy*, edited by Matthew Mendelsohn and Andrew Parkin. New York: Palgrave.

CHAVEZ, LYDIA. 1998. *The color bind: California's battle to end affirmative action*. Berkeley, CA: University of California Press.

CHRISTIN, THOMAS and SIMON HUG. 2002. Referendums and citizen support for European integration. *Comparative Political Studies* 35: 586–617.

CITRIN, JACK, BETH REINGOLD, EVELYN WALTERS and DONALD GREEN. 1990. The 'Official English' movement and the symbolic politics of language in the United States. *Western Political Quarterly* 43: 535–60.

COLLINS, RICHARD. 2001. Part II: New directions in direct democracy: How democratic are initiatives? *University of Colorado Law Review* 72: 983–1003.

CRAIG, STEVEN, AMIE KREPPEL and JAMES KANE. 2001. Public opinion and direct democracy: A case study. In *Referendum democracy: Citizens, elites, and deliberation in referendum campaigns*, edited by Matthew Mendelsohn and Andrew Parkin. New York: Palgrave.

CREE, NATHAN. 1892. *Direct legislation by the people*. Chicago: A.C. McClurg and Co.

CRONIN, THOMAS. 1989. *Direct democracy: The politics of initiative, referendum, and recall*. Cambridge: Harvard University Press.

CROUCH, WINSTON. 1950. *The initiative and referendum in California*. Los Angeles: The Haynes Foundation.

CUSHMAN, ROBERT. 1916. Recent experience with the initiative and referendum. *American Political Science Review* 10: 532–9.

DAO, JAMES. 2004. Flush with victory, grass-roots crusader against same-sex marriage thinks big. *New York Times*, 26 Nov: A28.

DONOVAN, TODD and SHAUN BOWLER. 1997. Direct democracy and minority rights: Opinions on antigay and lesbian ballot initiatives. In *Anti-gay rights: Assessing voter initiatives*, edited by S. Witt and S. McCorkle. Westport, CT: Praeger.

_____. 1998a. Direct democracy and minority rights: An extension. *American Journal of Political Science* 43: 1020–5.

_____. 1998b. Responsive or responsive government. In *Citizens as legislators: Direct democracy in the United States*, edited by Shaun Bowler, Todd Donovan and Caroline Tolbert. Columbus, OH: Ohio State University Press.

_____. 2004. *Reforming the republic: Democratic institutions for the new America.* Upper Saddle River, NJ: Prentice Hall.

DONOVAN, TODD, SHAUN BOWLER and DAVID MCCUAN. 2001. Political consultants and the initiative industrial complex. In *Dangerous democracy? The battle over ballot initiatives in America*, edited by Larry Sabato, Bruce Larson and Howard Ernst. Lanham, MD: Rowman and Littlefield.

DONOVAN, TODD, SHAUN BOWLER, DAVID MCCUAN and KENNETH FERNANDEZ. 1998. Contending players and strategies: Opposition advantages in initiative elections. In *Citizens as legislators: Direct democracy in the United States*, edited by Shaun Bowler, Todd Donovan and Caroline Tolbert. Columbus, OH: Ohio State University Press.

DONOVAN, TODD and JOSEPH SNIPP. 1994. Support for legislative term limitations in California: Group representation, partisanship, and campaign information. *Journal of Politics* 56: 492–501.

DONOVAN, TODD, CAROLINE TOLBERT and DANIEL SMITH. 2005. Do state-level ballot measures affect Presidential elections? Gay marriage and the 2004 election. Paper presented at the annual meeting of the American Political Science Association, Washington, DC.

DONOVAN, TODD, JAMES WENZEL and SHAUN BOWLER. 2000. Direct democracy initiatives after Romer. In *The politics of gay rights, edited by Craig Rimmerman, Ken Wald and Clyde Wilcox.* Chicago: University of Chicago Press.

ELLIS, RICHARD. 2002. *Democratic delusions: The initiative process in America.* Lawrence, KS: University Press of Kansas.

FREEDMAN, PAUL. 2004. The gay marriage myth. Slate, 5 Nov. Available online at http:// slate. msn.com/id/2109275/.

FREY, BRUNO and L. GOETTE. 1998. Does the popular vote destroy civil rights? *American Journal of Political Science* 41: 245–69.

FRIEL, BRIAN. 2004. Both sides claim ballot-issue victories. *National Journal* 36: 3415.

GAMBLE, BARBARA. 1997. Putting civil rights to a popular vote. *American Journal of Political Science* 41: 245–69.

GARRETT, ELIZABETH. 1997. Perspective on direct democracy: Who directs direct democracy? University of Chicago Law School Roundtable 4: 17–36.

_____. 1999. Money, agenda setting, and direct democracy. *Texas Law Review* 77: 1845–90.

_____. 2005 (forthcoming). Hybrid democracy. *George Washington Law Review.*

GARRETT, ELIZABETH and DANIEL SMITH. 2005. Veiled political actors and campaign disclosure laws in direct democracy. *Election Law Journal* 4: 295–328.

GARRETT, ELIZABETH and ELISABETH GERBER. 2001. Money in the initiative and referendum process: Evidence of its effects and prospects for reform. In *The battle over citizen lawmaking*, edited by M. Dane Waters. Durham, NC: Carolina Academic Press.

GERBER, ELISABETH. 1996. Legislative response to the threat of popular initiatives. *American Journal of Political Science* 40: 99–128.

_____. 1998. Pressuring legislatures through the use of initiatives: Two forms of indirect influence. In *Citizens as legislators: Direct democracy in the United States*, edited by Shaun Bowler, Todd Donovan and Caroline Tolbert. Columbus, OH: Ohio State University Press.

_____. 1999. *The populist paradox: Interest group influence and the promise of direct legislation.* Princeton, NJ: Princeton University Press.

GERBER, ELISABETH and SIMON HUG. 2001. Minority rights and direct legislation: Theory, method and evidence. In *Referendum democracy: Citizens, elites, and deliberation in referendum campaigns*, edited by Matthew Mendelsohn and Andrew Parkin. New York: Palgrave.

GERBER, ELISABETH and ARTHUR LUPIA. 1995. Campaign competition and policy responsiveness in direct political behavior. *Political Behavior* 17: 287–306.

_____. 1999. Voter competence in direct legislation elections. In *Democracy and citizen competence*, edited by Steven Elkin and Karol Soltan. University Park, PA: Penn State Press.

GERBER, ELISABETH, ARTHUR LUPIA and MATHEW MCCUBBINS. 2004. When does government limit the impact of voter initiatives? The politics of implementation and enforcement. *Journal of Politics* 66: 43–68.

GERBER, ELISABETH, ARTHUR LUPIA, MATHEW MCCUBBINS and RODERICK KIEWIET. 2001. *Stealing the initiative.* Upper Saddle River, NJ: Prentice Hall.

GOEBEL, THOMAS. 2002. *A government by the people: Direct democracy in America, 1890–1940.* Chapel Hill, NC: University of North Carolina Press.

GUBER, DEBORAH LYNN. 2001. Environmental voting in the American states: A tale of two initiatives. *State and Local Government Review* 33: 120–32.

HAIDER-MARKEL, DONALD. 1999. AIDS and gay civil rights: Politics and policy at the ballot box. *American Review of Politics* 20: 349–75.

_____. 2001. Shopping for favorable venues in the States: Institutional influences on legislative outcomes of same-sex marriage bills. *American Review of Politics* 22: 27–54.

HAIDER-MARKEL, DONALD and MARK JOSLYN. 2005. Attributions and the regulation of marriage: Considering the parallels between race and homosexuality. *PS: Political Science and Politics* 38(2): 233–39.

HAIDER-MARKEL, DONALD and KENNETH J. MEIER. 1996. The politics of gay and lesbian rights: Expanding the scope of the conflict. *Journal of Politics* 58: 332–49.

HAJNAL, ZOLTAN, ELISABETH GERBER and H. LOUCH. 2002. Minorities and direct legislation: Evidence from California ballot proposition elections. *Journal of Politics* 64: 154–177.

HASEN, RICHARD. 2000. Parties take the initiative (and vice versa). *Columbian Law Review* 100: 731–52.

HERO, RODNEY. 1998. *Faces of inequality: Social diversity in American politics.* New York: Oxford University Press.

HERO, RODNEY and CAROLINE TOLBERT. 1996. A racial/ethnic diversity interpretation of politics and policy in the states of the US. *American Journal of Political Science* 40: 851–71.

_____. 2004. Minority voices and citizen attitudes about government responsiveness in the American states: Do social and institutional context matter? *British Journal of Political Science* 34: 109–21.

HILLYGUS, SUNSHINE and TODD SHIELDS. 2005. Moral issues and voter decision making in the 2004 Presidential Election. *PS: Political Science and Politics* 38: 201–10.

HOFSTADTER, RICHARD. 1955. *The age of reform*. New York: Vintage Books.

HOWE, FREDERIC C. 1915. The constitution and public opinion. Proceedings of the Academy of Political Science in the City of New York 5: 7–19.

JOHNSTON, RICHARD, ANDRE BLAIS, ELISABETH GIDENGIL and NEIL NEVITTE. 1996. *The challenge of direct democracy: The 1992 Canadian referendum*. Montreal: McGill-Queen's University Press.

KARP, JEFFREY. 1998. The Influence of Elite Endorsements in Initiative Campaigns. In *Citizens as Legislators: Direct Democracy in the United States*, edited by Shaun Bowler, Todd Donovan, and Caroline Tolbert. Columbus: Ohio State University Press.

KOBACH, KRIS. 1993. *The referendum: Direct democracy in Switzerland*. Dartmouth, England: Aldershot.

KOUSSER, THAD and MATHEW MCCUBBINS. 2005. Social choice, crypto-initiatives, and policymaking by direct democracy. *Southern California Law Review* 78: 949–84.

LACEY, R. 2005. The electoral allure of direct democracy: The Effect of initiative salience on voting, 1990–1996. *State Politics and Policy Quarterly* 5(2): 168–81.

LASCHER, EDWARD, MICHAEL HAGEN and STEVEN ROCHLIN. 1996. Gun behind the door? Ballot initiatives, state policies and public opinion. *Journal of Politics* 58: 760–75.

LASSEN, DAVID. 2005 (in press). The effect of information on voter turnout: Evidence from a natural experiment. *American Journal of Political Science* 49.

LEDUC, LAWRENCE. 2003. *The politics of direct democracy*. Peterborough, Ontario: Broadview Press.

LEWKOWICZ, MICHAEL. 2006. The effectiveness of elite cues as heuristics in proposition elections. *American Politics Research* 34: 51–68.

LINDE, HANS. 1994. On reconstructing republican government. *Oklahoma City University Law Review* 19: 193–211.

LOWENSTEIN, DANIEL. 1982. Campaign spending and ballot propositions: Recent experience, public choice theory, and the first amendment. *UCLA Law Review* 505: 505–641.

LOWY, JOAN. 2004. DNC: Dems, GOP push ballot measures to influence voters, Naples News, 29 July. Available online at http://www.naplesnews.com/npdn/news/article/ 0,2071,NPDN_14940_3071424,00.html.

LUPIA, ARTHUR. 1994. Shortcuts versus encyclopedias: Information and voting behavior in California insurance reform elections. *American Political Science Review* 88: 63–76.

MADISON, JAMES. [1788] 1961. Federalist #10. In *The Federalist Papers*, edited by Clinton Rossiter. New York: New American Library.

MAGLEBY, DAVID. 1984. *Direct legislation: Voting on ballot propositions in the United States*. Baltimore, MD: Johns Hopkins University Press.

MAGLEBY, DAVID and KELLY PATTERSON. 1998. Consultants and direct democracy. *PS: Political Science and Politics* 31: 160–9.

MARSCHALL, MELLISSA and ANIRUDH RUHIL. 2005. Fiscal effects of the voter initiative reconsidered: addressing endogeneity. *State Politics and Policy Quarterly* 5: 327–55.

MATSUSAKA, JOHN. 1995. Fiscal effects of the voter initiative: Evidence from the last 30 years. *Journal of Political Economy* 103: 587–623.

_____. 2001. Problems with a methodology used to evaluate the voter initiative. *Journal of Politics* 63: 1250–6.

_____. 2004. *For the many or the few: The initiative, public policy, and American democracy.* Chicago: University of Chicago Press.

_____. 2005. Direct democracy works. Journal of Economic Perspectives 19: 185–206.

MATTSON, KEVIN. 1998. *Creating a democratic public: The struggle for urban participatory democracy during the Progressive Era.* University Park, PA: Penn State Press.

MCCUAN, DAVID, SHAUN BOWLER, TODD DONOVAN and KEN FERNANDEZ. 1998. California's political warriors: Campaign professionals and the initiative process. In *Citizens as legislators: Direct democracy in the United States,* edited by Shaun Bowler, Todd Donovan and Caroline Tolbert. Columbus, OH: Ohio State University Press.

MENDELSOHN, MATTHEW and ANDREW PARKIN, eds. 2001. *Referendum democracy: Citizens, elites, and deliberation in referendum campaigns.* New York: Palgrave.

MENDELSOHN, MATTHEW and FRED CUTLER. 2000. The effect of referenda on democratic citizens: Information, politicization, efficacy and tolerance. *British Journal of Political Science* 30: 669–98.

MUNRO, WILLIAM B., ed. 1912. *The Initiative, referendum, and recall.* New York: Appleton and Co.

NEW, MICHAEL. 2001. Limiting government through direct democracy: The case of state tax and expenditure limitations. In Cato Institute, Policy Analysis, December 13. Available online at http://www.cato.org.

NICHOLSON, STEVEN. 2003. The political environment and ballot proposition awareness. *American Journal of Political Science* 47: 403–10.

_____. 2005. *Voting the agenda: Candidates elections and ballot propositions.* Princeton, NJ: Princeton University Press.

NORQUIST, GROVER. 1993. Prelude to a landslide: How Republicans will sweep the Congress. Policy Review (Heritage Foundation) 66: 30–35.

PIOTT, STEVEN. 2003. *Giving voters a voice: The origins of the initiative and referendum in America.* Columbia, MO: University of Missouri Press.

PIPPEN, J., SHAUN BOWLER and TODD DONOVAN. 2002. Election reform and direct democracy: The case of campaign finance regulations in the American states. *American Politics Research* 30: 559–82.

PRICE, CHARLES. 1975. The initiative: A comparative state analysis and reassessment of a western phenomenon. *Western Political Quarterly* 28: 243–62.

QVORTRUP, MATT. 2002. *A comparative study of referendums: Government by the people.* Manchester: Manchester University Press.

SCHMIDT, DAVID. 1989. *Citizen lawmakers: The ballot initiative revolution.* Philadelphia, PA: Temple University Press.

SCHRAG, PETER. 1996. Take the initiative, please. *The American Prospect,* 1 Oct, pp. 1–3.

_____. 1998. *Paradise lost: California's experience, America's future.* New York: New Press.

SEARS, DAVID and JACK CITRIN. 1982. *Tax revolt: Something for nothing in California.* Cambridge, MA: Harvard University Press.

SHOCKLEY, JOHN. 1983. Money in politics: Judicial roadblocks to campaign finance reform. *Hastings Constitutional Law Quarterly* 10: 679–92.

_____. 1985. Direct democracy, campaign finance and the courts: Can corruption, undue influence, and declining voter confidence be found? *University of Miami Law Review* 39: 377–428.

SMITH, DANIEL. 1998. *Tax crusaders and the politics of direct democracy*. New York: Routledge.

_____. 2001a. Campaign financing of ballot initiatives in the American States. In *Dangerous democracy? The battle over ballot initiatives in America*, edited by Larry Sabato, Bruce Larson and Howard Ernst. Lanham, MD: Rowman and Littlefield.

_____. 2001b. Special interests and direct democracy: An historical glance. In *The battle over citizen lawmaking*, edited by M. Dane Waters. Durham, NC: Carolina Academic Press.

_____. 2001c. Homeward bound? Micro-Level legislative responsiveness to ballot initiatives. *State Politics and Policy Quarterly* 1: 50–61.

_____. 2003a. Overturning term limits: The legislature's own private Idaho? *PS: Political Science and Politics* 36: 215–20.

_____. 2003b. Ballot initiatives and the (sub)urban/rural divide in Colorado. In *Colorado's future: Meeting the needs of a changing state*, edited by Daphne T. Greenwood. Colorado Springs, CO: Center for Colorado Policy Studies.

_____. 2004. Peeling away the populist rhetoric: Toward a taxonomy of anti-tax ballot initiatives. *Public Budgeting and Finance* 24: 88–110.

SMITH, DANIEL A., MATTHEW DESANTIS and JASON KASSEL. 2006. Same-Sex Marriage Ballot Measures and the 2004 Presidential Election. *State and Local Government Review* 38(2).

SMITH, DANIEL and ROBERT HERRINGTON. 2000. The process of direct democracy: Colorado's 1996 parental rights amendment. *Social Science Journal* 37: 179–94.

SMITH, DANIEL and JOSEPH LUBINSKI. 2002. Direct democracy during the Progressive Era: A crack in the populist veneer? *Journal of Policy History* 14: 349–83.

SMITH, DANIEL and CAROLINE TOLBERT. 2001. The initiative to party: Partisanship and ballot initiatives in California. *Party Politics* 7: 738–57.

_____. 2004. Educated by initiative: *The effects of direct democracy on citizens and political organizations in the American states*. Ann Arbor, MI: University of Michigan Press.

SMITH, MARK. 2001. The contingent effects of ballot initiatives and candidate races on turnout. *American Journal of Political Science* 45: 700–6.

_____. 2002. Ballot initiatives and the democratic citizen. *Journal of Politics* 64: 892–903.

SULLIVAN, JAMES. 1892. *Direct legislation by the citizenship through the initiative and referendum*. New York: True Nationalist Publishing Co.

TOLBERT, CAROLINE. 1998. Changing rules for state legislatures: Direct democracy and governance policies. In *Citizens as legislators: Direct democracy in the United States*, edited by Shaun Bowler, Todd Donovan and Caroline Tolbert. Columbus, OH: Ohio State University Press.

_____. 2001. Public policy and direct democracy. In *The battle over citizen lawmaking*, edited by M. Dane Waters. Durham, NC: Carolina Academic Press.

_____. 2003. Cycles of democracy: Direct democracy and institutional realignment in the American states. *Political Science Quarterly* 118(3): 467–89.

TOLBERT, CAROLINE and JOHN GRUMMEL. 2003. White voter support for California's Proposition 209: Revisiting the racial threat hypothesis. *State Politics and Policy Quarterly* 3: 183–202.

TOLBERT, CAROLINE, JOHN GRUMMEL and DANIEL SMITH. 2001. The effects of ballot initiatives on voter turnout in the American states. *American Politics Research* 29: 625–48.

TOLBERT, CAROLINE and RODNEY HERO. 1996. Race/ethnicity and direct democracy: An analysis of California's illegal immigration initiative. *Journal of Politics* 58: 806–18.

_____. 2001. Facing diversity: Racial/ethnic context and social policy change. *Political Research Quarterly* 54: 571–604.

TOLBERT, CAROLINE, DANIEL LOWENSTEIN and TODD DONOVAN. 1998. Election law and rules for using initiatives. In *Citizens as legislators: Direct democracy in the United States*, edited by Shaun Bowler, Todd Donovan and Caroline Tolbert. Columbus, OH: Ohio State University Press.

TOLBERT, CAROLINE, RAMONA MCNEAL and DANIEL SMITH. 2003. Enhancing civic engagement: The effect of direct democracy on political participation and knowledge. *State Politics and Policy Quarterly* 3: 23–41.

TOLBERT, CAROLINE and DANIEL SMITH. 2005. The educative effects of ballot initiatives on voter turnout. *American Politics Research* 33: 283–309.

TOLBERT, CAROLINE and GERTRUDE STEUERNAGEL. 2003. Race/ethnicity and referenda on redistributive health care. In *Race, welfare, and the politics of reform*, edited by R. Fording, J. Soss and S. Schram. Ann Arbor, MI: University of Michigan Press.

ULFERTS, ALLISON. 2003. Lawmakers want hard road for initiatives. *St Petersburg Times*, 9 Dec.

WATERS, M. DANE, ed. 2001. *The battle over citizen lawmaking*. Durham, NC: Carolina Academic Press.

_____. ed. 2003. *The Initiative and Referendum Almanac*. Durham, NC: Carolina Academic Press.

WENZEL, JAMES, TODD DONOVAN and SHAUN BOWLER. 1998. Direct democracy and minorities: Changing attitudes about minorities targeted by initiatives. In *Citizens as legislators: Direct democracy in the United States*, edited by Shaun Bowler, Todd Donovan and Caroline Tolbert. Columbus, OH: Ohio State University Press.

WILCOX, DELOS. 1912. *Government by all the people (or The initiative, the referendum and the recall as instruments of democracy)*. New York: The Macmillan Company.

WITT, STEPHANIE L. and SUZANNE MCCORKEL. 1997. *Anti-gay rights: Assessing voter initiatives*. Westport, CT: Praeger.

ZIMMERMAN, JOSEPH. 1999. *The initiative: Citizen law-making*. Westport, CT: Praeger.

ZISK, BETTY. 1987. *Money, media, and the grass roots: State ballot issues and the electoral process*. Newbury Park, CA: Sage.

End Note

i. Representation, Vol. 42, No. 1, 2006 ISSN 0034–4893 print/1749-4001 online/06/010025-20 2006 McDougall Trust, London DOI: 10.1080/00344890600583743

CHAPTER 5
POLITICAL PARTIES

POLITICAL PARTIES AND THE RECRUITMENT OF WOMEN TO STATE LEGISLATURES[1]

KIRA SANBONMATSU

The Ohio State University

This article analyzes the role of political parties in shaping women's representation across the U.S. states. Using data from 1971 to 1999, I analyze several hypotheses about how party affects women's recruitment to the lower houses of state legislatures. I argue that the incentive structure facing potential women candidates is somewhat different for Democratic and Republican women. The social eligibility pool, legislative professionalism, and partisan composition of the legislature affect women's representation differently by party. Rather than assuming a single path for women to elective office, this research implies that it is necessary to disaggregate women by party in order to understand the pattern of where women run for and hold state legislative office.

The percentage of women in state legislatures has increased dramatically since the early 1970s, from about 6% of all state legislators to about 22% today (CAWP 2001). Often overlooked in these averages is the significant variation across states in women's representation-from a low of 8% in Alabama to a high of about 40% in Washington. Past scholars who have sought to explain this puzzle of women's representation usually analyze women as a group, without making comparisons between Democratic and Republican women.[2] Yet there are reasons to believe that women's path to office differs by political party. By disaggregating women by party, we can identify factors that influence women's recruitment and improve our understanding of women's political underrepresentation.

Previous explanations for the variation across states in women's representation have often focused on contextual factors such as social structure (e.g., ideology, political culture), electoral rules (e.g., multimember districts), and the institutional setting (e.g., the degree to which the legislature is professionalized). This study places the role of parties at the center of the analysis. In addition, unlike most previous studies, this study pools data over time.

I argue that the explanation for variation across states in women's representation differs by party. First, the state's social eligibility pool has a greater effect on Democratic women's representation than Republican women's representation. Second, party shapes the political opportunity structure facing women candidates. The effects of legislative professionalism and the partisan composition of the legislature differ for Democratic women compared to Republican women. This study suggests that aspects of the political opportunity structure facing women candidates are specific to each party.[3]

Political Parties and the Recruitment of Women to State Legislatures, Kira Sanbonmatsu, The Journal of Politics, 2002, 64:3, 791–809. Reprinted by permission of The University of Chicago Press Journals.

I next discuss the limitations of previous accounts of political parties and women's representation. I then test several hypotheses with an original data set that extends from 1971 to the present. Finally, I conclude and discuss implications for future research.

Past Research on Political Parties and Women's Representation

Understanding why more women do not hold elective office is an important normative question with implications for the legitimacy of our democracy. There are policy implications as well, since women legislators are much more likely than men to articulate and support issues of interest to women as a group (Burrell 1994; Dodson et al. 1995; Swers 1998; Thomas 1994).

One scholarly approach to women's representation has entailed studies of individual women's races for the legislature (Darcy, Welch, and Clark 1994; Seltzer, Newman, and Leighton 1997). Darcy, Welch, and Clark (1994, 63) argue that studying the state as the unit of analysis is a less direct research strategy and favor instead a focus on women's actual races. However, as Rule (1981, 60) argues, state-level analyses shed light on the eligibility of women and on their selection and election. Women continue to be underrepresented despite a significant body of research demonstrating that men and women fare similarly when they run for office; it is therefore necessary to look earlier in the recruitment process to understand women's continued underrepresentation (Rule 1981). Indeed, understanding the factors that lead women to run for office and why women are discouraged from running is a neglected area of research (Carroll 1993). We miss half the story of women's representation if we only study women who run for office and ignore the women who do not run.

An inquiry focusing on the state as the unit of analysis is appropriate because the state legislatures are in fact 50 different institutions. The hypotheses investigated here concern factors that are likely to affect women candidates at the state level. State-level studies can complement individual-level studies of women candidates.

Renewed scholarly interest in political recruitment makes this research timely (Moncrief 1999; Moncrief, Squire, and Jewell 2001; Moncrief, Squire, and Kurtz 1998; Squire and Moncrief 1999; Stone and Maisel 1999). Practitioners have recently focused their attention on recruitment as well (National Women's Political Caucus 1994).[4] The pattern of women in the state legislatures has implications for women's election to statewide and federal offices since women state legislators may run for higher office. The recent trend of greater devolution of federal power to the states also makes research on state legislatures increasingly important.

Studies of women and parties in comparative politics have often focused on the existence of affirmative action or quotas for women within party structures, which provide important mechanisms for women's election to office (Caul 1999; Lovenduski and Norris 1993). Parties have not been the primary focus of scholarship on women's election to state legislatures in the United States, perhaps because the gatekeeping powers of parties in the United States are weaker than in other advanced industrialized democracies (Burrell 1993; Norris 1993).[5] However, the parties may still play an important role in shaping women's representation.

I use two theories of political parties to develop hypotheses about how par ties may affect women's representation. These theories suggest several aspects of the path to office that might be different for women by party.

Hypotheses

The Social Eligibility Pool

One way to conceptualize political parties is as a pool of potential candidates for office. Baer and Bositis (1988) argue that the traditional tripartite view of party-party-in-the-electorate, party-in-the-organization, party-in government-fails to incorporate mass and elites within one model. The theory of parties as office-seekers construes parties as solely concerning elites, neglecting the public altogether. Instead, Baer and Bositis argue that parties can be thought of as linkages between the mass public and elites: parties have a representational aspect, connecting various social groups to public office.

This conceptualization means that each party's base of women adherents in the electorate is a source of candidates: the party can be thought of as a mechanism by which women can become political elites. This theory implies that if the parties' bases are comprised of different social groups, then the two parties' bases of women may differ as well. I therefore hypothesize that the effect of the state's social eligibility pool on women's representation differs by party.[6]

The social eligibility pool is recognized as an important determinant of women's representation: states with more working women, women executives, and women law students and lawyers are likely to have more women in the legislature than other states (Hill 1981; Nelson 1991; Norrander and Wilcox 1998; Rule 1990; Welch 1978; Williams 1990). But scholars have neglected the possible inter-action of party with the social eligibility pool. There are several rea sons to believe that Democratic and Republican women may constitute two different candidate pools. The greater involvement of Republican women in electoral politics in the late 1800s and through much of the 1900s may have been a by-product of the class difference between the two parties since Republican women may have had more time and resources for politics (Cox 1996; Diamond 1977; Freeman 2000). In the past, Democratic women elites have been less likely to be homemakers and more likely to be in the labor force (Baer and Bositis 1988; Kirkpatrick 1976).[7] Today, Democratic and Republican women state legislators come to office through different networks and with different bases of organizational support (Carey, Niemi, and Powell 1998; Car roll and Strimling 1983).[8] Yet there has been little research comparing the two groups of women.

Because Democratic and Republican women state legislators seem to have different backgrounds, the relevant eligibility pool for women candidates may be somewhat different for each party.[9] If Republican women elites are more likely to be homemakers than Democratic women elites, then women's labor force participation in the state may have a greater impact on Democratic women's representation than Republican women's representation.

The Political Opportunity Structure

A second way to conceptualize the party is as a group of office-seeking individuals (Downs 1957; Schlesinger 1985). In this view, parties consist of elites competing for electoral office. Parties develop organizations precisely to enhance their chances of winning office (Schlesinger 1985). This view calls our attention to the role of the party in shaping the political opportunity structure.

By political opportunity structure, I mean structural factors that shape candidate emergence. Schlesinger (1966) uses the term to describe the opportunities for elective office available to ambitious politicians. Subsequent scholars have studied progressive ambition and the factors that lead politicians to seek higher office (Abramson, Aldrich, and Rohde 1987; Rohde 1979). My use of the term is somewhat different. I have in mind systemic or institutional factors such as incumbency, electoral rules, and party organizations that shape the opportunities available to potential candidates.[10] Here, I examine three ways that parties may shape the political opportunity structure facing women candidates: legislative professionalism, partisan composition of the legislature, and party influence over nominations.

I hypothesize that legislative professionalism has a stronger effect on Democratic women's representation. If the parties' eligible pools of women candidates are different, then party may interact with the negative effect of legislative professionalism.[11] Past studies have found that women are less likely to hold office in the more professional legislatures and more likely to hold the office if it is less desirable-possibly because of increased competition among potential candidates for the office or the higher costs of campaigning in those states (Diamond 1977; Rule 1981). Women's presence is negatively related to salary, length of session, and staff, and positively related to turnover and the ratio of seats to population (Diamond 1977; Nechemias 1987; Norrander and Wilcox 1998; Rule 1981; Squire 1992).

More professional states are also thought to hold greater appeal for Democratic than Republican legislators (Ehrenhalt 1991; Fiorina 1994; Fiorina 1996). Fiorina argues that differences in the attitudes and demographic backgrounds of Democrats and Republicans are likely to affect their incentives to run for office. Republicans probably prefer legislatures that are less professional because they may be more likely to want the flexibility to pursue an occupation perhaps law or business-in addition to serving in the legislature. Democrats, however, probably find professional legislatures more appealing; they may be more likely to want to serve as a full-time occupation, and they may find the salary in professional legislatures more attractive than Republicans do. The opportunity costs of serving in the legislature may simply be higher for Republican candidates since Democratic legislators are more likely to pursue politics as a career. In addition, seeking reelection is increasingly time-consuming (Ehrenhalt 1991).

If more professionalized legislatures are more attractive to Democratic than Republican candidates, then professionalism may create more competition among potential Democratic candidates.[12] The impact of legislative professionalism on women's representation may therefore have a stronger effect on Democratic women than Republican women.

I also hypothesize that states with low pay and long sessions are positively related to Republican women's representation but have no effect on Democratic women's representation. I expect that there is an interactive effect for these two components of professionalism for Republican women, but not Democratic women. In some states, the legislature is in session much of the year, and yet the pay is not high enough for a breadwinner (Ehrenhalt 1991). If the legislative demands make it difficult to maintain a separate profession, then Republican men may be less interested in the office, creating opportunities for Republican women. The same opportunities may not exist for Democratic women. Democratic men's interest in serving may be less affected by the interaction of pay and session length than Republican men's interest because Democratic men may be less concerned about the opportunity costs. And Democratic women may be less likely than Republican women to be housewives. Thus legislatures with long sessions and low pay may create disproportionate opportunities for Republican women because of income and occupational differences between the two parties and differences in women's backgrounds. I also test the hypothesis that being in the majority negatively affects both Republican and Democratic women's representation. Thus Democratic control of the chamber should negatively affect Democratic women but positively affect Republican women, and vice versa. Scholars have found a negative relationship between women's representation and Democratic party dominance and a positive relationship with Republican party dominance (Diamond 1977; Rule 1981; Rule 1990; but see Nechemias 1987). Most women state legislators were also Republicans for most of the century (Cox 1996; Diamond 1977; Werner 1968). However, these past studies have not examined the effects of majority party status on women by party. [. . .]

[. . .] Analyses

Table 5.1 presents the results. The hypothesis concerning the social eligibility pool is confirmed: the variable working women is positively related to women's representation for both groups of women, but the effect is larger for Democratic women. These two coefficients are significantly different from

Table 5.1 Parameter Estimates of Women's Representation		
Variable	**Coefficient**	**Robust Standard Error**
Social eligibility pool, party interactions		
Working women		
× Republican women	.58**	.08
× Democratic women	.83**	.11
Political opportunity structure, party interactions		
Length of session		
× Republican women	−.001	.005
× Democratic women	−.008*	.004
Compensation		
× Republican women	−1.46	1.02
× Democratic women	−.44	.80
Long session, low pay		
× Republican women	3.70[a]	1.91
× Democratic women	2.58	2.55
Democratic margin, lagged		
× Republican women	−.85	2.02
× Democratic women	−7.37**	1.75
Traditional party organizations		
× Republican women	−1.36*	.61
× Democratic women	−2.10**	.67
Control variables		
Ideology	.51**	.10
Multimember districts	4.61**	1.72
Moral political culture	−2.24	2.00
South	−2.15	1.74
Democratic women	−8.27	6.59
Constant	−3.07	6.42

R^2 = .52
N = 1194
[a]$p \le .10$, *$p \le .05$, **$p \le .01$

each other (p < .05). The percentage of working women in the state is more strongly related to Democratic women's representation.

Legislative compensation is not statistically significant for either group of women.[13] However, length of session is negatively related to Democratic women's representation, though only marginally statistically significant (p < .10); length of session is not statistically significant for Republican women. Length of session seems to have a stronger effect on Democratic women, but the difference between the two coefficients is not statistically significant.

The dummy variable for states with long sessions and low pay is positive and marginally statistically significant for Republican women only (p = .06), as expected. Perhaps because Republican women legislators are somewhat more likely to be housewives, legislatures with demanding schedules but low compensation provide a favorable context for Republican women. The partisan composition of the legislature, measured by a lag of the Democratic margin in the lower house, is negatively related to Democratic women's representation but unrelated to Republican women's representation. Being in the majority does not have the negative effect on the recruitment of Republican women that it does on Democratic women.[14] [. . .]

[. . .] Discussion

This study has argued that there are two somewhat different paths to office for women by party. While it is not surprising that party matters to elections, I depart from past research in arguing that the incentive structures facing potential women candidates differ for Democratic and Republican women. First, the effect of the social eligibility pool on women's representation is conditional on party. Because the parties can be conceptualized as two different social groups, including different subgroups of women, the pool of eligible women candidates interacts with party. More research is needed on differences in the occupational backgrounds of Democratic and Republican women legislators.

Second, conceptualizing parties as groups of ambitious politicians calls our attention to the opportunities available within both parties. Women's political recruitment is more limited where party organizations have traditionally exercised more influence over nominations. Democratic party control is negatively related to Democratic women's representation but unrelated to Republican women's representation. This differential effect may mean that being in the majority generates more competition for nominations within the Democratic party than it does within the Republican party. The effects of legislative professionalism on women's representation differ by party as well.

This study has several implications for understanding women's election to the state legislatures. First, it suggests that political opportunities for potential candidates within each party may be structured by gender. For example, in a context where it is difficult for the parties to find candidates, the parties may actively recruit women.[15] In contrast, where the office is more desirable, the party role may be to referee political ambition rather than cultivate it, and the party may be less likely to seek out women candidates.

Term limits is another factor that may affect candidate interest in seeking office. Term limits are thought to create opportunities for women by generating more open seats. However, if term limits increase interest in running for the legislature, competition for nominations may increase, with a possible decline in opportunities for women candidates-the relative newcomers. Such a dynamic might explain why term limits have had a mixed effect on women's presence in the legislatures.

In short, we need to understand how men's opportunities for office interact with women's opportunities. More research is needed on how the desirability of the office within each party affects how active the party is in recruiting candidates and how that recruitment in turn affects women's opportunities. For example, future research could examine the role of legislative campaign committees. If legislative campaign committees disproportionately help nonincumbents, then women might benefit. However, if party leaders do not consider women to be as viable as men in the races that they target, then strong campaign committees could hurt women's opportunities. Thus the effect of these committees is unclear.

Second, rather than assuming a single path for women to elective office, this research implies that it is necessary to disaggregate women by party in order to understand the pattern of where women run for and hold state legislative office. Future research on women's election to office should consider whether the factors shaping women's candidacies work the same way for both groups of women. Factors that are expected to increase women's opportunities may not equally benefit women from both parties. For example, since there has been more mobilization of women's organizations on behalf of women candidates on the Democratic side, then it may not be surprising that Democratic women have come to outnumber Republican women in the state legislatures.

By comparing women by party, this study has sought to contextualize gender and move beyond comparisons of men with women in order to further our understanding of different subgroups of women (Carroll and Zerilli 1993; Dolan and Ford 1998). This approach is similar to recent analyses of gender within a partisan context (Swers 1999). Social and demographic differences between the two parties, and the intersection of party with other structural factors, lead to somewhat different recruitment patterns for Democratic and Republican women.

References

Abramson, Paul R., John H. Aldrich, and David W. Rohde. 1987. "Progressive Ambition among United States Senators: 1972–1988." *Journal of Politics* 49(1): 3–35.

Baer, Denise L., and David A. Bositis. 1988. *Elite Cadres and Party Coalitions: Representing the Public in Party Politics*. New York: Greenwood Press.

Bernstein, Robert A., and Anita Chadha. 2000. "The Effects of Term Limits on Representation: Why So Few Women'?" Paper presented at the Coping with Term Limits: Ohio and the Nation Conference, Columbus, Ohio.

Burrell, Barbara C. 1993. "Party Decline, Party Transformation and Gender Politics: The USA." In *Gender and Party Politics*, eds. Joni Lovenduski and Pippa Norris. London: Sage.

Burrell, Barbara C. 1994. *A Woman's Place Is in the House: Campaigning for Congress in the Feminist Era*. Ann Arbor: University of Michigan Press.

Carey, John M., Richard G. Niemi, and Lynda W. Powell. 1998. "Are Women State Legislators Different?" In *Women and Elective Office: Past, Present, & Future*, eds. Sue Thomas and Clyde Wilcox. New York: Oxford University Press.

Carey, John M., Richard G. Niemi, and Lynda W Powell. 2000. *Term Limits in the State Legislatures*. Ann Arbor: University of Michigan Press.

Carroll, Susan J. 1993. "The Political Careers of Women Elected Officials: An Assessment and Research Agenda." In *Ambition and Beyond*, eds. Shirley Williams and Edward L. Lascher, Jr. Berkeley: Institute of Governmental Studies Press, University of California.

Carroll, Susan J. 1994. *Women as Candidates in American Politics*. 2nd ed. Bloomington: Indiana University Press.

Carroll, Susan J., and Krista Jenkins. 2001. "Do Term Limits Help Women Get Elected?" *Social Science Quarterly* 82(1): 197–201.

Carroll, Susan J., and Wendy S. Strimling. 1983. Women's Routes to Elective Office: A Comparison with Mens. Rutgers, NJ: Rutgers University, Center for the American Woman and Politics, Eagleton Institute of Politics.

Carroll, Susan J., and Linda M. G. Zerilli. 1993. "Feminist Challenges to Political Science." In *Political Science: The State of the Discipline II*, ed. Ada W. Finifter. Washington, DC: American Political Science Association.

Caul, Miki. 1999. "Women's Representation in Parliament: The Role of Political Parties." *Party Politics* 5(1): 79–98.

CAWP (Center for American Women and Politics). 2001. "Women in State Legislatures 2001." Fact sheet. Eagleton Institute of Politics. Rutgers, NJ: Rutgers University, National Information Bank on Women in Public Office.

Council of State Governments. Various years. *The Book of the States*. Lexington, KY: Council of State Governments.

Cox, Elizabeth M. 1996. *Women State and Territorial Legislators, 1895–1995: A State-by-State Analysis, with Rosters of 6,000 Women*. Jefferson, NC: McFarland.

Darcy, R., Charles D. Hadley, and Jason F. Kirksey. 1997. "Election Systems and the Representa tion of Black Women in American State Legislatures." In *Women Transforming Politics: An Alternative Reader*, eds. Cathy J. Cohen, Kathleen B. Jones, and Joan C. Tronto. New York: New York University Press.

Darcy, R., Susan Welch, and Janet Clark. 1994. *Women, Elections, and Representation*. 2nd ed. Lincoln: University of Nebraska Press.

Diamond, Irene. 1977. *Sex Roles in the State House*. New Haven, CT: Yale University Press.

Dodson, Debra L., Susan J. Carroll, Ruth B. Mandel, Katherine E. Kleeman, Ronnee Schreiber, and Debra Liebowitz. 1995. Voices, Views, Votes. The Impact of Women in the 103rd Congress. Rutgers, NJ: Center for the American Woman and Politics.

Dolan, Kathleen, and Lynn E. Ford. 1998. "Are All Women State Legislators Alike?" In *Women and Elective Office: Past, Present, & Future*, eds. Sue Thomas and Clyde Wilcox. New York: Oxford University Press.

Downs, Anthony. 1957. *An Economic Theory of Democracy*. New York: Harper and Row.

Ehrenhalt, Alan. 1991. *The United States of Ambition: Politicians, Power, and the Pursuit of Office*. New York: Times Books.

Elazar, Daniel J. 1984. *American Federalism. A View from the States*. 3d ed. New York: Harper and Row.

Erikson, Robert S., Gerald C. Wright, and John P. Mclver. 1993. *Statehouse Democracy. Public Opinion and Policy in the American States*. Cambridge, UK: Cambridge University Press.

Fiorina, Morris P. 1994. "Divided Government in the American States: A Byproduct of Legislative Professionalism?" *American Political Science Review* 88(2): 304–16.

Fiorina, Morris P. 1996. *Divided Government.* 2nd ed. Boston: Allyn and Bacon.

Freeman, Jo. 2000. *A Room at a Time: How Women Entered Party Politics.* Lanham, MD: Rowman and Littlefield.

Gibson, James L., Cornelius P. Cotter, John F. Bibby, and Robert J. Huckshorn. 1985. "Whither the Local Parties?: A Cross-Sectional and Longitudinal Analysis of the Strength of Party Organiza tions." *American Journal of Political Science* 29(1): 139–60.

Hill, David B. 1981. "Political Culture and Female Political Representation." *Journal of Politics* 43(1): 159–68. Inter-university Consortium for Political and Social Research. 1992. State Legislative Election Returns in the United States, 1968–1989 [Codebook]. Fifth ICPSR ed. Ann Arbor: ICPSR.

Jewell, Malcolm E. 1984. *Parties and Primaries: Nominating State Governors.* New York: Praeger.

Jewell, Malcolm E., and Sarah M. Morehouse. 2001. *Political Parties and Elections in American States.* 4th ed. Washington, DC: CQ Press.

Kirkpatrick, Jeane. 1976. *The New Presidential Elite: Men and Women in National Politics.* New York: Russell Sage.

Kurtz, Karl T. 1992. "Understanding the Diversity of American State Legislatures." APSA Legislative Studies Newsletter Extension of Remarks 16: 2–5.

Lovenduski, Joni, and Pippa Norris, eds. 1993. *Gender and Party Politics.* London: Sage.

Mayhew, David R. 1986. *Placing Parties in American Politics: Organization, Electoral Settings, and Government Activity in the Twentieth Century.* Princeton, NJ: Princeton University Press.

Moncrief, Gary F 1999. "Recruitment and Retention in U.S. Legislatures." *Legislative Studies Quarterly* 24(2): 173–208.

Moncrief, Gary F, Peverill Squire, and Malcolm E. Jewell. 2001. *Who Runs for the Legislature?* Upper Saddle River, NJ: Prentice Hall.

Moncrief, Gary F, Peverill Squire, and Karl Kurtz. 1998. "Gateways to the Statehouse: Recruit ment Patterns among State Legislative Candidates." Paper presented at the annual meetings of the American Political Science Association, Boston.

NCSL Reapportionment Task Force. 1989. *Reapportionment Law: The 1990s.* Denver, CO: National Conference of State Legislatures.

National Women's Political Caucus. 1994. "Why Don't More Women Run?" A study prepared by Mellman, Lazarus, and Lake. Washington, DC: NWPC.

Nechemias, Carol. 1985. "Geographic Mobility and Women's Access to State Legislatures." *Western Political Quarterly* 38(2): 119–31.

Nechemias, Carol. 1987. "Changes in the Election of Women to U.S. Legislative Seats." *Legislative Studies Quarterly* 12(1): 125–42.

Nelson, Albert J. 1991. The Emerging Influentials in State Legislatures: Women, Blacks, and His panics. Westport, CT: Praeger.

Niven, David. 1998. *The Missing Majority: The Recruitment of Women as State Legislative Candidates.* Westport, CT: Praeger.

Norrander, Barbara, and Clyde Wilcox. 1998. "The Geography of Gender Power: Women in State Legislatures." In *Women and Elective Office: Past, Present, & Future*, eds. Sue Thomas and Clyde Wilcox. New York: Oxford University Press.

Norris, Pippa. 1993. "Conclusions: Comparing Legislative Recruitment." In *Gender and Party Politics*, eds. Joni Lovenduski and Pippa Norris. London: Sage.

Rohde, David W. 1979. "Risk-Bearing and Progressive Ambition: The Case of Members of the United States House of Representatives." *American Journal of Political Science* 23(1): 1–26.

Rosenthal, Alan. 1989. "The Legislative Institution: Transformed and At Risk." In *The State of the States*, ed. Carl E. Van Horn. Washington, DC: CQ Press.

Rule, Wilma. 1981. "Why Women Don't Run: The Critical Contextual Factors in Women's Legislative Recruitment." *Western Political Quarterly* 34(1): 60–77.

Rule, Wilma. 1990. "Why More Women Are State Legislators: A Research Note." *Western Political Quarterly* 43(2): 437–48.

Schlesinger, Joseph A. 1966. *Ambition and Politics: Political Careers in the United States*. Chicago: Rand McNally.

Schlesinger, Joseph A. 1985. "The New American Political Party." *American Political Science Review* 79(4): 1152–69.

Seltzer, Richard A., Jody Newman, and Melissa Vorhees Leighton. 1997. *Sex as a Political Variable: Women as Candidates & Voters in US. Elections*. Boulder, CO: Lynne Rienner.

Squire, Peverill. 1988. "Career Opportunities and Membership Stability in Legislatures." *Legislative Studies Quarterly* 13(1): 65–82.

Squire, Peverill. 1992. "Legislative Professionalization and Membership Diversity in State Legislatures." *Legislative Studies Quarterly* 17(1): 69–79.

Squire, Peverill. 1997. "Another Look at Legislative Professionalization and Divided Government in the States." *Legislative Studies Quarterly* 22(3): 417–32.

Squire, Peverill, and Gary F. Moncrief. 1999. "The Road Less Traveled: Recruitment Patterns among Women State Legislative Candidates." Paper presented at the annual meetings of the Western Political Science Association.

Stimson, James A. 1985. "Regression in Space and Time: A Statistical Essay." *American Journal of Political Science* 29(4): 914–47.

Stone, Walter J., and L. Sandy Maisel. 1999. "The Not-So-Simple Calculus of Winning: Potential U.S. House Candidates' Nomination and General Election Chances." Paper presented at the annual meetings of the American Political Science Association.

Swers, Michele. 1998. "Are Women More Likely to Vote for Women's Issue Bills than Their Male Colleagues?" *Legislative Studies Quarterly* 23(3): 435–48.

Swers, Michele. 1999. "Placing Women's Issues on the National Agenda: An Analysis of Gender Differences in Women's Issue Bill Sponsorship for the 103rd and 104th Congress." Paper presented at the annual meetings of the Midwest Political Science Association, Chicago.

Thomas, Sue. 1994. *How Women Legislate*. New York: Oxford University Press.

U.S. Bureau of the Census. 1972. Census of Population: 1970; General Social and Economic Characteristics. Final Report. United States Summary. Washington, DC: Government Printing Office.

U.S. Bureau of Economic Analysis. 2001. "Bureau of Economic Analysis, Regional Accounts Data, State Personal Income." U.S. Department of Commerce. http://www.bea.doc.gov/bea/regional/spi/

U.S. Department of Labor. Bureau of Labor Statistics. Various years. Geographic Profile of Employment and Unemployment. Washington, DC: Government Printing Office.

Welch, Susan. 1978. "Recruitment of Women to Public Office." *Western Political Quarterly* 31(3): 372–80.

Werner, Emmy E. 1968. "Women in the State Legislatures." *Western Political Quarterly* 19(1): 40–50.

Williams, Christine B. 1990. "Women, Law and Politics: Recruitment Patterns in the Fifty States." *Women and Politics* 10(3): 103–23.

End Notes

1. Sanbonmatsu, Kira. "Political Parties and the Recruitment of Women to State Legislatures." *The Journal of Politics* 64, no. 3 (2002): 791–809. http://www.jstor.org/stable/1520113.
2. Nelson (1991) is an exception.
3. Rohde (1979) and Abramson, Aldrich, and Rohde (1987) also discuss party differences in the political opportunity structure.
4. The National Women's Political Caucus has tried to encourage more women to run and has sought to understand why more women do not run, arguing that "when women run, women win."
5. Neither the Democratic party nor the Republican party has rules mandating the slating of women candidates.
6. Nelson (1991) found that women's labor force participation affected the representation of both Democratic and Republican women, but he did not directly compare the effect for the two groups.
7. Kirkpatrick (1976) found that 30% of Democratic women delegates to the 1972 party conventions were housewives, compared to 49% of Republican women delegates. Baer and Bositis (1988) found that 25% of Republican women county chairs were housewives, compared to 12% of Democratic women county chairs. Some 26% of Republican women convention delegates were house wives, compared to 7% of Democratic women delegates; 30% of Democratic women delegates represented a women's group, compared to 15% of Republican women delegates; and 16% of Democratic county chairs represented a women's group, compared to 2% of Republican women county chairs. These data are from 1984.
8. For example, Carroll and Strimling (1983) found that Democratic women state representatives were more likely to be members of at least one major women's organization (84% compared to 70% for Republican women), and more likely to be members of at least one feminist organization (60% compared to 31% for Republican women). In the state senates, 90% of Democratic women were members of at least one major women's organization, compared to 69% of Republican women; 74% of Democratic women were members of at least one feminist organization, compared to 40% of Republican women.
9. For example, in a 1988 study of women state legislators conducted by the Center for American Women and Politics (CAWP), Republican women state legislators were less likely than Democratic women to have worked outside the home before serving in the legislature (85% to 94%). I thank Susan Carroll for sharing these data with me.

10. Carroll (1994, 5) uses political opportunity structure to mean any factors external to women candidates. Carroll's definition is broader than mine because it includes voter attitudes as well as the recruitment practices of the parties.

11. Legislative professionalism-the length of session, salary, and staff-has increased over time, with many states coming to more closely resemble Congress (Kurtz 1992; Rosenthal 1989; Squire 1988; Squire 1992; Squire 1997).

12. Nelson (1991) found that legislative compensation negatively affected the representation of Democratic women, but did not affect the representation of Republican women. However, since Nelson's analysis was limited to several elections in the 1980s, it is not clear if the relationship persists across time.

13. I also examined the effect of base pay as opposed to total compensation (including extras). The base pay measure also was not statistically significant for either.

14. An alternative operationalization of partisan composition-using a simple dummy variable for Democratic control-confirmed this result. Also, in order to determine if the negative effect of Democratic party dominance was limited to the past, as Nechemias (1987) has argued, I interacted Democratic party control with a dummy variable for the 1970s. This interaction term was not statistically significant, meaning that the negative effect of Democratic party control is not limited to the past.

15. An example of this may be Maine, where it is reportedly difficult to recruit candidates because the legislature is not very professionalized (Carey, Niemi, and Powell 2000, 22–3). Today, Maine is one of the highest ranking states with regard to women's representation (CAWP).

PRESIDENTIAL ADDRESS: SOUTHERN PARTIES IN STATE AND NATION

JOHN H. ALDRICH
Duke University

No Abstract*

One-half century ago, V. O. Key, Jr., published his masterpiece, *Southern Politics in State and Nation*. Key's analysis of the failure of democracy in the South must count as one of the great achievements of our discipline. His explanation is rich and complex. Certainly the anti-liberal basis of society in the mid twentieth-century South was crucial-"Whatever phase of the southern political process one seeks to understand, sooner or later the trail of inquiry leads to the Negro," he wrote (1984[1949], 5). But it was not only that the South was an illiberal society, what really mattered was that the South was also non-democratic. The failure of democracy can be traced to the absence of party competition and, according to Key, the consequent failure of a coherent and organized party system to emerge. His explanation is that the lack of organized partisan competition to win the support of the great body of the people, as James Madison might have put it, by itself accounts for the failure of democracy. In this account, therefore, if only there was regularized competition, there would be organized parties, and if only there were at least two organized political parties, democracy would inevitably follow. A cottage industry then arose to study, first, the possibility of partisan realignment in the South (e.g., Converse 1966; Phil lips 1970), subsequently it sought to assess the inroads Republicans were making in their ability to compete in the South (e.g., Beck 1977; Black and Black 1987), and most recently that industry turned to examine the culmination of the process, ending with a fully competitive (perhaps even dominant) GOP in the South (e.g., Aistrup 1996; Black 1998; Lamis 1990). The attraction of this stream of research is understandable. These are scholars considering whether trends are pointing toward sustained, organized partisan competition. If that were to be so, we would then conclude that the full flowering of democracy would at last be expected to appear in the South.

Here I reexamine Key's arguments and findings a half-century later. Much that Key believed has come to pass. The South, we know, has become a partisan battleground. Concomitantly, the two parties have achieved a substantial extent of organizational development in the South perhaps more so than in any other region. Democracy, we might say, has arrived in the South for the first time in a century. There are, I hope to show, some aspects to this development that suggest that competition between organized parties might not by itself ensure a truly democratic polity, but required social as well as political changes. Key cannot, of course, be held responsible for failure to foresee the problems that might be weakening the links between sustained, organized partisan competition and democratic outcomes in contemporary America. He could, however, have looked back to an earlier era. He could have seen that there were times of high competition between the two national parties in the South and yet the level of organizational development of the parties in the South lagged considerably and for a long time behind

Presidential Address: Southern Parties in State and Nation, John H. Aldrich, The Journal of Politics 2000 62:3, 643–670. Reprinted by permission of University of Chicago Press.

that of other equally competitive states. This was particularly evident in virtually all of the antebellum period, and it is especially pertinent in the second party system (1832–1860). It thus appears that electoral competition is not sufficient to ensure the development of regularized parties. Therefore, it follows that the system of parties Key so powerfully argued for may not be sufficient to ensure the development and maintenance of an effective and successful democracy.

Why, then, did competition in Jacksonian America fail to lead to the kind of organized parties in the South and apparently nowhere else that Key felt so central? My speculation is that during Jacksonian Democracy, slavery became peculiarly southern, became its "peculiar institution" (see Berlin 1998). It was, therefore, the attempt to keep an illiberal social institution embedded in a putatively democratic polity that required that the development of democratic institutions be stunted to the point of failure to achieve the required results. If so, it was at least potentially not the case that the absence of organized partisan competition kept the South nondemocratic in the 1940s. Rather, it might well have been the case that the perpetuation of an illiberal society thwarted the development of a democratic polity, and that the absence of partisan competition was the instrument used by an illiberal society to restrict the development of democratic practices in New Deal as well as in Jacksonian Democracy.

Key's Argument

As noted above, Key recognized that the "solid South" was centered on race. The problem was that those who, in the post-Reconstruction South, built the machinery of the one-party system and of Jim Crow segregation were seeking a unified South in national politics.

> From another standpoint, two-party competition would have meant the destruction of south ern solidarity in national politics-in presidential elections and in the halls of Congress. Unity on the national scene was essential in order that the largest possible bloc could be mobilized to resist any national move toward interference with southern authority to deal with the race question as was desired locally. And the threat of federal intervention remained, as the furore over the Lodge force bill of 1890 demonstrated. (1984, 8–9)

This need for strict southern unity was, therefore, the same need the South felt before the Civil War, and for the same reasons (see Aldrich 1995; Weingast 1998). They needed a veto to ensure freedom from northern interference, and they required southern unity to employ the veto effectively. The creation of this solid South certainly worked in the large (that is, in Congress) and in the small (that is, at the microlevel of the individual voter). The familiar image of the "yellow dog Democrat" is most often used to describe the politics of the relatively un informed, but it applied just as well to the more involved, active, and sophisticated. C. Vann Woodward, for example, quotes from the Jackson Clairion Ledger, September 18, 1890:

> Edward Mayes, chancellor of the University of Mississippi and a historian of some distinction, proudly announc[ing] that "in all my life I have never voted any other ticket, I have never failed to vote, I have never scratched a ticket, and I would not, no matter whom the party might nominate for its candidate." ([1951]1971, 51–52)

And this was even before the institutions of Jim Crow were in place. If the central purpose in building the solid South was to have a unified national presence, the trade-off was, to Key, the acceptance of factionalism, frag mentation, and fundamentally nondemocratic politics locally. To Key, national unity and local fragmentation were as closely tied as the two sides of a coin. As he put it:

> The one-party system is purely an arrangement for national affairs. The legend prevails that within the Democratic party in the southern states factional groups are the equivalent of political parties elsewhere. In fact, the Democratic party in most states of the South is merely a holding-company for a congeries of transient squabbling factions, most of which fail by far to meet the standards of permanence, cohesiveness, and responsibility that characterize the political party. . . . In the conduct of campaigns for control of legislatures, for control of governorships, and for representatives in the national Congress, the South must depend for political leadership not on political parties, but on lone-wolf operators, on fortuitous groupings of individuals usually of a transient nature, on spectacular demagogues odd enough to command the attention of considerable numbers of voters, on men who have become persons of political consequence in their own little bailiwicks, and on other types of leaders whose methods to attract electoral attention serve as substitutes for leadership of a party organization. (1984, 16)

The consequences of the politics of faction were to Key thoroughly negative and precisely the negative of the politics of party (see 1984, 302–306). Factions, he claimed, lack continuity in name and in the makeup of their leader ship and the political candidates they present to the public. As a result, factions lack continuity in voter support. The electorate becomes confused because it does not have as clear a set of options, sustained over time, as with parties. Par ties, he believed, are able to be held responsible and, therefore, exercise at least a modicum of responsibility. Factions cannot be held responsible and, therefore, will not exercise responsibility. With factions, there is no consistent out group. Such a loyal and regularized opposition will search for issues to raise in their attempt to oust the governing party, unlike irregular factions, which, as he had just demonstrated held true for the southern states, generally cast issueless appeals. They lack collective spirit, a sense of duty and obligation, and any sense of joint responsibility between governor and legislature as well. In sum, fac tional politics undermines each part of his triad of party structures, both in the short term and, more worrisome, in the long term.

The solution to the problem of factions was clear-organized and sustained competition.

> When two distinct groups with some identity and continuity exist, they must raise issues and appeal to the masses if for no other reason than the desire for office. Whether the existence of issues causes the formation of continuing groups of politicians or whether the existence of competing groups causes issues to be raised is a moot point. Probably the two factors inter act. Nevertheless, in those states with loose and short-lived factions campaigns often are the emptiest sorts of debates over personalities, over the means for the achievement of what everybody agrees on. . . . [A] disorganized politics makes impossible a competition between recognizable groups for power. (1984, 304)

Thus, when writing of southern politics in state, he insisted in calling it the "nonparty South," reserving the term "one-party South" for discussing south ern politics in nation. To him, it was a "bald fact" that party machinery was an "impotent mechanism" and that southern party organizations "appear devoid of significance . . . in contrast to party organizations of states with dual party competition" (Key 1984, 387). He continued:

When the party does not have to fight campaigns-i.e., when it is not a vote-getting institution party organization departs radically from the usual conception of it. Democratic nominees in the South win with only the most feeble electioneering in the general elections. Lacking op position, no external pressure drives the party toward internal unity and discipline. Patronage does not function as a cohesive force; it remains beyond the reach of party functionaries as such: the party has little to do with putting into office those who control patronage. The party organization, therefore, becomes merely a framework for intra-party factional and personal competition. It has the usual complement of conventions, committees, and officials, but the resemblance to genuine party organization is purely formal. (1984, 387–88).

Factional politics lacks every positive virtue he felt partisan politics offered. Most serious among these were its effects on the ability of the public to exercise their sovereignty effectively. For Key, democracy worked from bottom up (his own words) while southern politics operated from the top down, and it was the creation and maintenance of factional rather than party politics that intentionally destroyed the ability of the public to govern.

The Emergence of Republican Competition in the South

Woodward (1971) makes clear that the dominance of the Democratic party arose in a "top-down" fashion (that is, from elites to the masses) in the late nineteenth century. Whites residing in the black belt secured political dominance over the whole South by ensuring that the overwhelming proportion of general election votes was counted in the Democratic column. They might be able to reduce, sometimes dramatically, the number of voters eligible, registered, and/or turning out. They might commit fraud in counting ballots. But no matter how they might shape the electorate and count the votes, in the end, they still needed to secure the support of most of the voters, most of the time. The most certain way to do so over the long haul was to assure that virtually all of the ambitious current and prospective politicians would spend their careers as Democrats. If all elites, even prominent educators and historians such as Edward Mayes, were Democrats and if all competition among them could be contained within the Democratic party, then what could the public do but choose among Democrats?

One threat they could not control, of course, was national politics: the possibility of the southern voter being attracted to the national Republican party or repelled from the national Democratic party. The party of Lincoln, especially if led by such as Theodore Roosevelt, attracted rather few southern voters, at least once blacks were disenfranchised. Eventually, however, Republicans would nominate presidential candidates, if not Eisenhower then Goldwater, considerably more attractive to the typical southern white voter than the Democratic opponent. Eventually, too, national (that is northern) Democrats would seek to pass a mid- to late-twentieth century analogue to a "force" bill-one might note the similarity between the Lodge force bill (a bill with little force) and the 1964 Civil Rights and 1965 Voting Rights acts. Most remarkable of all, it would be the southern, Democratic, accidental president who would have the inclination and the ability to break the implicit pact between the two regional wings of the party-sufficiently so that southerners would break with their party, seriously and in large numbers, at the presidential level. While the full story is more complex, the break of the solid South was top-down, but one effected primarily by the actions of national rather than regional politicians as it impacted the south ern electorate.

The rise of Republican voting in the South is well documented (e.g., Aistrup 1996). It has been a long, slow process. By now, as Figure 5.1 shows, the Republican party has become a serious and sustained competitor to the Democrats for essentially any and all national and state-level offices, and quite often at lower levels as well. By beginning in the first election after Brown v. Board, Figure 5.1 displays the generally slow rise of office holding by the GOP. Election to all of these offices began at under 10%. The effect of the civil rights movement and then the Civil Rights and Voting Rights acts marked the first increase in Republican victories in the South, especially at the top end (i.e., for governor and the national offices). But even these did not exceed one in four until the 1970s an era when attacks on Democrats could be phrased in terms of McGovern and Kennedy liberalism (a favorite tactic of Senator Jesse Helms, Republican from North Carolina, elected first in 1972). From there, GOP successes in seeking these offices increased in a highly variable but fundamentally upwards fashion. By the 1990s, the Republicans had reached the point where they consistently win more elections to these offices than the Democrats.

The Republicans had greater difficulty in breaking through in state legislative elections. While there was an increase in legislative electoral victories in the wake of the civil rights era, that was a jump to between only 10% and 15% and a jump that was virtually level from 1966 until the Reagan era. From that point on, GOP success in state legislative elections increased steadily, reaching approximately two victories in five contests in the last two elections. At one in ten losses, the Democratic legislative majorities were not in serious jeopardy in the 1970s. At one in three or more since then, those majorities were under serious threat and sometimes, as in North Carolina and Virginia, actually lost. This account, then, is of successes in Republican voting and outright electoral victories coming from the highest levels first. Aistrup (1996) has offered a recent and compelling account of the top-down nature of the emergence of Republican electoral success in the South. Here I offer a somewhat different, systematic, quantitative analysis.

[. . . Statistical evidence presented elsewhere in articles suggests a bottom-up approach, which] seems to be in stark contrast with what we have observed directly and as seen in Figure 5.1. How can both

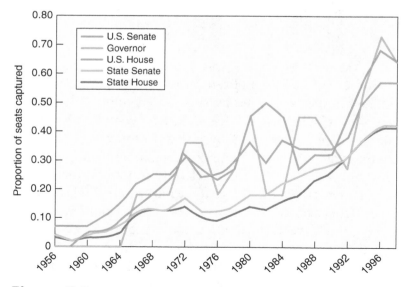

Figure 5.1

be true? The evidence is not yet weighed. If both kinds of evidence are correct, there is at least one plausible explanation. The electoral breakthroughs did in fact begin at the presidential level, of course, and move to high-profile Senate races, and so on "down." These broke the southern Democratic dominance, to be sure. They undoubtedly emboldened those who might run for office as Republicans. But they were just that breakthroughs. They did not signal a systematic development of Republican voting patterns, but idiosyncratic responses of southern voters to particular candidates. The statistical evidence . . . however, is estimating the systematic turn to support for Republican candidates. These are the accumulation of regularized provision of supportable candidates. That is, they describe the coming of the systematic appearance of ambitious politicians. As Schlesinger argued, they would enter politics as Republicans and climb systematically up the opportunity structure. What is being captured . . . then, is the systematic opening of these opportunities and the seizing of them by ambitious candidates.

Whichever the direction of influence, Key's more general question can be answered affirmatively. Southern Democrats, both in state and nation, face serious and by now sustained electoral competition from an organized and broad based party. Indeed, while the seriousness of the challenge undoubtedly varies considerably from district to district, two-party electoral competition is by now a fact of life throughout the South at a level not seen since the eras of competition between Jacksonian Democrat and Whig and again between Republican or Fusion and Redeemer for dominance.

Conclusion

[. . .] The empirical case has now been made. The development of southern parties in the twentieth century follows rather closely the lines Key's analysis suggested. The emergence of serious and sustained opposition at all levels of office to Democratic candidates by Republicans is closely associated in time with the development of perhaps the strongest and most effectively organized dual party system in southern history and at least at levels currently found outside the South, if not even higher.

The South has become a hotly contested region, reaching a peak not seen since the Jacksonian era and the two decades during which Conservative Democrats fought northern and Black Republicans for control of southern counties and states. As we have seen, in the former case, competition did not lead to organization. The latter case is even clearer. Competition in post-Reconstruction South led not to stronger party organizations as they sought votes among the mass public, but to the restrictions on the electorate, such that the Republican and even the potential Populist party base was not just undermined but effectively disenfranchised (Woodward 1971). Only in this manner, through the implementation of the political arms of Jim Crows laws, could the Democrats hold the South unified.

This solid southern Democracy was the creation primarily of a minority the black-belt, largely land-owning whites. They were a minority in several senses. Some were a racial minority in their own counties (see Key 1984, 7, Table 1), although in only Mississippi and South Carolina were there a majority of whites residing in counties with more than a 40% black population (a percentage central to the contemporary majority-minority district debate), and only in Georgia in addition was the percentage over one third. Thus, the white planter class was sometimes a local minority, racially, the black belt was a geographic minority in most of the South, and these whites at issue were everywhere and always a minority economically.

It is, thus, in some sense surprising that Key associated organized and competitive parties with healthy democratic rule. The case for these various links being necessary conditions is questioned by the nineteenth-century history of the South itself. Clearly, Key's argument has force. Competition is likely to lead to greater efforts to organize to win in the face of that competition. And when that competition is itself organizing to seek to win and hold majorities in the electorate and in the government, then one way to compete is to try to out organize to win those contests for majority allegiance. That is the consequence of majority-seeking in a majority system that favors two-party competition in the sense of Duverger's Law (see Aldrich 1995; Cox 1997).

That link may be strong but it is not inevitable. There is an alternative. Instead of competing within the structure of majority-rule based, republican democracy, one can try to alter the system of majority rule. The problem of politics is that those who seek to use the rules to govern are at the same time those who can write and rewrite the rules. One does so in a way that undermines the Madisonian republican principle only when the commitment to democratic principles is less than the commitment to something else. In the South in the nineteenth as in the twentieth century, the problem the whites faced was that they were (or, earlier, were soon to become) a minority a permanent minority. The majoritarian principle was to be feared at the founding if slaves were to be a part of the electorate. The majoritarian principle was to be feared in the second party system, as even with the founding compromise the South was becoming a minority in the nation. The necessity of national veto power described by Aldrich (1995) and Weingast (1998) was only one part of the solution sought in the second party system. Blocking northern interference was the key in that period, whether through veto, through the struggle over nullification, or eventually, through secession. The problem in the late nineteenth century was that the white upper class was a minority even within the South. The Populist threat of an alliance between the white farmer and worker and their black counterparts was the threat that if an alliance were successfully struck, it would form a majority. Thus, the minority could hold power only by undermining majority rule and that could be done only by undermining democratic principles.

It was, therefore, the maintenance of an illiberal society the withholding of the rights of citizenship from a sufficiently large number to assure minority elections in a putatively majority system that was the goal. It was the undermining of competition in the public that was the means, and that meant the failure of party organizations. The problems of factional politics that Key, following Madison, so decried was the tradeoff. The problems of personalization of politics that Van Buren sought to solve through the creation of the original mass party (see Aldrich 1995 for details) was the tradeoff for southern unity nation ally and minority control locally. It was the case, in other words, just as Key began his study, that "whatever phase of the southern political process one seeks to understand, sooner or later the trail of inquiry leads to the Negro" (1984[1949], 5).

References

Abramson, Paul R., John H. Aldrich, and David W Rohde. 1999. *Change and Continuity in the 1996 and 1998 Elections*. Washington, DC: CQ Press.

Aistrup, Joseph A. 1996. *The Southern Strategy Revisited: Republican Top-Down Advancement in the South*. Lexington: University Press of Kentucky.

Aldrich, John H. 1995. *Why Parties: The Origin and Transformation of Party Politics in America*. Chicago: University of Chicago Press, 1995.

Aldrich, John H., Brad Gomez, and John Griffin. N.d. "The State of State Party Organizations, 1999." Forthcoming manuscript.

Aldrich, John H. and John D. Griffin. 2000. "Ambition in the South: The Development of Republican Electoral Support, 1948–1998." Prepared for the Citadel Symposium on Southern Politics, Charleston, SC.

Beck, Paul Allen. 1977. "Partisan Dealignment in the Postwar South." *American Political Science Review* 71(2): 477–97.

Berlin, Ira. 1998. Man *Thousands Gone: The First Two Centuries of Slavery, in North America.* Cambridge, MA: Belknap Press of Harvard University Press.

Black, Earl. 1998. "The Newest Southern Politics." *Journal of Politics* 60(3): 591–612.

Black, Earl, and Merle Black. 1987. *Politics and Society in the South.* Cambridge, MA: Harvard University Press.

Converse, Philip E. 1966. "On the Possibility of Major Political Realignment in the South." In Angus Campbell, Philip E. Converse, Warren E. Miller, and Donald E. Stokes, eds. *Elections and the Political Order.* New York: John Wiley and Sons.

Cox, Gary W. 1997. *Making Votes Count: Strategic Coordination in the World's Electoral Systems.* Cambridge, UK: Cambridge University Press.

Gibson, James L., Cornelius P. Cotter, and John F. Bibby. 1983. "Assessing Party Organizational Strength." *American Journal of Political Science* 27 (2): 193–222.

Key, VO., Jr. [1949] 1984. *Southern Politics in State and Nation.* Reprint. Knoxville: University of Tennessee Press.

Lamis, Alexander P. 1990. *The Two Party South.* 2nd expanded ed. Oxford: Oxford University Press.

McCormick, Richard P. 1966. *The Second American Party System: Party Formation in the Jacksonian Era.* Chapel Hill: University of North Carolina Press.

Phillips, Kevin P. 1970. *The Emerging Republican Majority.* Garden City, NY: Doubleday.

Schlesinger, Joseph A. 1966. *Ambition and Politics: Political Careers in the United States.* Chicago: Rand McNally.

Wattenberg, Martin P. 1996. *The Decline of American Political Parties, 1952–1994.* Cambridge, MA: Harvard University Press.

Weingast, Barry R. 1998. "Political Stability and Civil War: Institutions, Commitment, and American Democracy." in Robert H. Bates, Avner Greif, Margaret Levy, Jean-Laurent Rosenthal, and Barry R. Weingast, eds., *Analytical Narratives.* Princeton, NJ: Princeton University Press.

Woodward, C. Vann. [1951] 1971. *Origins of the New South: 1877–1913.* Baton Rouge: Louisiana State University Press.

CHAPTER 6
INTEREST GROUPS

CITIZENS UNITED V. FEC

SUPREME COURT OF THE UNITED STATES
558 U.S. 310 (2010)

Justice **Kennedy** delivered the opinion of the Court.

Federal law prohibits corporations and unions from using their general treasury funds to make independent expenditures for speech defined as an "electioneering communication" or for speech expressly advocating the election or defeat of a candidate. 2 U.S.C. § 441b. Limits on electioneering communications were upheld in *McConnell* v. *Federal Election Comm'n*, 540 U.S. 93, 203–209 (2003). The holding of *McConnell* rested to a large extent on an earlier case, *Austin* v. *Michigan Chamber of Commerce*, 494 U.S. 652 (1990). *Austin* had held that political speech may be banned based on the speaker's corporate identity.

In this case we are asked to reconsider *Austin* and, in effect, *McConnell*. It has been noted that "*Austin* was a significant departure from ancient First Amendment principles," *Federal Election Comm'n* v. *Wisconsin Right to Life, Inc.*, 551 U.S. 449 (2007) (Scalia, J., concurring in part and concurring in judgment). We agree with that conclusion and hold that *stare decisis* does not compel the continued acceptance of *Austin*. The Government may regulate corporate political speech through disclaimer and disclosure requirements, but it may not suppress that speech altogether. We turn to the case now before us.

[. . .]

III

The First Amendment provides that "Congress shall make no law . . . abridging the freedom of speech." Laws enacted to control or suppress speech may operate at different points in the speech process. . . .

The law before us is an outright ban, backed by criminal sanctions. Section 441b makes it a felony for all corporations—including nonprofit advocacy corporations—either to expressly advocate the election or defeat of candidates or to broadcast electioneering communications within 30 days of a primary election and 60 days of a general election. Thus, the following acts would all be felonies under § 441b: The Sierra Club runs an ad, within the crucial phase of 60 days before the general election, that exhorts the public to disapprove of a Congressman who favors logging in national forests; the National Rifle Association publishes a book urging the public to vote for the challenger because the incumbent U. S. Senator supports a handgun ban; and the American Civil Liberties Union creates a Web site telling the public to vote for a Presidential candidate in light of that candidate's defense of free speech. These prohibitions are classic examples of censorship.

Section 441b is a ban on corporate speech notwithstanding the fact that a PAC created by a corporation can still speak. . . . A PAC is a separate association from the corporation. So the PAC exemption from § 441b's expenditure ban, § 441b(b)(2), does not allow corporations to speak. Even if a PAC could somehow allow a corporation to speak—and it does not—the option to form PACs does not alleviate the First Amendment problems with § 441b. PACs are burdensome alternatives; they are expensive to administer and subject to extensive regulations. For example, every PAC must appoint a treasurer, forward donations to the treasurer promptly, keep detailed records of the identities of the persons making donations, preserve receipts for three years, and file an organization statement and report changes to this information within 10 days. . . .

And that is just the beginning. PACs must file detailed monthly reports with the FEC, which are due at different times depending on the type of election that is about to occur. . . .

PACs have to comply with these regulations just to speak. This might explain why fewer than 2,000 of the millions of corporations in this country have PACs. . . . PACs, furthermore, must exist before they can speak. Given the onerous restrictions, a corporation may not be able to establish a PAC in time to make its views known regarding candidates and issues in a current campaign.

Section 441b's prohibition on corporate independent expenditures is thus a ban on speech. As a "restriction on the amount of money a person or group can spend on political communication during a campaign," that statute "necessarily reduces the quantity of expression by restricting the number of issues discussed, the depth of their exploration, and the size of the audience reached." *Buckley* v. *Valeo*, 424 U.S. 1, 19 (1976). Were the Court to uphold these restrictions, the Government could repress speech by silencing certain voices at any of the various points in the speech process. . . . If § 441b applied to individuals, no one would believe that it is merely a time, place, or manner restriction on speech. Its purpose and effect are to silence entities whose voices the Government deems to be suspect.

Speech is an essential mechanism of democracy, for it is the means to hold officials accountable to the people. . . . The right of citizens to inquire, to hear, to speak, and to use information to reach consensus is a precondition to enlightened self-government and a necessary means to protect it. The First Amendment "has its fullest and most urgent application' to speech uttered during a campaign for political office." *Eu* v. *San Francisco County Democratic Central Comm.*, 489 U.S. 214, 223, (1989). . . .

For these reasons, political speech must prevail against laws that would suppress it, whether by design or inadvertence. Laws that burden political speech are "subject to strict scrutiny," which requires the Government to prove that the restriction "furthers a compelling interest and is narrowly tailored to achieve that interest." While it might be maintained that political speech simply cannot be banned or restricted as a categorical matter . . . the quoted language . . . provides a sufficient framework for protecting the relevant First Amendment interests in this case. We shall employ it here.

Premised on mistrust of governmental power, the First Amendment stands against attempts to disfavor certain subjects or viewpoints. Prohibited, too, are restrictions distinguishing among different speakers, allowing speech by some but not others. As instruments to censor, these categories are interrelated: Speech restrictions based on the identity of the speaker are all too often simply a means to control content.

Quite apart from the purpose or effect of regulating content, moreover, the Government may commit a constitutional wrong when by law it identifies certain preferred speakers. By taking the right to speak from some and giving it to others, the Government deprives the disadvantaged person or class of the right to use speech to strive to establish worth, standing, and respect for the speaker's voice. The Government may not by these means deprive the public of the right and privilege to determine for itself what speech and speakers are worthy of consideration. The First Amendment protects speech and speaker, and the ideas that flow from each.

The Court has upheld a narrow class of speech restrictions that operate to the disadvantage of certain persons, but these rulings were based on an interest in allowing governmental entities to perform their functions. . . . The corporate independent expenditures at issue in this case, however, would not interfere with governmental functions, so these cases are inapposite. These precedents stand only for the proposition that there are certain governmental functions that cannot operate without some restrictions on particular kinds of speech. By contrast, it is inherent in the nature of the political process that voters must be free to obtain information from diverse sources in order to determine how to cast their votes. At least before *Austin*, the Court had not allowed the exclusion of a class of speakers from the general public dialogue.

We find no basis for the proposition that, in the context of political speech, the Government may impose restrictions on certain disfavored speakers. Both history and logic lead us to this conclusion.

A

1

The Court has recognized that First Amendment protection extends to corporations. . . .

This protection has been extended by explicit holdings to the context of political speech. Under the rationale of these precedents, political speech does not lose First Amendment protection "simply because its source is a corporation." Corporations and other associations, like individuals, contribute to the 'discussion, debate, and the dissemination of information and ideas' that the First Amendment seeks to foster" (quoting *Bellotti,* 435 U.S. at 783).

The Court has thus rejected the argument that political speech of corporations or other associations should be treated differently under the First Amendment simply because such associations are not "natural persons. . . ."

At least since the latter part of the 19th century, the laws of some States and of the United States imposed a ban on corporate direct contributions to candidates. Yet not until 1947 did Congress first prohibit independent expenditures by corporations and labor unions. . . .

For almost three decades thereafter, the Court did not reach the question whether restrictions on corporate and union expenditures are constitutional. . . .

B

The Court is . . . confronted with conflicting lines of precedent: a pre-*Austin* line that forbids restrictions on political speech based on the speaker's corporate identity and a post-*Austin* line that permits them. No case before *Austin* had held that Congress could prohibit independent expenditures for political speech based on the speaker's corporate identity. Before *Austin*, Congress had enacted legislation for this purpose, and the Government urged the same proposition before this Court. . . .

In its defense of the corporate-speech restrictions in § 441b, the Government. . .argues instead that [an]other compelling interests support *Austin's* holding that corporate expenditure restrictions are constitutional: an anticorruption interest. . . .

[. . .]

What we have said also shows the invalidity of other arguments made by the Government. . . . [T]he Government falls back on the argument that corporate political speech can be banned in order to prevent corruption or its appearance. In *Buckley*, the Court found this interest "sufficiently important" to allow limits on contributions but did not extend that reasoning to expenditure limits. . . .

The practices *Buckley* noted would be covered by bribery laws . . . if a *quid pro quo* arrangement were proved. The Court, in consequence, has noted that restrictions on direct contributions are preventative, because few if any contributions to candidates will involve *quid pro quo* arrangements. The *Buckley* Court, nevertheless, sustained limits on direct contributions in order to ensure against the reality or appearance of corruption. That case did not extend this rationale to independent expenditures, and the Court does not do so here.

[. . .]

When *Buckley* identified a sufficiently important governmental interest in preventing corruption or the appearance of corruption, that interest was limited to *quid pro quo* corruption. . . . The fact that speakers may have influence over or access to elected officials does not mean that these officials are corrupt. . . .

The appearance of influence or access, furthermore, will not cause the electorate to lose faith in our democracy. By definition, an independent expenditure is political speech presented to the electorate that is not coordinated with a candidate. . . . The fact that a corporation, or any other speaker, is willing to spend money to try to persuade voters presupposes that the people have the ultimate influence over elected officials. This is inconsistent with any suggestion that the electorate will refuse "'to take part in democratic governance'" because of additional political speech made by a corporation or any other speaker.

[. . .]

[I]t is our law and our tradition that more speech, not less, is the governing rule. An outright ban on corporate political speech during the critical preelection period is not a permissible remedy. Here Congress has created categorical bans on speech that are asymmetrical to preventing *quid pro quo* corruption.

DISSENT

Justice **Stevens,** with whom Justice Ginsburg, Justice Breyer, and Justice Sotomayor join, concurring in part and dissenting in part.

The real issue in this case concerns how, not if, the appellant may finance its electioneering. Citizens United is a wealthy nonprofit corporation that runs a political action committee (PAC) with millions of dollars in assets. Under the Bipartisan Campaign Reform Act of 2002 (BCRA), it could have used those assets to televise and promote *Hillary: The Movie* wherever and whenever it wanted to. It also could have spent unrestricted sums to broadcast *Hillary* at any time other than the 30 days before the last primary election. Neither Citizens United's nor any other corporation's speech has been "banned." All that the parties dispute is whether Citizens United had a right to use the funds in its general treasury to pay for broadcasts during the 30-day period. The notion that the First Amendment dictates an affirmative answer to that question is, in my judgment, profoundly misguided. Even more misguided is the notion that the Court must rewrite the law relating to campaign expenditures by *for-profit* corporations and unions to decide this case.

The basic premise underlying the Court's ruling is its iteration, and constant reiteration, of the proposition that the First Amendment bars regulatory distinctions based on a speaker's identity, including its "identity" as a corporation. While that glittering generality has rhetorical appeal, it is not a correct statement of the law. Nor does it tell us when a corporation may engage in electioneering that some of its shareholders oppose. It does not even resolve the specific question whether Citizens United may be required to finance some of its messages with the money in its PAC. The conceit that corporations must be treated identically to natural persons in the political sphere is not only inaccurate but also inadequate to justify the Court's disposition of this case.

In the context of election to public office, the distinction between corporate and human speakers is significant. Although they make enormous contributions to our society, corporations are not actually members of it. They cannot vote or run for office. Because they may be managed and controlled by nonresidents, their interests may conflict in fundamental respects with the interests of eligible voters. The financial resources, legal structure, and instrumental orientation of corporations raise legitimate concerns about their role in the electoral process. Our lawmakers have a compelling constitutional basis, if not also a democratic duty, to take measures designed to guard against the potentially deleterious effects of corporate spending in local and national races.

The majority's approach to corporate electioneering marks a dramatic break from our past. Congress has placed special limitations on campaign spending by corporations ever since the passage of the Tillman Act in 1907. . . . The Court today rejects a century of history when it treats the distinction between corporate and individual campaign spending as an invidious novelty born of *Austin* v. *Michigan Chamber of Commerce*, 494 U.S. 652 (1990).

III

[. . .]

The ruling rests on several premises. First, the Court claims that *Austin* and *McConnell* have "banned" corporate speech. Second, it claims that the First Amendment precludes regulatory distinctions based on speaker identity, including the speaker's identity as a corporation. Third, it claims that *Austin* and *McConnell* were radical outliers in our First Amendment tradition and our campaign finance jurisprudence. Each of these claims is wrong.

The So-Called "Ban"

Pervading the Court's analysis is the ominous image of a "categorical ba[n]" on corporate speech. This characterization is highly misleading, and needs to be corrected.

In fact it already has been. Our cases have repeatedly pointed out that, "[c]ontrary to the [majority's] critical assumptions," the statutes upheld in *Austin* and *McConnell* do "not impose an *absolute* ban on all forms of corporate political spending." For starters, both statutes provide exemptions for PACs, separate segregated funds established by a corporation for political purposes. . . .

Administering a PAC entails some administrative burden, but so does complying with the disclaimer, disclosure, and reporting requirements that the Court today upholds. . .and no one has suggested that the burden is severe for a sophisticated for-profit corporation. . . . Like all other natural persons, every shareholder of every corporation remains entirely free under *Austin* and *McConnell* to do however much electioneering she pleases outside of the corporate form. The owners of a "mom & pop" store can simply place ads in their own names, rather than the store's.

[. . .]

So let us be clear: Neither *Austin* nor *McConnell* held or implied that corporations may be silenced; the FEC is not a "censor". . . [T]he majority's incessant talk of a "ban" aims at a straw man.

CHAPTER 7
LEGISLATURES

WHO PASSES BUSINESS'S "MODEL BILLS"? POLICY CAPACITY AND CORPORATE INFLUENCE IN U.S. STATE POLITICS[1]

ALEXANDER HERTEL-FERNANDEZ
Harvard University

Which policymakers are most likely to enact legislation drafted by organized business interests? Departing from the business power scholarship that emphasizes structural, electoral, or financial mechanisms for corporate influence, I argue that lawmakers are likely to rely on businesses' proposals when they lack the time and resources to develop legislation on their own, especially when they also hold an ideological affinity for business. Using two new datasets of "model bills" developed by the American Legislative Exchange Council (ALEC), a policy group that promotes pro-business legislation across the states, I find strong support for this theory. These results indicate that ALEC provides private policy capacity to state legislators who would otherwise lack such support, and relatedly, that low state policy capacity may favor certain organized interests over others—namely the business interests affiliated with ALEC. My findings have implications for the study of business influence in policymaking, as well as for state politics.

[. . .]

After assuming the governorship of Wisconsin in 2011, Scott Walker worked with his state's legislature to enact a controversial budget reform agenda that, among other measures, sharply limited the collective bargaining rights of many public sector workers. Progressive advocacy groups and journalists noted that many of the provisions in Walker's budget bill bore a striking resemblance to policy proposals from a business-backed, conservative group called the American Legislative Exchange Council (ALEC). The budget bill was not the only instance of ALEC legislation in Wisconsin. Both tort reform and telecommunications deregulation bills signed into law by Governor Walker in 2011 drew heavily from model bills developed by ALEC.[2] By ALEC's account, Wisconsin is just one example of the group's influence. ALEC claimed that states enacted 115 bills in 2009 that were based on ALEC proposals (826 were introduced), covering areas as diverse as elections, health care, education, the environment, taxes, and gun rights. As media coverage over the past several years has established, ALEC provides companies the opportunity to work with state lawmakers to draft model bills that are distributed to state legislatures across the country—often with great success for the companies. The New York Times, for example, has concluded that ALEC acts as a "stealth" lobbyist for business,[3] Bill Moyers opined on an episode of his show dedicated to the group that ALEC is the "most influential corporate-funded political force most of America has never heard of," Bloomberg Business Week characterized ALEC as a "bill laundry" for corporate policy proposals,[4] and Fortune called ALEC the big corporate political player "you've never heard of."[5] I examine ALEC's influence, arguing that the group provides an important window into business power in American politics, a

Alexander Hertel-Fernandez, *Who Passes Business's "Model Bills?" Policy Capacity and Corporate Influence in U.S. State Politics,* Perspectives on Politics, 12(3), 582–602, reproduced with permission.

topic that has long generated debates within political science.[6] The primary reason ALEC makes such an interesting case is that it is a major avenue through which companies pursue policy change. Businesses as diverse as Amazon, UPS, pharmaceutical firms, private prison operators, Enron, insurance companies, and tobacco manufacturers have all worked through ALEC over its forty-year history to develop and pass legislation across the country. In addition, ALEC operates at the state level, providing an opportunity to examine variation in the legislative success of business across governments embedded in different social, economic, and political contexts. Finally, the structure of ALEC is relatively unusual, providing a case of lobbying that is distinct from other business associations or labor groups since ALEC does not give political contributions or engage in electoral politics. Because of this, ALEC offers a chance to look beyond political campaigning and donations to other mechanisms that businesses use to influence the policymaking process. In particular, I argue that business interests can take advantage of low policy capacity in state legislatures, offering private policy resources to legislators. By providing pre-written model bills, talking points, and extensive research assistance, businesses can attract support from harried, part-time state officials who are in need of precisely such services. Business influence through low policy capacity should be magnified for lawmakers who are already supportive of business interests. This sort of power is different from the pathways typically described in the business politics literature, which often revolve around campaign donations and other financial inducements, or the structural power that business enjoys in a capitalist economy. I argue that leveraging weak state policy capacity is precisely the strategy that ALEC has employed to influence legislation. Using a new dataset I have constructed that combines leaked internal ALEC documents with the results of a survey of state legislators (both from 1995), I test this argument and find strong support for my claims. ALEC model legislation was more likely to become law when legislators spent relatively more time on non-policy activities (like campaigning) and less time working on legislation, and had access to fewer legislative resources. "Citizen" legislatures thus appear much more likely to rely on business-drafted bills compared with more professionalized legislatures. ALEC bills were also much more likely to been acted when legislators viewed business, rather than labor, as their political constituency and when states were governed by conservative lawmakers. I find consistent results in an analysis of another new dataset I assembled of individual legislators who sponsored ALEC model bills in 1995. Ideologically conservative legislators and Republicans were much more likely to propose ALEC bills, as were junior lawmakers who were not in policy leadership positions and thus had access to fewer policy resources. My quantitative results are further buttressed by qualitative evidence I have assembled from a variety of sources, including archival ALEC documents, interviews, and the media record.

[. . .]

What Is ALEC and What Does It Do?

Founded in 1973 by conservative activists, including Paul Weyrich (a co-founder of the Heritage Foundation and the Moral Majority coalition), ALEC was conceived as a group that could promote conservative, pro-business legislation at the state level by bringing private companies together with state legislators.[7] Today, ALEC reports a membership of about 2,000, largely Republican, state lawmakers (this represents about one-third of all current state lawmakers).[8] These legislators are joined by several hundred private companies, as well as conservative think tanks and philanthropies. ALEC does not publish the names of its private sector members, but the companies listed on its private-sector board of advisors include PhRMA, Pfizer, Diageo, AT&T, Koch Companies Public Sector, Altria, Exxon, State Farm, and UPS. ALEC's public- and private-sector members convene in task forces each year to draft model bills ranging across a diverse set of issue areas. Once a task force authors and approves a model bill, and that model bill is in turn approved by ALEC's board of directors, ALEC disseminates these proposals through publications, annual events, and its website.

[. . .]

Though ALEC argues that state legislators always have the final say over what model legislation is adopted by the organization[9], the *New York Times* has reported that

> The organization's rules give corporations a great deal of influence on the task forces, where model legislation must first clear a preliminary vote before going to the board. As a result, meeting minutes show, draft bills that are preferred by a majority of lawmakers are sometimes killed by the corporate members at the table . . . ALEC's bylaws also grant its corporate members greater power over task force appointments. They say lawmakers can be removed from a task force leadership position for any reason, while private-sector members can be removed only "with cause," like nonpayment of dues.[10]

Private sector members thus appear to have an important veto over what is ultimately drafted and promoted by the group. Indeed, ALEC itself has acknowledged that the main authors of the model legislation are frequently lawyers from its private sector members. According to ALEC's senior director of policy, "[m]ost of the bills are written by outside sources and companies, attorneys, [and legislative] counsels."[11] In general, ALEC's task forces have recommended model bills to reduce the regulation of business; privatize public sector services; cut taxes, especially for wealthier individuals and companies; and restrict the collective bargaining power and organizing capacity of labor unions, particularly in the public sector.[12] ALEC's bills generally coincide closely with the interests of its private sector members. For example, the corporate members of the public safety and criminal justice task force, including the largest private prison firms, have worked to develop and promote legislation that would create mandatory minimum sentences, "three strikes" laws, and "truth in sentencing" laws—all of which would increase the number of incarcerated individuals and thus increase the demand for prison facilities.[13] Similarly, online educational services providers have drafted ALEC bills requiring public school students to take online-only courses as part of their graduation requirements.[14] Ammunition and gun distributers also worked through ALEC to promote controversial "stand your ground" legislation legalizing the use of deadly force for self-defense; this same legislation would be referenced in the Trayvon Martin shooting controversy.[15] And energy companies have pushed for states to weaken their environmental regulations and to hamper efforts to address climate change.[16] ALEC's activities are largely financed through its private sector members, who pay between $7,000 and $25,000 in tax-deductible annual dues. State legislators, in contrast, pay $50 each year.[17]

[. . .]

In sum, ALEC provides businesses with an opportunity to articulate and promote their preferences for public policy across the states, and provides state legislators an opportunity to gain access to policy ideas and legislative assistance provided by those business interests. In the following section, I describe how this relationship serves as an important mechanism for corporate influence and discuss how it fits into debates over business power in American politics.

What ALEC Can Teach Us about Business Power

Political scientists have long been attracted to the study of business power in American politics. A recurring theme is the tension between pluralist and elitist perspectives on business power. Represented best by some of the earlier work of Robert Dahl,[18] the pluralists argued that business is an interest group like any other, and receives no special treatment within the political arena; other interests and actors can provide a check on the influence of corporations.

Contemporary work in the pluralist tradition includes Mark Smith[19] and Gunnar Trumbull.[20] Smith argues that organized business interests tend to win in American politics only when they enjoy support from the public. The issues that business tends to unite around, Smith argues, are precisely the issues that tend to receive the most public attention, and therefore are policy debates in which citizens are well-equipped to hold their public officials accountable. To Smith's mind, organized business possesses independent power only in so much as it can shape public attitudes. Trumbull makes a congruent claim, arguing that businesses need the support of broad-based citizen groups to succeed in politics.

In contrast to the optimistic assessments of the pluralists is the scholarship from elitists, who argue that business holds a privileged place in politics and is unlike other interest groups. One important reason for this power, according to Fred Block[21] and the later work of Robert Dahl and Charles Lindblom,[22] is that businesses are responsible for employment and investment in a capitalist economy. Politicians thus need to appease business interests to maintain a healthy economy. In addition, business also possesses a greater number of easily deployable power resources, especially financial contributions, which it can bring to bear on the policymaking process.[23] A final important lever that business can exploit, according to elite theorists, is limiting the terms of political debate to avoid even discussing issues that go against business interests.[24] Jeffrey Winters and Benjamin Page's work captures the elitist perspective in more recent years; the authors argue that the United States can currently be characterized as a political oligarchy, with wealthy Americans exerting vastly greater control than ordinary Americans in key domains of policy.[25]

Between these two poles is a third set of scholars who argue that neither the pluralist nor elitist perspectives capture the full range of American politics. Rather, this third set of researchers contends that the pluralist tradition describes American politics in some periods and arenas of politics, while elitists are correct in other periods and policies. David Vogel, for example, has argued that business power ebbs and flows, corresponding to the public's perception of the economy.[26] Business gains strength when the public perceives the economy as weak, while business loses strength when the public perceives the economy as strong and thus can tolerate more intervention and regulation. Jacob Hacker and Paul Pierson concur with Vogel that business power is a variable, not a constant, arguing that it is conditioned by institutional and economic factors.[27] Business influence, for example, is maximized when firms can threaten capital flight, such as in a decentralized system of policymaking.[28] In later work, Hacker and Pierson have also stressed the importance of a strong organized labor movement in checking the power of business.[29]

Here I follow the third set of authors in charting a middle course between elitist and pluralist approaches. Like the elitists, I argue that business power may well be asymmetric, especially when organized labor or other comparable groups are weak and incapable of generating countervailing pressure against business or when legislators are predisposed to supporting business interests. At the same time, following the pluralist perspective, I see business power as flowing not just from business's structural position in the economy, but also from other more traditional strategies employed by interest groups.

Drawing on the work of Richard Hall and Alan Deardorff[30] and other interest group scholars,[31] I argue that one powerful way that businesses can influence the policymaking process is by providing policy resources to legislators who might otherwise lack such resources. Halland Deardorff argue that lobbying is not about trying to exchange money for votes, or to persuade opposing legislators to change their positions. Rather, effective lobbyists provide "matching grants" of information, talking points, polling, and policy resources to similar-minded legislators to support policy development. Despite offering a persuasive argument consistent with observed interest group behavior, the business power literature has largely not engaged with Hall and Deardorff's claim about the importance of policy resources and capacity. While rightly calling on researchers to focus more on policy and less on "electoral spectacle," Hacker and Pierson's recent work, for example, still emphasizes financial and electoral pressures as the main mechanisms for business influence.[32] My argument starts from the premise that legislators seek to enact laws, especially if those laws correspond to the preferences of legislators' constituents, interest group supporters, and their own personal beliefs. Crafting legislation, however, requires a series of costly inputs. These inputs include ideas for legislation, references to relevant scholarly work, research assistance examining the implications of proposed legislation, expert witnesses who can testify in favor of (or against) bills, and polling data about public opinion towards different proposals. I hypothesize that businesses can therefore influence the policymaking process by providing those policy inputs to legislators who would otherwise lack such resources. Corporate interests, in essence, are lowering the cost of passing business-friendly bills relative to the cost of passing non-business friendly bills.[33] Provided with cheaper business-friendly bills, we ought to see resource-constrained legislators enact more of those bills.

[. . .]

In sum, while the interests that ALEC represents are similar to other business groups in politics, it functions very differently from those organizations. ALEC thus matters as an interesting case of business mobilization in its own right, given its success over the past four decades and its unique political structure. It also is an interesting case since it presents an opportunity for closely examining how policy resources matter for business influence.

[. . .]

When Do Legislators Rely on Business's Model Bills?

If my theory regarding policy resources were correct, we ought to observe that ALEC was most successful where legislators had fewer resources to dedicate towards policymaking, particularly where legislators were also already supportive of business interests. I assess these predictions across three different datasets I have assembled: a quantitative analysis of the correlates of ALEC bill enactments across the states, a quantitative analysis of the characteristics of individual legislators who authored and sponsored ALEC model bills, and a review of qualitative materials from the group's members, leadership, and critics.

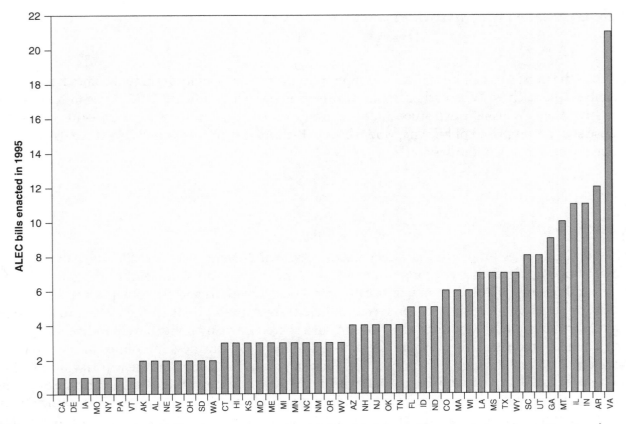

Figure 7.1 ALEC bill enactments in 1995. Neither Rhode Island or Kentucky enacted bills from ALEC in 1995.

ALEC Bill Enactments across the States

My first analysis looks at the characteristics of states that enacted ALEC bills. My outcome measure in this analysis comes from an internal ALEC publication that lists which states enacted legislation based on ALEC's model bills in 1995.[34] Figure 7.1 shows these bill totals for each state in 1995. In all, ALEC could claim 231 state enactments that year. The states with the most ALEC bill enactments in 1995 included Virginia (with 21 bills), Arkansas (12), Indiana (11), Illinois (11), and Montana (10). The states with the most ALEC bill introductions included Illinois (52 bills), California (41), Hawaii (38), New York (37) and Louisiana (33). The states with especially high success rates—ALEC bill enactments as a share of introductions—included Indiana, Montana, Virginia, and Idaho.

[...]

[...]

In sum, the analysis of individual legislator behavior closely matches the findings across states, and strongly supports my argument that business influence, as exercised through ALEC, is high when legislators lack policy resources, and especially when those legislators are also more receptive to businesses' interests.

Evidence from the Historical Record

[. . .]

Perhaps the most compelling evidence in support of the policy capacity argument comes from ALEC members themselves. When asked about his involvement with ALEC in 2012, Oregon state representative Gene Whisnant explained that the group "is 'a great resource' for a part-time legislator whose staff is comprised of his wife, who works half-time, and an aide who works three days a week when lawmakers are not in session."[35]

[. . .]

Conclusion

How do businesses influence the policymaking process? Much of the past literature on business power has suggested that corporate interests hold sway over American politics because of their structural position in the economy or because of tactical donations and electoral pressures that push legislators to support businesses' preferred policies. These perceptions in the academic literature, especially the emphasis on political giving, are also shared by many politicians, pundits, journalists, and citizens, who regularly attribute the outsized influence of business in politics to corporations' large capacity for campaign donations.[36] The focus on money in politics as the primary mechanism for business influence has only been reinforced by the 2010 Citizens United decision by the Supreme Court, which permitted unlimited (independent) political spending by corporations, associations, and labor unions, as well as the ensuing progressive backlash to the Court's decision. As political journalist Matt Bai summarized, "The oft-repeated narrative . . . goes like this: Citizens United unleashed a torrent of money from businesses and the multi-millionaires who run them, and as a result we are now seeing the corporate takeover of American politics."[37]

Without directly challenging these perspectives, I illustrate the importance of another, underappreciated mechanism for business influence, especially across the states: weak policy capacity. Faced with constraints on their time and resources, legislators turn to private groups for policy ideas, research assistance, and administrative support. By offering these bundles of policy resources—especially in an appealing manner through free trips and conferences—businesses can have great legislative success, particularly when legislators are already ideologically oriented towards the policies business is promoting. This strategy is likely to be especially successful when groups offering perspectives opposed to those of business are weak or absent.

I have tested this argument by studying the behavior of one specific business group—ALEC—that primarily engages in policy capacity-related lobbying across the states, allowing me to isolate these mechanisms from other avenues of influence through elections or donations. Indeed, the appeal of ALEC to many corporate interests was a realization that the states represented an untapped opportunity for businesses to build relationships with lawmakers who were looking for new legislation and in need of policy resources.[38] I find strong support for the policy capacity arguments in the new datasets I have assembled: ALEC bills were more likely to been acted in states where legislators had access to fewer policy resources, and ALEC bills were more likely to be introduced and authored by junior legislators with less policy expertise. Consistent with the notion that policy capacity interacts with prior ideological convictions, I also find that ALEC bills were more likely to be introduced and enacted by conservative legislators under conditions of low policy capacity.

Together, my findings suggest that citizens, advocacy groups, and journalists interested in understanding the role of business in politics ought to focus on policy capacity, in addition to the usual suspects of political contributions and electoral campaigns. They also suggest that scholars and citizens concerned with economic and political inequality ought to pay just as much attention to the states as to the federal government. As ALEC demonstrates quite vividly, the battles between organized business and labor are just as pitched—and consequential—in American statehouses as they are in Washington, DC. The need for greater attention to businesses' role in state policymaking is further underscored by the fact that the decision by corporations to mobilize in state government was a strategic one; corporate representatives and ALEC staff recognized that they possessed strategic advantages in state houses that they otherwise lacked in national politics (recall, for example, the quote from ALEC's national chairman describing how state legislators were more receptive to business interests than national lawmakers).

[. . .]

References

ALEC. 1981. "Fundraising letter from Lawrence D. Pratt for ALEC." Berkeley, CA: University of California, Berkeley Bancroft Library: People for the American Way Collection, Carton 6, Folder 16.

ALEC. 1983. "First Reading: Interview with ALEC National Chairman Buz Lukens." University of California, Berkeley Bancroft Library: People for the American Way Collection, Carton 6, Folder 27.

ALEC. 1989. "Attention Legislative Spouses." University of California, San Francisco: Legacy Tobacco Archives.

ALEC. 1990. "Criminal Justice Reporter." University of California, San Francisco: Legacy Tobacco Archives.

ALEC.1995. "FYI:A Bulletin for ALEC Leaders, July 12, 1995." University of California, San Francisco: Legacy Tobacco Archives.

ALEC. 2002. "Annual Report." University of California, Berkeley Bancroft Library: People for the American Way Collection of Conservative Political Ephemera and Broadcasting, 1980–2004.

ALEC. n.d.a. "ALEC: A Grant Proposal for Focus on Tax Policy." University of California, San Francisco: Legacy Tobacco Archives.

ALEC. n.d.b. "Private Sector Membership Renewal Letter to the Tobacco Institute." University of California, San Francisco: Legacy Tobacco Archives.

Ansolabehere, Stephen, John M. de Figueiredo, and James M. Snyder. 2003. "Why Is There so Little Money in U.S. Politics?" *Journal of Economic Perspectives* 17(1): 5–30.

Arnold, R. Douglas. 1990. *The Logic of Congressional Action.* New Haven, CT: Yale University Press.

Austen-Smith, David. 1993. "Information and Influence: Lobbying for Agendas and Votes." *American Journal of Political Science* 37(3): 799–833.

Bachrach, Peter, and Morton S. Baratz. 1962. "Two Faces of Power." *American Political Science Review* 56(4): 947–52.

Bai, Matt. 2012. "How Much Has Citizens United Changed the Political Game?" *New York Times Magazine*, July 17.

Balla, Steven J. 2001. "Interstate Professional Associations and the Diffusion of Policy Innovations." *American Politics Research* 29(3): 221–45.

Bartels, Larry. 2008. *Unequal Democracy: The Political Economy of the Gilded Age.* Princeton, NJ: Princeton University Press.

Berkman, Michael B. 2001. "Legislative Professionalism and the Demand for Groups: The Institutional Context of Interest Population Density." *Legislative Studies Quarterly* XXVI(4): 661–79.

Berry, William D., Richard C. Fording, Evan J. Ringquist, Russell L. Hanson, and Carl E. Klarner. 2010. "Measuring Citizen and Government Ideology in the U.S. States: A Re-appraisal." *State Politics and Policy Quarterly* 10(2): 117–35.

Biewen, John. 2002. "Corporate-Sponsored Crime Laws (Part I of Corrections, Inc.)." American Radio Works, April.

Block, Fred. 1977. "The Ruling Class Does Not Rule." *Socialist Revolution* 33: 6–28.

Bottari, Mary. 2011. "ALEC Bills in Wisconsin." Madison, WI: The Center for Media and Democracy.

Bottari, Mary, and Brendan Fischer. 2013. "Efforts to Deliver 'Kill Shot' to Paid Sick Leave Tied to ALEC." The Huffington Post, April 3.

Broockman, David. 2012. "The 'Problem of Preferences': Medicare and Business Support for the Welfare State." *Studies in American Political Development* 26: 83–106.

Buttice, Matthew K., and Benjamin Highton. 2013. "How Does Multilevel Regression and Post stratification Perform with Conventional National Surveys?" *Political Analysis* 21(4): 449–67.

Carey, John M., Richard G. Niemi, and Lynda W. Powell. 2000a. "State Legislative Survey and Contextual Data, 1995." Ann Arbor, MI: Inter-university Consortium for Political and Social Research.

_____. 2000b. *Term Limits in the State Legislatures.* Ann Arbor: University of Michigan Press.

Clawson, Dan, Alan Neustadtl, and Denise Scott. 1992. *Money Talks: Corporate PACs and Political Influence.* New York: Basic Books.

Cole, Michelle. 2012. "ALEC gains foothold in Oregon, with one-fourth of legislators as members." *The Oregonian*, May 26.

Conservative Digest. 1985. "ALEC—The Most Dangerously Effective Organization." University of California, Berkeley Bancroft Library: People for the American Way Collection, Carton 6, Folder 17.

Council of State Governments. 1994–1995. *The Book of the States, Volume 30.* Lexington, KY: Council of State Governments.

Culpepper, Pepper D. 2010. *Quiet Politics and Business Power: Corporate Control in Europe and Japan.* New York: Cambridge University Press.

Dagan, David, and Steven M. Teles. 2012. "The Conservative War on Prisons." *The Washington Monthly*, November 13.

Dahl, Robert A. 1959. "Business and Politics: A Critical Appraisal of Political Science." *American Political Science Review* 53(1): 1–34.

_____. 1961. *Who Governs? Democracy and Power in an American City.* New Haven, CT: Yale University Press.

Dahl, Robert, and Charles Lindblom. 1976. *Politics, Economics and Welfare.* New York: Harper.

Edsall, Thomas B. 1989. *The New Politics of Inequality.* New York: W.W. Norton & Company.

Elk, Mike, and Bob Sloan. 2011. "The Hidden History of ALEC and Prison Labor." *The Nation*, August 1.

Fang, Lee. 2013. *The Machine: A Field Guide to the Resurgent Right.* New York: The New Press.

Fenno, Richard. 1973. *Congressmen in Committees.* Boston, MA: Little, Brown.

Ferguson, Thomas, and Joel Rogers. 1987. *Right Turn: The Decline of the Democrats and the Future of American Politics.* New York: Hill and Wang.

Fischer, Brendan. 2012. "WI Legislators Receive $24K in Campaign Contributions after Pushing ALEC Predatory Lending Bill." Madison, WI: Center for Media and Democracy.

Fortune Magazine. 2011. "The Big Political Player You've Never Heard Of." January 10.

Francis, Wayne L. 1989. *The Legislative Committee Game: A Comparative Analysis of Fifty States.* Columbus, OH: Ohio State University Press.

Gilens, Martin. 2012. *Affluence and Influence: Economic Inequality and Political Power in America.* Princeton, NJ: Princeton University Press.

Gilligan, Thomas W., and Keith Krehbiel. 1990. "Organization of Informative Committees by a Rational Legislature." *American Journal of Political Science* 34(2): 531–64.

Graves, Lisa, Jennifer Page, Brendan Fischer, and Mary Bottari. 2011. A Comparison of ALEC and NCSL. Madison, WI: Center for Media and Democracy.

Graves, Lisa. 2012. "Buying Influence: How the American Legislative Exchange Council Uses Corporate-Funded "Scholarships" to Send Lawmakers on Trips with Corporate Lobbyists." Common Cause, Center for Media and Democracy, and DBA Press.

Gray, Virginia, and David Lowery. 2000. *The Population Ecology of Interest Representation: Lobbying Communities in the American States.* Ann Arbor: University of Michigan Press.

Greeley, Brendan, and Alison Fitzgerald. 2011. "Pssst … Wanna Buy a Law?" *Bloomberg Business Week*, December 11.

Hacker, Jacob S., and Paul Pierson. 2002. "Business Power and Social Policy: Employers and the Formation of the American Welfare State." *Politics and Society* 30(2): 277–325.

_____. 2010. *Winner-Take-All Politics: How Washington Made the Rich Richer—and Turned Its Back on the Middle Class.* New York: Simon & Schuster.

Hall, Richard L., and Alan V. Deardorff. 2006. "Lobbying as Legislative Subsidy." *American Political Science Review* 100(1): 69–84.

Hamm, Keith E., Ronald D. Hedlund, and Stephanie Shirley Post. 2011. "Committee Specialization in U.S. State Legislatures during the 20th Century: Do Legislatures Tap the Talents of Their Members?" *State Politics & Policy Quarterly* 11(3): 299–324.

Hansen, John Mark. 1991. *Gaining Access: Congress and the Farm Lobby, 1919–1981.* Chicago, IL: University of Chicago Press.

Hawkins, Beth. 2012. "ALEC and Corporate Fingerprints Are All Over National Push for Online Learning." *The Minnesota Post*, March 26.

Huevel, Katrina vanden. 2012. "Building a Progressive Counterforce to ALEC." *The Nation*, April 11.

Isaac, Jeffrey C. 1987. "Beyond the Three Faces of Power: A Realist Critique." *Polity* 20(1): 4–31.

Jackman, Molly. 2013a. "ALEC & State Legislation: Who, What & Where." Washington, DC: The Brookings Institution.

_____. 213b. "ALEC's Influence over Lawmaking in State Legislatures." Washington, DC: Brookings Institution.

Judis, John. 2001. *The Paradox of American Democracy: Elites, Special Interests, and the Betrayal of the Public Trust*. New York: Routledge Press.

Karch, Andrew. 2007. *Democratic Laboratories: Policy Diffusion among the American States*. Ann Arbor: University of Michigan Press.

Kastellec, Jonathan, Jeffrey Lax, and Justin Phillips. 2010. "Estimating State Public Opinion with Multi-level Regression and Poststratification using R." Princeton, NJ: Princeton University Department of Politics Working Paper.

Kelly, Nathan J., and Christopher Witko. 2012. "Federalism and American Inequality." *Journal of Politics* 74(2): 414–26.

Korpi, Walter. 1985. "Power Resources Approach vs. Action and Conflict." *Sociological Theory* 3(2): 31–45.

Kurtz, Karl T., Gary Moncrief, Richard G. Niemi, and LyndaW.Powell.2006. "Full-Time, Part-Time, and Real Time: Explaining State Legislators' Perceptions of Time on the Job." *State Politics & Policy Quarterly* 6 (3):322–38.

Lafer, Gordon. 2013. "The Legislative Attack on American Wages and Labor Standards, 2011–2012." Washington, DC: The Economic Policy Institute.

Lax, Jeffery R, and Justin H. Phillips. 2009. "Gay Rights in the States: Public Opiniona and Policy Responsiveness." *American Political Science Review* 103(3): 367–86.

_____. 2012. "The Democratic Deficit in the States." *American Journal of Political Science* 56(1): 148–66.

Lessig, Lawrence. 2011. *Republic, Lost: How Money Corrupts Congress - and a Plan to Stop It*. New York: Twelve.

Lichtblau, Eric. 2012. "Martin Death Spurs Group to Readjust Policy Focus." *The New York Times*, April 17.

Lindblom, Charles. 1977. *Politics and Markets: The World's Political Economic Systems*. New York: Basic Books.

Lukes, Stephen. 1974. *Power: A Radical View*. London, UK: Macmillion.

Martin, Cathie Jo. 2000. *Stuck in Neutral: Business and the Politics of Human Capital Investment Policy*. Princeton, NJ: Princeton University Press.

Martin, Cathie Jo, and Duane Swank. 2012. *The Political Construction of Business Interests: Coordination, Growth, and Equality*. New York: Cambridge University Press.

McIntire, Mike. 2012. "Conservative Non-Profit Acts as a Stealth Business Lobbyist." *The New York Times*, April 21.

Mizruchi, Mark S. 2013. *The Fracturing of the American Corporate Elite.* Cambridge, MA: Harvard University Press.

Nichols, John. 2011. "ALEC Exposed." *The Nation*, July 12.

Nownes, Anthony J. 1999. "Solicited Advice and Lobbyist Power Evidence from Three American States." *Legislative Studies Quarterly* 24(1): 113–23.

Nownes, Anthony J., and Patricia Freeman. 1998. "Interest Group Activity in the States." *Journal of Politics* 60(1): 86–112.

National Resources Defense Council and Defenders of Wildlife. 2002. "Corporate America's Trojan Horse in the States: The Untold Story Behind the American Legislative Exchange Council." Washington, DC: National Resources Defense Council and Defenders of Wildlife.

People for the American Way. 2011. "ALEC: The Voice of Corporate Special Interests in State Legislatures." Washington, DC: People for the American Way Foundation.

Powell, Lynda W. 2012. *The Influence of Campaign Contributions in State Legislatures: The Effects of Institutions and Politics.* Ann Arbor: The University of Michigan Press.

Progress VA. 2012. "ALEC Exposed: Who is Writing Virginia's laws? ". Available online: http://www.progressva.org/alec/ProgressVA%20-%20ALEC%20in%20Virginia.pdf (accessed June 15, 2014).

Robinson, William. 1950. "Ecological Correlations and the Behavior of Individuals." *American Sociological Review* 15(3): 351–7.

Schattschneider, Elmer Eric. 1960. *The Semi-Sovereign People: A Realist's View of Democracy in America.* New York: Holt, Rinehart and Winston.

Schlozman, Kay Lehman, and John T. Tierney. 1983. "More of the Same: Washington Pressure Group Activity in a Decade of Change." *Journal of Politics* 45(2): 351–77.

Schlozman, Kay Lehman, Sidney Verba, and Henry E. Brady. 2012. *The Unheavenly Chorus: Unequal Political Voice and the Broken Promise of American Democracy.* Princeton, NJ: Princeton University Press.

Shor, Boris, and Nolan McCarty. 2011. "The Ideological Mapping of American Legislatures." *American Political Science Review* 105(3): 530–51.

Silver, Charlotte. 2013. "US Criminal Justice System: Turning a Profit on Prison Reform?" *Al Jareeza America*, September 27.

Smith, Mark. 2000. *American Business and Political Power: Public Opinion, Elections, and Democracy.* Chicago, IL: University of Chicago Press.

Snyder, James M. 1992. "Long-Term Investing in Politicians; Or, Give Early, Give Often." *Journal of Law and Economics* 35(1): 15–43.

Squire, Peverill. 2007. "Measuring State Legislative Professionalism: The Squire Index Revisited." *State Politics & Policy Quarterly* 7(2): 211–27.

Sullivan, Laura. 2010. "Shaping State Laws With Little Scrutiny." NPR Morning Edition, October 29.

Swenson, Peter. 2004. "Varieties of Capitalist Interests: Power, Institutions, and the Regulatory Welfare State in the United States and Sweden." *Studies in American Political Development* 18(Spring): 1–29.

The New York Times. 2012. "The Big Money Behind State Laws." February 12.

Trumbull, J. Gunnar. 2012. *Strength in Numbers: The Political Power of Weak Interests*. Cambridge, MA: Harvard University Press.

Underwood, Julie, and Julie F. Mead. 2012. "A smart ALEC threatens public education." Phi Delta Kappan 93(6): 51–5.

Vogel, David. 1989. *Fluctuating Fortunes: The Political Power of Business in American Politics*. Washington, DC: Beard Books.

Weinstein, Adam. 2012. "How the NRA and Its Allies Helped Spread a Radical Gun Law Nationwide." *Mother Jones*, June 7.

Wilce, Rebekah. 2013. "A Reporters' Guide to the '"State Policy Network'." Madison, WI: Center for Media and Democracy.

Williams, Erica, and Nicholas Johnson. 2013. "ALEC Tax and Budget Proposals Would Slash Public Services and Jeopardize Economic Growth." Washington, DC: Center on Budget and Policy Priorities.

Winters, Jeffrey, and Benjamin Page. 2009. "Oligarchy in the United States?" *Perspectives on Politics* 7(4):731–51

End Notes

1. Hertel-Fernandez, A. (2014). Who Passes Business's "Model Bills"? Policy Capacity and Corporate Influence in U.S. State Politics. *Perspectives on Politics*, 12(3), 582–602. doi:10.1017/S1537592714001601
2. See, e.g., Bottari 2011.
3. McIntire 2012.
4. Greeley and Fitzgerald 2011.
5. Fortune Magazine 2011.
6. See, e.g., Dahl 1959, 1961; Lindblom 1977; Schattschneider 1960.
7. Interview with ALEC staffer, June 11, 2013.
8. ALEC has maintained this level of membership since the early 1990s; interview with ALEC staffer, June 11, 2013. See Graves et al. 2011 on the partisan orientation of ALEC legislative members, especially those in leadership positions. See also the analysis in Jackman 2013 b, 2013 a.
9. Interview with ALEC staffer, June 11, 2013; ALEC "FAQ": http://www.alec.org/about-alec/frequentlyasked-questions/.
10. McIntire 2012.
11. Quoted in Sullivan 2010.
12. Nichols 2011; People for the American Way 2011; Williams and Johnson 2013.
13. Elk andSloan2011.Inrecent years, however, ALEC has switched to promoting policies that would reduce the incarcerated population (see especially Dagan and Teles 2012),but that may benefit bail companies and other firms providing rehabilitation services to state governments; Silver 2013.
14. Hawkins 2012.
15. Lichtblau 2012; Weinstein 2012. Since the Martin shooting, and subsequent backlash from a coalition of progressive groups, a number of companies dropped their ALEC membership, including Kraft Foods, McDonald's, and Coca-Cola. ALEC also halted its law enforcement activities in the wake of the Martin controversy.

16. The New York Times 2012.
17. McIntire 2012; Underwood and Mead 2012.
18. Dahl 1961, but see Dahl 1959 for an alternative perspective that emphasizes the need to focus academic attention explicitly on business influence (especially section IV).
19. Smith 2000.
20. Trumbull 2012.
21. Block 1977.
22. See Dahl and Lindblom 1976; see also Lindblom 1977.
23. see, e.g., Lessig 2011; Clawson, Neustadtl, and Scott 1992. For a skeptical interpretation of business influence through contributions see, e.g., Ansolabehere, de Figueiredo, and Snyder 2003.
24. Lukes 1974; Bachrach and Baratz 1962. See also Schattschneider 1960 for the canonical concept of "mobilization of bias."
25. Winters and Page 2009.
26. Vogel 1989.
27. Hacker and Pierson 2002.
28. Hacker and Pierson 2002, 290.
29. Hacker and Pierson 2010. Mizruchi 2013 makes a similar argument as well. Judis 2001 adds that an independent elite class is also essential to checking the power of business interests.
30. Hall and Deardorff 2006.
31. Nownes 1999; Nownes and Freeman 1998; Schlozman and Tierney 1983; Berkman 2001; Austen-Smith 1993.
32. See, e.g., Hacker and Pierson 2010, especially 121–2 and 201–211, though see 123–4 for a reference to the rise of conservative think tanks. One important exception in the business power literature is the work of Pepper Culpepper (2010), who argues that business is likely to be most successful on issues of low public salience, since legislators are more likely to rely on business for technical advice and recommendations, and the public is unlikely to be able to follow the policy debate. Still, Culpepper generally focuses on variation in the salience of a policy issue, rather than variation in the policy capacity of legislators, which is what I consider in this paper.
33. I thank Ben Gruenbaum for this helpful formulation.
34. Obtained from the Legacy Tobacco Documents Archive at the University of California, San Francisco.
35. Quoted in Cole 2012.
36. This perspective is reflected in Lessig 2011, for example.
37. Bai 2012.
38. See especially ALEC 1983. See also ALEC n.d.-b.

CHAPTER 8
GOVERNORS

DO GOVERNORS MATTER?
BUDGETING RULES AND THE POLITICS
OF STATE POLICYMAKING[1]

CHARLES BARRILLEAUX
Florida State University

MICHAEL BERKMAN
Pennsylvania State University

Whether and how governors influence public policies in the U.S. is open to question. This research tests a model of gubernatorial influence on public policymaking in which gubernatorial power is conceived of the governor's power over the budgetary process relative to that of the state legislature. We argue that governors with greater control over the budget process will use those powers to deliver a higher proportion of policies that confer benefits to statewide versus more localized constituencies. As governors' electoral security increases, their willingness to support legislatively desired localized spending increases. Empirical results derived from pooled cross-sectional models largely support the models tested.

American state governments vary in the extent to which governors or legislators dominate the budgetary process and state policymaking, but overall state governors are stronger than ever before (Gosling 1994; Beyle 1996; Hedge 1998). Bureaucracies are more centralized, formal powers have been enhanced, governors enjoy a larger role in setting state priorities (Rosenthal 1998; Hedge 1998; Clynch and Lauth 1991), and domestic policy devolution offers them and their policy innovations national visibility. Further, the quality of the individuals who become governors has improved (Sabato 1978: 57) and contemporary governors are celebrated for their "pragmatism" and skill (Stanfield 1996). The National Governors' Association is increasingly prominent and influential, and governors regularly make major party presidential and vice-presidential short-lists.

Yet, we know little about the consequences of all this institution building. Models of American state policymaking tend to focus on legislatures at the expense of executives.[2] In some cases, such as when measuring governmental capability (Brace 1993), information on the two is even combined into a single indicator. Although governors may appear to be central players in American politics, political scientists' models of state policymaking provide only limited tests of their roles. Whether governors influence state policymaking is important for at least three reasons. First, for students of democratic politics, the variations in the design of executive and legislative institutions that exist among the American states provide a unique opportunity to assess the distributive consequences of differing governmental designs. Institutional designs do not occur by happenstance but more often are put in place to achieve some political, managerial, or policy goal (Knott and Miller 1987). Second, research on American state politics portrays governors as either extremely influential (e.g., Beyle 2001) or as inconsequential (e.g., Erikson, Wright, and McIver 1993). Given that governors are among the most visible officeholders in any state, a clearer understanding of whether, how, and under what circumstances they affect public policy is justified.

Third, at least one prominent scholar, Paul Peterson (1995), argues that the states, because of the parochialism of legislatures, are particularly bad vehicles for achieving statewide policy goals. This is of particular concern in the present era, where policy responsibility for welfare, health care, and other policies are commonly referred to the states by the national government. If, as we shall argue below, governors have incentives to produce public policies whose benefits have statewide, rather than district, incidence, the argument against states as vehicles for redistribution may not be as clear cut as Peterson suggests.

Governors and legislators bring to state policymaking distinct preferences shaped by the composition of their constituencies. While legislators are "pulled by local geographic constituencies" governors must consider the interests of a "larger and more diverse group" (Crain and Miller 1990: 1030). We argue that governors seek higher levels of spending for redistributive programs that benefit their geographically diffuse constituencies in ways similar to legislators' pursuit of geographically concentrated distributive benefits. Thus, our core assumption is that governors have distinct, identifiable, institutionally based preferences. The budgetary process shapes the extent to which governors are able and strategically motivated to pursue these spending priorities. The rules that govern the budgetary process are contested and biased, and the governor has greater power over the process in some states than others (Gosling 1994). These powers can be used to direct resources toward their desired type of policy while limiting legislators' pursuit of their spending priorities. [...]

Of course, governors pursue more than just these embedded institutional interests. They are also part of, and even leaders of, a team—their political party—and their interests and preferences therefore extend to those of the team as well. We argue that their willingness to act as leader by promoting the interests of the legislative team members is conditioned by the electoral environment faced by legislators and the governor. Many state-level studies treat both branches as though they are facing the same competitive threat (e.g., Dye 1984) or competitive milieu (e.g., Ranney 1971). Drawing upon Schlesinger's (1994) "Revised Party Theory" we argue that cooperation is based upon the distinct competitive threat faced by each. Governors can be expected to cooperate with legislators' policy priorities when legislative elections in a state are close and the governor is secure politically. Absent this security, governors will pursue their policy interests at the expense of legislators within their same party. [...]

Following Peterson (1995) and others (Baumgartner and Jones 1993) we divide state spending into two types: developmental spending where benefits are concentrated in specific geographic sections of the states, and redistributive spending where benefits are spread around the entire the state. We offer hypotheses about the ratio of one type of spending to the other. The results strongly support our core hypotheses that budgeting rules and competitive threat shape the ability of each branch to pursue their institutional interests. The policymaking models we develop allow us to fully incorporate both the legislature and governor, and offer a way to capture the tension between the branches inherent in state and the federal constitutions.

[...]

Governors and Policymaking in the States

Systematic tests of executive effects on state policymaking take two approaches. The first casts the governor as the leader of a party team whose success is a function of the governor's leadership and political skills. The second focuses on the institutional powers of the governor, suggesting that the ability to lead depends upon the resources and design of the governorship.[3]

Governors as Team Leaders

As a member of a party team, a governor's success or failure is viewed as a function of his ability to lead that team (Morehouse 1998). The strength and cohesion of the party organization is a crucial tool at a governor's disposal, but individual ability to use those resources largely establishes whether a governor will succeed or fail. Related to this view, governors are cast as the "legislator in chief" and their effectiveness a reflection of their individual ability to work with the legislature (Bernick and Wiggins 1981). This view is supported by evidence from studies of redistributive policies that find that Democratic governors, like Democratic legislators, promote more redistribution (Dye 1984; Winters 1976). The team-leader approach, in general terms, leads to a focus on the party of the governor, and tends to see the governor's constituency in terms very similar to that as a legislator from the same party.

Clearly the governor's leadership of her legislative party is important. But it also the case that within any party each individual office has its own constituency and organization; [. . .]This means that not only may different officeholders within the same party have different policy interests, but also that the notion of a team is variable and conditional. We suggest below it is possible to identify when governors have the incentives to act independently or otherwise.

Governors' Power

A second approach emphasizes the governor's formal and informal powers (Mueller 1985; Beyle 1996; Schlesinger 1971) conditioned by political circumstances. For example, powerful governors are more successful when they enjoy strong electoral margins and legislative majorities (Sigelman and Dometrius 1988) and the same party controls both branches (Clarke 1998). But commonly used measures of gubernatorial power are not designed to discriminate when particular powers matter because they mix budgetary powers with others (such as appointment powers; see for example Schlesinger 1971 and Beyle 1996). Therefore, they can obscure the issue of influence and fail to measure power over the legislature in the stage at which the legislature is most involved—the formulation of budget totals and priorities. [. . .]

Electoral Incentives and Policy Preferences

Our model borrows from both of these approaches. But we put in the forefront gubernatorial preferences embedded within the institution. To derive these we draw upon legislative studies, which offer a theoretically rigorous analysis of institutionally derived preferences that are advanced and mediated by institutional capacity. Influential studies of Congress recognize that legislators' electoral incentives cannot be explained solely in terms of the demography, partisanship, and the ideological profile of their constituencies. Legislators, irrespective of party, are parochial in their preferences (Mayhew 1974) eager to deliver particularized benefits to their constituencies (Tullock 1962;

Weingast, Shepsle, and Johnsen 1981). While our understanding of how distributive politics operates would not be possible without an appreciation of how legislators' preferences are rooted in geographically defined constituencies, this approach has had more limited influence on state-level studies.[4]

Governor's preferences, too, should be rooted in their geographic constituencies. Governors cannot spread the costs of particularized programs for their constituents among others' constituents, the way legislators can; their constituency is statewide, or "at-large" so their "benefit-cost calculus for appraising government programs" is not the same (Crain and Miller 1990: 1030). Therefore, they may seek to lower legislative spending, which may reduce overall spending totals (Crain and Miller 1990). Yet governors may have constituency driven preferences of their own that go beyond their desire to suppress spending by the legislature and their own budget-maximizing agencies. Thus, in contrast to legislators' interest in policies "with district-specific benefits" (Crain 1999: 678), governors should prefer to fund policies with statewide benefits.

Peterson, who characterizes policies as "redistributive or developmental" based upon their geographic impact, has advanced this argument. Developmental programs, (frequently called distributive) provide "physical and social infrastructure" (1995: 17) and "are generally perceived to be a concentrated benefit" (Peterson 1995: 41). Redistributive programs "reallocate societal resources from the 'haves' to the 'have-nots'" (Peterson 1995: 17), are structured by class rather than geography (Wong 1989), and have costs and benefits that are "geographically diffuse" (Peterson 1995:43).[5] Providing statewide benefits best rewards governors, who must appeal to statewide constituencies (Schlesinger 1994). If governors are politically ambitious (as many seem to be), their focus should be on the U.S. Senate—a statewide office—or other national office, so they are again best served by providing benefits to a broad constituency. But evidence for this is scarce. Mark Peterson (1990) finds that presidents introduce more redistributive proposals than any other kind, and Winters (1976) finds that governors push for re distributive measures. But we find no direct tests of hypotheses based upon the assumption that governors and legislators are motivated to support diff e rent types of policies. These hypotheses are developed in the next section.

Hypotheses

Following Peterson (1995), we distinguish between redistributive and developmental policies because links between these types of policies and different constituencies are most easily drawn. Redistributive and developmental spending decisions may often be dependent on choices in the other area—in other words, spending for one category of program forces a government to make a tradeoff. We conceive of this tradeoff as a simple ratio of developmental to redistributive spending. In other words, our interest is in explaining the extent to which one category of spending is rewarded relative to the other.

Institutional Characteristics

Budgeting Rules: There is "considerable diversity" among the states (Gosling 1994) in the extent to which the governor or legislature has greater power over the budgetary process, which may be critical to budgetary outcomes (Poterba 1996; Clarke 1998). From Gosling (1994) and the detailed case-studies of twelve states in Clynch and Lauth (1991) we identify how budgetary rules can reasonably be expected to distribute power. [. . .]

H1: The more power the governor has over the budgetary process the smaller the ratio of developmental to redistributive spending.

Legislative Professionalism: We expect professional legislators to have a "vested interest in the expansion of government" (Peterson 1995: 101) and therefore to favor higher spending of all types (Carmines 1974; Hedge 1998). But between the two types of policies, we expect that legislators promote developmental over redistributive policies. As legislatures become increasingly professionalized, the value of a seat increases and members have stronger incentives to produce benefits that are apparent to the voters at home than do members in a less professionalized body (Fiorina 1994; Peterson 1995).

H2: The more professional the membership the greater the ratio of developmental to redistributive spending.

Institutional Characteristics

Parties: Democrats support larger government and more spending than Republicans (Alt and Lowry 1994). But, as Peterson (1995) notes, developmental spending with its emphasis on subsidizing economic growth, and redistributive spending, with its emphasis on shifting resources from haves to have-nots, each favor different constituencies. Democratic legislators, therefore, should support higher levels of spending on everything, but when there is an explicit tradeoff, they should favor redistribution.

H3: The presence of a Democratic governor will be associated with a lower ratio of developmental to redistributive spending.

H4: Higher percentages of Democrats in the legislature will be associated with a lower ratio of developmental to redistributive spending.

Electoral Competition: Greater electoral competition is generally thought to lead legislators to enact more generous redistributive policies (Plotnick and Winters 1985). Redistributive policies confer benefits to a broader bloc of voters than developmental policies, and competitive elections are expected to have the aggregate effect of leading politicians and parties to seek to provide benefits that appeal to more voters, including those who might not normally participate in politics. Following that logic, we expect greater competition to produce more redistributive spending as legislators are forced to seek to provide rewards for a broader set of constituents.[6]

H5: Increased competition for legislative seats should lower the ratio of developmental to redistributive spending.

With regard to competitiveness of gubernatorial races, we conceive of votes won as political capital governors may use to accomplish their policy and political goals. The greater the electoral margin the more political capital at a governor's disposal (Berry and Berry 1992). The incentive may exist under certain conditions to use this capital for the benefit of the governor's legislative party. We expect governors and legislatures to cooperate under conditions of electoral threat. We expect the governor to use her political capital to assist threatened members of her party. Although we are

Table 8.1   Prais-Winsten Regression Estimates of the Ratio of state Government Developmental to Redistributive Spending, 1990, 1992, 1994 and 1996 (N = 188[b])

Independent Variable	Unstandardized Regression Coefficient	Standard Error	t/probability t (two-tailed)
Institutional Characteristics			
Budget Powers Index	−.13	.04	−3.44/.001
Legislative Salary	.07	.03	2.54/.01
Behavioral Characteristics			
Citizen Ideology	−.01	.01	−2.95/.007
Electoral Competition	−.04	.02	−2.18/.029
% Democratic Legislators	−.00	.01	−.78/.43
Democratic Governor	.01	.07	.10/.92
Governor's Vote Margin	−.03	.01	−2.13/.033
Competition X Gov. Vote	.0007	.000	2.98/.003
Demographic, Economic, Spatial, and Temporal Controls			
Population	−.000	.000	−6.85/.000
Tax Capacity	−.01	.005	2.69/.007
South	.03	.15	.19/.848
Alaska	2.45	.55	4.47/.000
1990	.55	.05	11.97/.000
1992	.19	.01	4.13/.000
1994	.11	.04	2.84/.004
Intercept	7.01	1.21	5.81/.000
Adj. R²	.66		
Wald chi²/prob. > chi²	15471163.4/.0000		

[b] Louisiana, Nebraska, and Virginia are dropped from the analysis because their institutions or election laws do not conform to the rest of the states.

unable to observe this directly using aggregate data, we expect it to show up as help for the legislature in general, which means higher developmental spending relative to redistribution. We expect that this spending is distributed unevenly across districts to favor those of the governor's party, but cannot observe this.

H6: Increases in governors' winning margins yield lower values on the ratio of developmental to redistributive policy.

H7: In states with competitive legislative elections, the value of the ratio of developmental to redistributive spending will be greater as the size of the governor's winning margin in the previous election increases. [...]

Results

Results are reported in Table 8.1. The model explains about 66 percent of the variation in the ratio of developmental to redistributive spending in the states during the years 1990, 1992, 1994 and 1996 and is statistically significant. [. . .] So, consistent with our expectations, governors use their institutional advantages to produce policies that benefit their constituencies and institutionally stronger legislatures produce policies that benefit theirs.

[. . .]

The political parties of governors and legislators show no meaningful effects in the model. Contrary to our expectations in hypothesis 3, Democratic governors do not perform differently than non-Democrats vis-à-vis the ratio of developmental to redistributive spending. The percentage of legislative seats held by Democrats, likewise, has not significant effect on the dependent variable, leading us to reject hypothesis 4.

The remaining three of our seven hypotheses have to do with the effects of electoral competition and the governor's use of political capital. Hypothesis 5 is confirmed: Increased electoral competition has the expected negative effect on the ratio of developmental to redistributive spending[. . .]Hypothesis 6 is also supported. Greater winning percentages for governors significantly lessen the ratio of developmental to redistributive spending[. . .]Results of the test of hypothesis seven, in which we contend that governors use political capital to assist legislators of their party where legislators face competitive elections, suggest they do the opposite.

[. . .]

Conclusion

Our findings confirm that the institutional design of executive and legislative powers in state budgeting have meaningful effects on public policy. Governors affect state policymaking in a systematic and theoretically predictable way. We introduced a model of state policymaking designed to capture any effects of differing powers of governors versus legislatures in the formal budgetary process. The model we devised is explicitly integrative in that it draws elements from two prevailing, and seemingly disparate, traditions in research on American governors: that which focuses on formal institutional powers and that which focuses on the governor's partisan role. Our research shows each of these views to have merit. At times, it is the institutional effects that matter but at others governors mediate their individual interests in response to the competition for legislative seats. Governors appear to temper their preferences for redistribution when competition for legislative seats is high, but their bias remains toward redistribution. It may also be the case, although we are unwilling to make normative calls here, that governors may use their powers to enact what they believe since rely to be optimal public policies.

Of course, both governors and legislatures influence policymaking in the states, as is intended in systems with powers shared across institutions. Governors with greater control of the budgetary process are rewarded with an increased emphasis on spending that confers statewide benefits, which we expect to aid governors' political ambitions. The partisanship of the governor does not appear to affect the extent to which states pursue developmental versus redistributive policies, and neither does that of the legislature. We do not take this as sign that parties do not matter, but as sign that legislatures and governors have strong preferences for policies with specific incidences of benefits regardless of their partisanship.

The professionalism of state legislatures also directly influences states' emphasis on developmental versus redistributive spending. And, the competitiveness of legislative elections produced a boost in redistributive spending. The relationships among competitiveness of elections, legislative professionalism, and partisanship are likely quite complex. Professional legislatures are likely to have more Democrats than unprofessional legislatures (Fiorina 1994) and to be competitive. They also more likely to have progressively ambitious members whose policy preferences are consistent with their ambitions (Maestas 2000). These relationships bear additional investigation.

Paul Peterson's (1995) work may be read as a brief in favor of the nationalization of redistribution. The crux of the argument lies in his observation, based upon the assumption that legislators have no incentive to redistribute, that state governments are poor vehicles for redistributive policy. Our results suggest that strong state institutions that function within competitive electoral systems will focus on redistribution. Put otherwise, state legislators and governors can be given tools that will lead them beyond district-level parochialism to consider statewide needs. Whether their perception of equitable and appropriate levels of service will comport with what might flow from a nationalized system is unknown, but our evidence suggests that they will at least focus on redistribution.

References

Abney, Glenn, and Thomas P Lauth. 1995. "The Line Item Veto in the States: An Instrument for Fiscal Restraint or an Instrument for Partisanship?" *Public Administration Review* 45: 372–79. 1997.

_____. "The Item Veto and Fiscal Responsibility" *Journal of Politics* 59: 882–92.

Achen, Christopher. 2000. "Why Lagged Dependent Variables Can Suppress the Explanatory Power of Other Independent Variables." Working paper available at http://web.polmeth.ufl.edu/working00.alpha.html.

Alt, James E., and Robert C. Lowry. 1994. "Divided Government, Fiscal Institutions, and Budget Deficits: Evidence from the States." *American Political Science Review* 88: 811–28.

Barrilleaux, Charles. 1997. "A Test of the Independent Influences of Electoral Competition and Party Strength in a Model of State Policy-Making." *American Journal of Political Science* 41: 1462–66.

Baumgartner, Frank R., and Bryan D. Jones. 1993. *Agendas and Instability in American Politics.* Chicago: University of Chicago Press.

Beck, Nathaniel, and Jonathan N. Katz. 1995. "What To Do (And Not To Do) With Time-Series Cross-Section Data." *American Political Science Review* 89: 634–47.

Bemrnick, E. Lee, and Charles W Wiggins. 1981. "Executive-Legislative Power Relationships." *American Politics Quarterly* 9: 467–77.

Berry, Frances S., and William D. Berry. 1992. "Tax Innovation in the States: Capitalizing on Political Opportunity." *American Journal of Political Science* 36: 715–42.

Berry, William D., E. J. Ringquist, R. C. Fording, and R. L. Hanson. 1998. "Measuring Citizen and Government Ideology in the American States, 1960–93." *American Journal of Political Science* 41: 337–48.

Berry, William D., and Richard Fording. 1997. "Measuring State Tax Capacity and Effort." *Social Science Quarterly* 78: 158–66.

Beyle, Thad. 1996. "Governors: The Middleman and Women in Our Political System." In Virginia Gray and Herbert Jacob, eds., *Politics in the American States: A Comparative Analysis*, 6th ed., pp. 207–52. Boston, MA: Little Brown.

Brace, Paul. 1993. *State Government and Economic Development*. Baltimore, MD: Johns Hopkins University Press.

Carey, John M., Richard G. Niemi, and Lynda W. Powell. 2000. "Incumbency and the Probability of Reelection in State Legislative Elections." *Journal of Politics* 62: 671–700.

Carmines, Edward G. 1974. "The Mediating Influence of State Legislatures on the Linkage Between Interparty: Competition and Welfare Policies." *American Political Science Review* 68 (3) September: 1118–24.

Clarke, Wes. 1998. "Divided Government and Budget Conflict in the U.S. States." *Legislative Studies Quarterly* 23 (1): 5–22.

Clynch, Edward J., and Thomas P. Lauth. 1991. *Governors Legislatures, and Budgets: Diversity Across the American States*. New York: Greenwood Press.

Council of State Governments. Various Years. The Book of the States. Lexington, KY: CSG.

Crain, W. Mark. 1999. "Districts, Diversity, and Fiscal Biases: Evidence From The American States." *Journal Of Law and Economics* 42 (2): 675–98.

Crain, W. Mark, and James C. Miller III. 1990. "Budget Process and Spending Growth." *William and Mary Law Review* 31: 1021–46.

Dometrius, Nelson C. 1987. "Changing Gubernatorial Power: The Measure vs. Reality." *Western Political Quarterly* 40: 320–28.

Dye, Thomas. 1984. "Party and Policy in the States." *Journal of Politics* 46: 1097–1116.

Erikson, R., G. Wright, and J. McIver. 1993. *Statehouse Democracy*. New York: Cambridge University Press.

Fiorina, Morris. 1994. "Divided Government in the American States: A Byproduct of Legislative Professionalism." *American Political Science Review* 88: 304–16.

Gosling, James J. 1994. "Budget Procedures and Executive Review in State Legislatures." In Joseph Silbey, ed., *The Encyclopedia of American Legislatures*. New York: Scribners.

———. 1997. *Budgetary Politics*, 2nd ed. New York: Garland.

Green, William H. 1993. *Econometric Analysis*, 2nd ed., New York: McMillan.

Gross, Donald A. 1989. "Governors and Policymaking: Theoretical Concerns and Analytic Approaches." *Policy Studies Journal* 17: 764–87.

Hedge, David M. 1998. *Governance and the Changing American States*. Boulder, CO: Westview.

Holbrook, Thomas, and Emily Van Dunk. 1993. "Electoral Competition in the American States." *American Political Science Review* 87: 955–62.

Jaccard, James, Robert Turrisi, and Choi K. Wan. 1990. "Interaction Effects in Multiple Regression." Sage University Paper Series on Quantitative Applications in the Social Sciences, pp. 7–72. Newbury Park, CA: Sage.

Knott, Jack H., and Gary J. Miller. 1987. *Reforming Bureaucracy: The Politics of Institutional Choice*. Englewood Cliffs, NJ: Prentice-Hall.

Lowi, Theodore. 1979. *The End of Liberalism: The Second Republic of the United States*. New York: Norton.

Maestas, Cherie. 2000. "Courting the Future: The Effect of Ambition on the Behavior of State Legislatures." Presented at the American Political Science Association Meetings, Washington, D.C., August 30-September 4.

Mayhew, David. 1974. *Congress: The Electoral Connection*. Cambridge, MA: Harvard University Press.

Morehouse, Sarah. 1998. *The Governor as Party Leader*. Ann Arbor: University of Michigan.

Mueller, Keith. 1985. "Explaining Variation and Change in Gubernatorial Powers, 1960–1982." *Western Political Quarterly* 38: 424–31.

National Association of State Budget Officers. Various Years. Budget Processes in the States. Washington, DC: NASBO.

Peterson, Mark A. 1990. *Legislating Together: The White House and Capitol Hill from Eisenhower to Reagan*. Cambridge, MA: Harvard University Press.

Peterson, Paul E. 1995. *The Price of Federalism*. Washington, DC: Brookings Institution.

Plotnick, Robert D., and Richard F. Winters. 1985. "A Politicoeconomic Theory of Income Redistribution." *American Political Science Review* 79: 458–73.

Poterba, James M. 1996. "Budget Institutions and Fiscal Policy in the US States." *American Economic Review* 86: 395–400.

Ranney, Austin. 1971. "Parties in State Politics." In Herbert Jacob and Kenneth N. Vines, eds., *Politics in the American States: A Comparative Analysis*, 2nd ed., pp. 82–121. Boston, MA: Little, Brown.

Rosenthal, Alan. 1998. *The Decline of Representative Democracy: Process, Participation and Power in State Legislatures*. Washington, DC: Congressional Quarterly Press.

Sabato, Larry. 1978. *Goodbye to Good-Time Charlie: The American Governor Transformed, 1950–1975*. Lexington, MA: Lexington Books.

Schlesinger, Joseph A. 1971. "The Politics of the Executive." In H. Jacob and K. Vines, eds., *Politics in the American States*, 2nd ed., pp. 210–37. Boston, MA: Little, Brown.

_____. 1985. "The New American Political Party." *American Political Science Review* 79: 1152–69.

_____. 1994. *Political Parties and the Winning of Office*. Ann Arbor: University of Michigan Press.

Sharkansky, Ira. 1968. "Agency Requests, Gubernatorial Support, and Budget Success in State Legislatures." *American Political Science Review* 62: 1220–31.

Sigelman, Lee, and Nelson Dometrius. 1988. "Governors as Chief Administrators." *American Politics Quarterly* 16: 157–70.

Smith, Steven. 1995. *The American Congress*. Boston, MA: Houghton Mifflin.

Squire, Peverill. 1992. "The Theory of Legislative Institutionalization and the California Assembly." *Journal of Politics* 54:1026–54 .

Stanfield, Rochelle L. 1996. "Just Do It." *National Journal* 28 (13): 681–748.

Thurber, James A. 1997. "Centralization, Devolution, and Turf Protection in The Congressional Budget Process." In Lawrence Dodd and Bruce Oppenheimer, eds., *Congress Reconsidered*, 6th, eds, pp. 325–46. Washington, DC: Congressional Quarterly Press.

Tullock, Gordon. 1962. *The Politics of Bureaucracy*. New York: Public Affairs Press.

Weingast, Barry, Kenneth A. Shepsle, Christopher Johnsen. 1981. "The Political Economy of Benefits and Costs: A Neoclassical Approach to Distributive Politics." *Journal of Political Economy* 89 (4): 642–64.

Winters, Richard F. 1976. "Partisan Control and Policy Change." *American Journal of Political Science* 20: 597–636.

Wong, Kenneth K. 1989. "Policy-Making in the American States: Typology, Process, and Institutions." *Policy Studies Review* 8: 527–48.

End Notes

1. Barrilleaux, Charles, and Michael Berkman. "Do Governors Matter? Budgeting Rules and the Politics of State Policymaking." *Political Research Quarterly* 56, no. 4 (2003): 409–17. doi:10.2307/3219802.

2. For example Erikson, Wright, and McIver (1993) exclude the executive from their models. Where both institutions are considered, it is often in light of whether their partisan control is divided (e.g., Alt and Lowry 1994; Fiorina 1994) rather than on the powers of either institution.

3. Another important approach less applicable to our study of aggregate spending differences across states concerns the budgetary requests of executive agencies (e.g., Sharkansky 1968; Clarke 1998).

4. Examples include Wong (1989), Crain and Miller (1990), Crain (1999), and Peterson (1995).

5. Peterson's policy typology is similar to Lowi's (1979), but it ignores the means by which policy is carried out, is applied only to spending programs, and does not emphasize the conflict generated by policy types. It is also similar to the classification scheme offered by Baumgartner and Jones (1993), who differentiate investment from consumption policies because the former promote economic growth and the latter detract from the growth process. In practical terms their classification also brings together policies that target investment in particular geographic areas and those that spread benefits statewide.

6. This does not imply that competition will reduce the amount of developmental spending but that, in competitive situations, redistributive spending will be relatively higher than it would absent competition. Our hypothesis implies nothing about the level or change in developmental spending that occurs under competitive races.

CHAPTER 9
COURTS

IS JUDICIAL FEDERALISM ESSENTIAL TO DEMOCRACY? STATE COURTS IN THE FEDERAL SYSTEM

PAUL R. BRACE AND MELINDA GANN HALL

When it comes to american courts, many people have a perspective like the famous *New Yorker* magazine rendering of a New Yorker's view of the world. According to this view, a New Yorker looking west sees the George Washington Bridge, a vast wasteland, and a tiny Los Angeles in the distance. Similarly, in popular, journalistic, and even scholarly treatments of courts and law in the United States, there is the massive United States Supreme Court building in Washington, D.C., populated by nine towering figures, with only a huge, unknown, and under-appreciated wasteland beyond. On one level, this is not too surprising. Supreme Court justices have at times been towering legal intellects, and many of the Court's decisions are publicly salient and dramatic, with far-reaching consequences. At the same time, however, just as there is much of consequence going on between the George Washington Bridge and Los Angeles (or so some believe), there also is a tremendous amount of legal terrain beyond the United States Supreme Court that needs to be recognized, understood, and appreciated. State courts are at heart of this enterprise.

This chapter considers the fascinating realm of state judicial politics, dividing discussion into two separate but highly related parts. First, the historical development of state courts is described within the context of several core issues in democratic theory that state courts have helped to resolve. Second, more practical matters are examined through a discussion of the operating characteristics of contemporary state court systems, including the extraordinary diversity among these institutions. These discussions highlight the direct impact of state courts, especially state courts of last resort, on the landscape of contemporary American politics.

Because of the presentation below of some exciting new data on state supreme courts, this chapter is quite distinct from others in the volume. Using the recently released State Supreme Court Data Project, which contains an extraordinary array of information about the decisions reached in every state's highest court from 1995 through 1997, this chapter will present a series of graphs to depict a wide variety of ways in which these institutions resolve the cases on their dockets. This decidedly empirical focus will serve to illustrate dramatic state-to-state differences and will place in stark relief the legal and political significance of state judiciaries in the federal system.

Overall, this comprehensive examination of historical, theoretical, and contemporary issues about state judicial politics argues that state court systems in the United States have promoted democracy in two

INSTITUTIONS OF AMERICAN DEMOCRACY: THE JUDICIAL BRANCH edited by Kermit L. Hall & Kevin T. McGuire (2005): Chapter 7: "Is Judicial Federalism Essential to Democracy? State Courts in the Federal System" by Paul R. Brace and Melinda Gann Hall (pp. 174–199) "By permission of Oxford University Press, USA"

fundamental and interrelated ways. First, courts, especially state courts, provide an important forum for dispute resolution in a manner generally viewed as legitimate and authoritative. Without this, especially in large democracies, the dissatisfaction that arises from injustice or unresolved disputes would only serve to fuel conditions for rebellion or government oppression. Second, for the various reasons detailed below, courts prevent more conventional majoritarian processes from being overtaxed, which would result in factionalism or cyclical and unstable outcomes. Throughout U.S. history, state courts have played an important role in reducing the volume of disputes and the number of alternatives in conventional majoritarian politics. In the end, by virtue of the volume of disputes they resolve and the comparatively high esteem they receive from the public, state courts promote respect for the rule of law and the rights of citizens, two critical components of the fabric of a functioning democracy.

By design, very few conflicts in society spill over into the realm of majoritarian politics. However, this does not mean these conflicts do not exist, nor does it mean that they are not addressed to a reasonable degree of satisfaction. For many Americans involved in important conflicts over property, rights, or privileges, justice is sought not at the ballot box but in court, and overwhelmingly the forum for resolution of these significant conflicts is state courts. In a typical year, state trial courts handle *over three hundred times* as many cases as federal district courts. State intermediate appellate courts process *over three times* as many appeals as the U.S. Courts of Appeals. And state supreme courts address *over seven hundred times* as many cases as the United States Supreme Court. Clearly, when it comes to the volume of disputes handled in the United States, the state court systems are the backbone of the American judicial system.

By settling a huge number of important disputes each year (currently over 100 million filings per year in the trial courts alone), state court systems effectively remove many issues from majoritarian electoral or legislative politics. Courts generally, and state courts specifically, resolve disputes over important economic, social, and explicitly political issues. From tort litigation to privacy rights to ballot access and the permissibility of ballot measures, these courts influence our more traditional electoral political agenda. Specifically from the perspective of democratic theory, it has been well understood for about three centuries now that majoritarian processes suffer inherent problems that promote instability, and that these problems become even more pronounced when many alternatives are addressed. If unsettled grievances spilled over into majoritarian processes, society would be much more fractious, jeopardizing the stability and predictability necessary for democratic governance.

Undoubtedly, state court systems operate with certain biases. Certainly gaining access to these courts is not a minor affair, and there are many in our society with grievances against the government, a firm, or a private individual who never have their day in court. Yet, even though many never find themselves in courts, state or federal, huge proportions of the population, certainly more than have ever been in court, express tremendous confidence in their state court systems, as documented below. If citizens did not have confidence in these courts they would not abide by their rulings, which would put further burdens on other government institutions.

State courts, like their federal counterparts, have no power of enforcement. As a consequence, courts have found it crucial to nurture and maintain mass support. Because state courts have a high degree of legitimacy in the public's eyes, these institutions can address the huge volume of disputes before them authoritatively. By gaining and maintaining the public's confidence, state courts are able to solve many problems in democratic society in nonmajoritarian ways. State courts have, in essence, gained majoritarian support for a process, not an outcome, and this is a critical contribution to American democracy.

A Brief History of Courts in American Political Development

To appreciate better the contemporary role of state courts in American democracy, it is useful to trace the historical development of courts in the political processes. Writing about the America of the 1830s, Alexis de Tocqueville appreciated the instability of majoritarian processes and the importance of courts in American democracy.[1] He saw legislatures as very responsive to majoritarian impulses and commented extensively on the instability in law that this could produce. Alternatively, courts could affect law only within the context of particular cases before them. By rendering decisions that would bear upon the interests of the particular parties before them, courts would thus slight the law only incidentally. Consequently, laws produced through majoritarian impulse could be diminished slightly or completely if there were repeated cases before courts. Courts united the trial of the individual with the trial of the law, subjecting law to narrow corrections but protecting it from wholesale assault. To Tocqueville, it was this practice of American courts that operated to protect liberty and secure public order. Similarly, it is worthy to note that Tocqueville thought the insulation of courts from majoritarian pressures was vital, and thus Tocqueville was highly critical of the "experiments" of states to elect rather than appoint judges.

Stephen Skowronek reiterated the importance of courts to American political and economic development in his influential *Building a New American State*.[2] Skowronek saw courts as playing a very fundamental and even decisive role in our early political development. In the antebellum period, the state of the republic was defined by political parties and federal courts. Political parties, through aggressive use of patronage and distributing other spoils, were massively effective in gaining control of the apparatus and rewards of government. State and local political organizations defined a clear and irresistible discipline for gaining and manipulating political power and would ultimately provide the cement to hold together the highly fragmentary government designed by the Constitution. Political parties were successful in mobilizing majorities that facilitated working relationships within and among the branches and levels of government and sewed diverse geographical and institutional elements together in the pursuit of the distribution of the government's valuable goods and services. However, courts were the only institutions that stood outside direct party domination and, according to Skowronek, provided the essential counterbalance to the voracious electoral machines of the era. In many important ways, courts put the brakes on the highly partisan operation of politics in this period. Courts at each level of government nurtured and defined the state's prerogatives over the economy and society, promoting the sanctity of contracts and defining the grounds for corporate charters. Eventually, American judges embraced a pragmatic and positive view of themselves as policymakers, adopting an instrumental outlook.

While Skowronek emphasized the importance of the federal bench in this period, several authoritative studies point to the growing power and scope of state court systems. Morton Horowitz notes that decision by decision, state court judges in the early nineteenth century began the process of making new law and new legal rules that he characterizes as "instrumentalism," reshaping private law so that it may serve as "a creative instrument for directing men's energy toward social change."[3] Hence, to effect social change within a common law tradition inherently biased against change required both a transformation of legal rules and the role of judge-made law in society. He believed that courts generally, and state courts particularly, shed their passivity to the point of assuming a quasi-legislative role. He argues that early nineteenth-century judges understood that legal rules matter and that "different sets of legal rules would have differential effects on economic growth, depending both on the distribution of wealth they produced and the level of investment they encouraged."[4]

Kermit Hall also notes the emergence of legal instrumentalism that came to displace the older conception of law as precedent bound rules that judges applied mechanically.[5] Appellate courts emerged as both lawmaking and lawfinding institutions as states retreated from the post-revolutionary emphasis on legislatures. It was also in this era that state constitutions shifted from organic law to voluminous treatises intended to reign in legislatures. As Lawrence Friedman notes, the wordy and excessive text of state constitutions that would appear in this era were made to order for an aggressive judiciary. The many constitutional controls over sloppy, corrupt, and selfish legislation played into the hands of litigants and courts.

By the Civil War, judges were not only administering the rule of law but were increasingly called upon to mediate among the growing number of competing interests crowding the political scene. The appellate judiciary built upon this legacy after the Civil War, expanding its power in response to the distributive political decisions of the party period beginning in the 1830s.[6] This period witnessed a dramatic growth in the range and scale of judicial activity, with courts deciding an ever-increasing number of private disputes and determining public policy. As Hall notes, "judges had a large and active hand in the governance of a rapidly changing society."[7] To deal with burgeoning case loads, state court systems would grow more dense and complex in this period, commonly adopting a three-tiered system with trial, intermediate appellate, and an appellate court of last resort.

Friedman also notes that the period between the Civil War and the end of the century was characterized by the prevalence of activist judges. The variety of jurisdictions offered by American federalism induced responsiveness in the law. While the states might act as laboratories of social legislation, they were also competing sellers of jurisprudence in a vast federal matrix, and easy laws drove out harsh ones. Like their federal counterparts, state appellate courts would develop a doctrine of substantive due process to place limits on legislative power. In some instances, they would use this doctrine to strike down state legislation that had the effect of creating monopolies. At other times, it might be used to overturn state legislation intended to regulate health, safety, or welfare. Horowitz argues that courts transformed the law after the Civil War by developing new common law doctrines that subsidized American economic expansion and benefited the wealthy. It is in this period that legal formalism emerged, which held that judges should restrict themselves to abstract reasoning rooted in laissez-faire economic principles.

By the beginning of the twentieth century, a more sociological and liberal approach to judging began to develop. Judges began to recognize that extra-judicial materials could be useful in understanding intentions of legislators or the social implications of law. As a judge of the New York Court of Appeals, Benjamin Cardozo would write *The Nature of the Judicial Process*, in which he stated that judges were more than simple machines.[8] Cardozo believed that judges created laws, but he remained wedded to the notion that justice demanded respect for precedent or litigants would lose faith in the courts. Faced with vexing social problems, the duty of judges was not to find law but to create it in a manner that was bound by then-contemporary views of science. Cardozo called for a scientific analysis of social needs to pursue the law's ultimate end of achieving social justice. Like-minded judges in the 1920s and 1930s remained devoted to precedent but also pressed for a new social vision to avoid injustice. These judges would work to undermine the classical legal order that protected property and modified the law to fit emerging social needs. Nineteenth-century attitudes would disintegrate as judges came to view their role as one of social policymaking.

The broadened role of state courts called for heightened concerns about their integrity. Commenting on the changes in New York, William Nelson believes the "disintegration of shared values and the collapse of the doctrine of precedent . . . made it necessary to convince the public, and perhaps even the judges themselves, of the special dignity and integrity of the bench."[9] To be viewed as legitimate, the courts had to take ethics and discipline very seriously, and Nelson observes a dramatic increase in disciplinary actions in the 1960s and 1970s. The public might not always believe in the correctness of court decisions, but with attention to ethics, they could at least have faith in the integrity of the decision-making process.

Without institutional legitimacy, courts could not function as consequential partners in governance. State courts have pursued legitimacy throughout U.S. history but the approach has differed from one era to the next. In the contemporary era, much ink is spilled regarding the politics of judicial selection, the increasing role of money in judicial elections, and judicial ethics. Judges need to be seen as above conventional politics at a time when their decisions reach beyond precedent to create law. In another era, the quest for legitimacy was also pervasive but, as Friedman notes,

> late 19th century judges stressed very strongly that they did not make law. . . . There were ample reasons why the judges assumed so docile a posture. For one thing, it provided magnificent camouflage. It disclaimed responsibility for unpopular opinions. It was the one reason why judges, even though elected, did not stand naked before the partisan public. . . . The flight into technicality and personality was only apparently a flight toward a more humble, self-effacing role. . . . They claimed the expert's privilege of monopoly control of their business and insisted that what they did, like all experts' work, was value-free. These were valuable postures of self-defense.[10]

Because they have nurtured their legitimacy over time, state courts, like their federal counterparts, have been able to be active participants in governance, withstanding partisan tides while taking controversial stands. For much of U.S. history, state courts have performed like safety valves, taking on mediating functions between competing or conflicting social and economic interests, and they have done so authoritatively because they have promoted an image of propriety and legitimacy. This image has allowed them to make adjustments in policy in less visible ways than conventional majoritarian politics, reducing the agenda of more open political processes to manageable proportions.

State Courts: Part of the Method of Democracy

The choice to become a democratic republic over two centuries ago raised many important issues about governance that still are unresolved to this day. The term "republic" is derived from the Latin term *res publica*, or "public affair," and implies ownership or control of the state by the population at large. From this perspective, democracy is a system that promotes participatory decision making, either directly or through elections. Democracy is much more than this, however. William Riker observed that there is no single, authoritative definition of democracy. Instead, democracy is comprised of properties "found in these documents . . . [that are] elements of the democratic method . . . [and that] are means to render voting practically effective and politically significant, and all the elements of the democratic ideal [that] are moral extensions and elaborations of the features of the method that make voting work."[11]

From this perspective, democracy is not simply the opportunity to vote in elections but also is a broader methodology that renders voting practically effective and politically significant. For this to occur, not all issues can be subject to voting. Agendas must be set and alternatives must be narrowed.

Creating opportunities for voting and participation was not the primary pre-occupation of the framers of the U.S. Constitution. Quite the contrary, most of the framers were much more concerned with the instability and factionalism that could arise from mass participation in governance. Most notably, James Madison, commonly considered the architect of the Constitution, was preoccupied with the instability that could accompany a democratic system. He is perhaps most remembered for his observations concerning the mischief of faction: since conflict is sewn in the nature of man, how do we manage conflicts without destroying liberty? Like other theorists of democracy, Madison also was troubled that a key element of most democratic systems—majority rule—has some undesirable properties other than rampant factionalism. Madison was very familiar with the Marquis de Condorcet's seminal *Essai* where the French philosopher observed that for any option that might be chosen by a majority of voters, there is usually some other option, preferred by a different majority, which can upset it.[12]

For Madison and the other framers, there were thus both practical and theoretical reasons to devise a government that did not depend on simple majority rule. Factionalism could undermine the rights of all, and cyclical voting could produce destructive instability. It was imperative that very few issues were subject to majority rule. The result was a system of checks and balances between branches of government and a division of power between levels of government. It is a system of government that allows expression of popular sentiment on a limited number of issues at differing levels of government while, at the same time, removing many issues and alternatives from the public agenda. The resulting system places greater emphasis on stability than on responsiveness to mass preferences. As Madison noted in *Federalist* 37, "stability in government is essential to national character."[13]

It was not until almost two centuries later that scholars came to appreciate the vital role of government's structural arrangements in promoting stability. Nobel Prize economist Kenneth Arrow sought to discover which democratic voting rules or procedures for collective decision-making would be able to aggregate existing individual preference rankings into a single consistent collective outcome. He demonstrated that no such rules or procedures appear to be available and showed that democratic decision-making processes cannot be both fair and rational. Arrow's core insight is known as the voters' paradox. That paradox, the one initially noted by Condorcet and familiar to Madison, lay dormant until Arrow and others rediscovered it in the 1950s. The paradox indicates that decision making by the time-honored democratic practice of majority vote can produce nothing but perpetual cycling among the various options. The problem only worsens when expanded to large, real world settings where there are many more than three policy options available and far more than three individuals entitled to participate.

Given Arrow's insight, it is clear that democratic processes alone cannot produce definitive stable outcomes, and one must wonder what imparts the high degree of stability observed in the United States. Left only to majoritarian processes, rampant instability or factionalism should result. So why does this does not occur? The answer is simple: because the structure, rules, and procedures of the democracy reduce, divide, and distribute conflicts between branches and levels of government, subjecting only a small proportion of issues to anything like broad majoritarian processes.

Americans vote for their legislators from geographic subunits, not from the nation at large. As the nation was reminded in 2000, the president is selected by electors and not by the popular vote. Statewide voting for the United States Senate, state officials (including some state supreme court justices), and referenda or initiatives are the majoritarian processes of the largest scale in American politics. The evolution of the U.S. two-party system has, for the most part, narrowed the viable alternatives down to two candidates for most offices. One need only to reflect on the presidential election of 2000 to appreciate how more alternatives (e.g., Pat Buchanan, Ralph Nader) contribute to uncertainty or instability. Ballot measures in states with initiative processes remind us, too, that there are impassioned groups in American society striving to impose their values on the values of others. Even in the twenty-first century, there are indications that chaos might lurk just below the surface of the seeming stability.

State Courts and Democratic Processes

What if Americans had more alternatives to consider? As far back as the election of 1800 to as recently as the election of 2000, having more than two candidates for an office has lead to confusion and ambiguity in outcomes. In large measure, the U.S. two-party system narrows choices for elective office down to the nominees of the two major parties. They do not do this without a little help, however. State party organizations have succeeded over the years in passing legislation that makes ballot access difficult for any but the two major parties. Ballot access requirements make it difficult for third party or independent candidates to run in many states. However, ballot access laws are litigated, frequently finding their way into both federal and state courts. State courts thus play a major role in shaping the terms of engagement for political parties in this country and the number of alternative candidates from which voters can choose. This process of controlling alternatives can determine outcomes, precisely in the same manner understood by Condorcet, Madison, and Arrow.

To appreciate this fundamental point, consider this example about the 2004 presidential election. Recently, state or county court judgments in Arizona, Florida, Iowa, Michigan, Nevada, New Hampshire, Oregon, Pennsylvania, and West Virginia determined whether Ralph Nader appeared on the presidential ballot in these states. If the 2004 election were even remotely like the 2000 election, Nader's presence or absence on one or a few state ballots would have played a decisive role in determining the president of the United States.

What if Americans participated more in direct democracy? As it is, there is considerable activity in this area but there might well be much more if not for the courts. For example, in the 2002 election, there were 202 statewide ballot measures in forty states. Voters approved approximately 62 percent of them. In 2004, ballot measures on issues as varied as gay marriage, the minimum wage, and immigration appeared on state ballots. Voters considered whether to place caps on medical malpractice awards in a number of states. Florida voters cast ballots regarding parental notification before a minor receives an abortion and whether to raise the minimum wage above the national standard.

Over time, initiative and referenda processes bring many rights and privileges of Americans into play, and state courts frequently are being asked to invalidate these initiatives before or after they are passed. State courts also are being asked to rule on conflicts over the conditions for allowing initiatives to gain entry to the ballot in the first place. For example, a simple Lexis-Nexis search of California cases involving "ballot measure" reveals that these types of issues have appeared in over one hundred court cases since 1984. Of course, California may be an extreme example, but the fundamental point remains. State courts shape the frequency and scope of ballot initiatives in states where initiatives are allowed, thereby ultimately influencing the character of public policy in doing so.

Throughout U.S. history, state courts have played a fundamental role in keeping a lid on majoritarian impulses. They have tinkered with the particulars of majoritarian outcomes by resolving disputes and restricting alternatives. State courts have done this commonly in obscurity but with the confidence of the American people. It could reasonably be argued that this lid is too tight because political processes in America do not offer alternatives that are attractive to many Americans.[14] Alternatively, a much more expansive but chaotic process could ensue if barriers to the ballot were reduced, if opportunities to use the initiative process were more open, or if courts were more deferential to laws passed through ballot measures. Depending on one's values, the limits to third parties and initiative measures enforced by state courts may be viewed as a good or a bad thing. Most assuredly they cannot be ignored as unimportant. Directly or indirectly, state court actions shape the scope and direction of popular participation in American politics and play a decisive role in the democratic methodology. At best, settling disputes concerning ballot access or the acceptability of ballot initiatives is a rare but nonetheless important aspect of state court activity. Much more of their effort is devoted to handling routine criminal cases and civil disputes. To be effective, a democratic system must allow the peaceful articulation of demands and resolution of competing claims in a manner that promotes a sense of justice and social unity.

If public opinion polls are any indication, state court systems perform this role very well. In a 2002 national survey, 77 percent of those polled expressed some to a great deal of confidence in their state court system, while only 22 percent said they had just a little or no confidence in these courts. Only between 6 to 12 percent felt their state courts were doing a poor job, 61 percent thought the judges were independent, and 79 percent believed they were qualified.[15] While somewhat short of the support expressed for the United States Supreme Court, these levels exceed support for high courts in European countries, suggesting that state courts enjoy a high degree of legitimacy.[16]

Based on the sheer bulk of criminal and civil disputes addressed in state courts, it is evident that these courts provide the dominant means through which many demands are articulated and many rights are protected. Citizens obey the law based on perceptions of fairness or unfairness.[17] This respect for the rule of law is essential for democracy, and state courts play a vital role in this process not only by dispensing with a mountain of legal disputes, but doing so in a manner that promotes the widespread perception of fairness and legitimacy. It is easy to imagine how the seeds of rebellion could be sewn if significant numbers of citizens felt they were treated unfairly and quit obeying laws. Anarchy or ever-harsher government actions would seem to be a likely consequence. Clearly, state court systems are a vital component of the delicate balance of democracy.

All this is not to suggest that the public never challenges the authority of state courts. However, these incidents have been rare. For example, presumably because voters felt that judges were too lenient, voters in Washington passed a referendum in 1993 calling for "three strikes and you're out" mandatory sentencing. In practice, the referendum was designed to remove judges' discretion when sentencing criminal defendants ever convicted of three cumulative felonies by requiring mandatory life sentences for these defendants. In 1994, California followed suit with similar legislation, and by 2004 twenty-six states had some form of sentencing law like the one initially enacted in Washington in 1993. Thus, even though state courts generally enjoy substantial support from the public, the widespread fear of crime prompted the residents of many states to reduce the latitude of state courts in sentencing decisions.

Similarly, but within the context of civil law, in response to the perception that liability insurance coverage was becoming more costly and less available, most states enacted legislation in the mid-1980s that reformed common law rules and other court procedures involving tort litigation. Further, tort reform remains an active issue in many states.

In sum, "three strikes" rules and recent forms of tort reform indicate that even though the public expresses high amounts of general trust and confidence in their state court systems, the fear of crime and perceptions of leniency or excessive generosity can, and have, fueled popular efforts to circumscribe court actions. Nonetheless, while popular movements to make courts tougher on crime or to end the so-called lawsuit lotteries have gained voter support in many states, courts have remained very trusted and esteemed institutions. By sizable majorities, the American public believes that state courts administer justice in a fair and impartial manner, and mass movements to circumscribe judicial choice are rare. It is easy to imagine a distrustful public passing many laws to limit state court discretion if Americans did not have confidence in these tribunals. In practice, state courts have substantial latitude in most areas of law, making relatively quiet and minute adjustments to democratic outcomes or procedures in relative obscurity.

Courts in Practice

As discussed, state courts play a critical role in resolving disputes for individual litigants but also serve to stabilize the democratic political system. Now it is important to shift to a detailed description of some important dimensions of state judicial politics related to the earlier discussion. At this point, the focus is on state supreme courts, for a number of important theoretical and practical reasons.

First, as described, state courts are enormously important legal and political institutions, with the awesome responsibility for resolving the vast majority of the nation's legal disputes. As the courts of last resort, state supreme courts have the final authority on these issues most basic to citizens' daily lives. Furthermore, in rendering decisions, state supreme courts exercise extraordinary discretion. They interpret not only state laws but also federal laws and, in the process, contribute significantly to public policy. Finally, as power continues to devolve from the federal government to the states, state courts are assuming an increasingly central role in litigation and politics, making discussions of these institutions particularly timely.[18] Assessing the nature of state courts, their idiosyncrasies, and the latest developments within, is an important task. In fact, the failure to understanding the states results in a very incomplete understanding of American politics. From a practical standpoint, the recently completed State Supreme Court Data Project provides comprehensive and systematic data about the decisions of the states' highest courts from 1995 though 1997, a resource that simply does not exist for other state courts.

The exercise that follows with the State Supreme Court Data Project involves simple description and should not be mistaken for commentary or criticism. Also, the patterns to be presented are fascinating and clearly beg for explanation. Nonetheless, while critically important to seek to explain why the various patterns and variations to be described actually occur and with what political implications, such a task is well beyond the scope of this chapter. In fact, such an enterprise will demand considerable time and scholarly focus over the next several years if not the next decade.

With those caveats duly noted, consider the fact that within state supreme courts are individual decision makers with highly diverse backgrounds, experiences, and values. Moreover, because of the sheer volume of cases, these courts address virtually every legal issue and fact pattern likely to arise at the appellate level. Similarly, in resolving this vast array of issues, state supreme court justices interpret and apply a variety of constitutional provisions, statutes, and other types of law. State supreme courts also present a wide array of institutional features and configurations, both in terms of structures, and external and internal rules and procedures. Finally, the American states, the environments within which state supreme courts operate, are diverse politically, economically, and culturally. Therefore, within the context of state supreme courts, the range of judicial authority in the United States and the variety of ways in which these important institutions contribute to democracy can clearly be seen.

The Work of State Supreme Courts in the American Democracy

State supreme courts manifest extraordinary differences in the nature of their dockets, the propensity to favor or disfavor certain categories of litigants, the extent to which they supervise and correct the lower courts, their willingness to engage in the process of separation of powers by invalidating the actions of the other branches of government and citizen initiatives on constitutional grounds, and the degree to which individual justices are willing to step in front of the purple curtain and dissent from decisions of the court majority. These important and often dramatic variations across states reflect significant differences in the fundamental functions of these courts and in the exact nature of the role of the judiciary in state and national politics. In the aggregate, these variations have substantial impacts on access to government and on the distribution of wealth and power in the United States.

State Supreme Court Dockets

Consider Figure 9.1, for example, which describes state supreme court dockets from 1995 through 1997 (n = 21,296). In this graph, miscellaneous cases consist of a variety of specialized issues, such as juvenile cases and certification, that fall outside the usual range of criminal and civil disputes.

As Figure 9.1 illustrates, state supreme courts on average decide more civil cases than criminal. In fact, civil litigation occupies 60 percent or more of the dockets in all but thirteen supreme courts. However, state supreme courts vary dramatically in the extent to which they specialize in matters of criminal or civil law.

At one extreme, the high court in Alaska hears virtually no criminal cases and instead focuses its attention almost exclusively on civil matters. Less than 5 percent of the docket in Alaska involves criminal law and other cases, while about 96 percent of the docket is civil. Alabama is a close second,

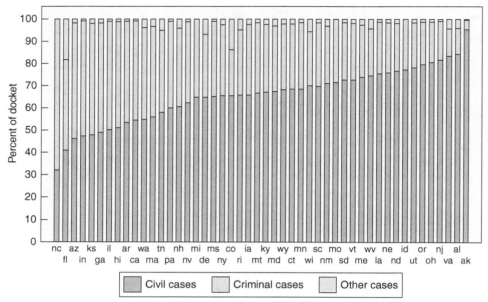

NOTE: Oklahoma and Texas have two supreme courts and have been excluded from this graph.

Figure 9.1

SOURCE: State Supreme Court Data Project 1995–1997.

devoting 85 percent of its docket space to civil litigation. At the other extreme, almost 70 percent of the cases in North Carolina are criminal, with only 31 percent devoted to civil issues. Florida is quite similar to North Carolina, dedicating only about 40 percent of its docket to civil matters. These dramatic differences in docket composition across the states suggest that supreme courts play very different functional roles within their respective judicial systems and states. State supreme courts can function largely either to strengthen or weaken the coercive arm of the state against convicted criminals, or to interject judicial authority into the relationships among a variety of classes of public and private litigants. These choices have the consequence of providing varying levels of access to judicial power to different groups in society and, depending on the nature of the decisions, play a decisive role in determining how power and wealth are allocated in the states.

These different roles are further evidenced in the specific components of the criminal and civil dockets. Figure 9.2 illustrates the proportion of criminal cases that involve murder, the most serious and publicly salient crime, and also distinguishes murder cases in which the death penalty actually was imposed by the trial court from all other murder cases.

Generally, seven state supreme courts devote over 50 percent of their criminal dockets to murder cases, while nine states spend less than 10 percent. At the extremes, North Carolina dedicates a whopping 91 percent of the criminal docket to murder cases, making these about the only type of criminal case reviewed by this court, while Maine hears almost none. Recall from the previous figure that only about 31 percent of North Carolina's docket involves civil matters; thus, taken together, North Carolina emerges as a state supreme court which largely is a forum for reviewing murder cases, which constitute 63 percent of the court's overall docket.

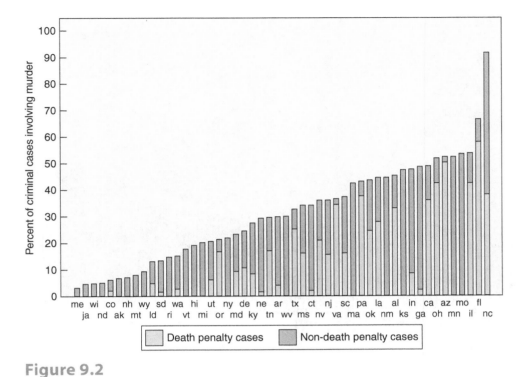

Figure 9.2

SOURCE: State Supreme Court Data Project 1995–1997.

Regarding the death penalty, seventeen states have no death penalty cases on their dockets, either because the state did not authorize capital punishment from 1995 through 1997 (Alaska, Hawaii, Iowa, Maine, Massachusetts, Michigan, Minnesota, North Dakota, Rhode Island, Vermont, West Virginia, and Wisconsin) or because there are no capital cases to review (Kansas, New Hampshire, New Mexico, New York, and Wyoming). On the other hand, states like Virginia and Arizona hear mostly capital cases, of the murder cases on their dockets. In fact, in Florida and Arizona, about half of the criminal docket involves capital murder. In these states, among other things, the justices, who are retained in elections, should be in a more precarious position with voters in their states, who could react negatively at election time to prior decisions overturning death sentences.

When considering the characteristics of civil dockets, recall from Figure 9.1 that most state supreme courts focus on civil litigation. Figure 9.3 illustrates the extent to which civil actions, which compose over 60 percent of most supreme courts' dockets, involve torts. Again, the substantial diversity among states is apparent. At one end of the spectrum, states like Georgia, Florida, Indiana, and Oregon devote only a small fraction of their civil dockets to tort cases, while Alabama, Illinois, Michigan, and Tennessee focus about half of their total civil dockets on torts. In fact, given the large percentage of civil cases on the Alabama Supreme Court docket and the considerable percentage of tort cases therein, the Alabama Court spends much of the time operating as a distributive arena. Recall that this stands in stark contradistinction to North Carolina at the other end of the spectrum, which is heavily loaded with capital cases. In fact, it appears that the job of supreme court justice is vastly different between these two states, along with the types of interests drawn to these courts and the typical stakes involved in the cases.

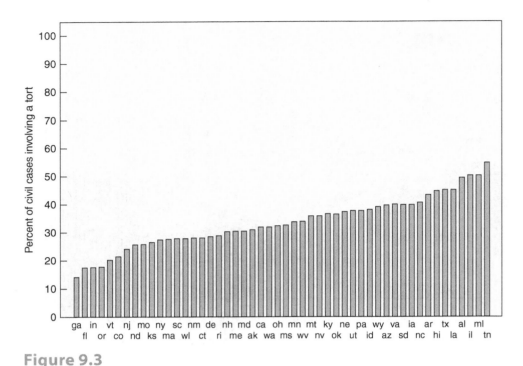

Figure 9.3

SOURCE: State Supreme Court Data Project 1995–1997.

Who Wins in State Supreme Courts

The extent to which courts favor "haves" (i.e., businesses, governments, groups) over "have-nots" (i.e., individuals) in civil litigation has been debated extensively in the scholarly literature, with lots of claims and counterclaims about the ability of courts to protect the downtrodden versus protecting the wealth and power of the entrenched economic and political elite. Figure 9.4 illustrates the extent to which have-nots win in state supreme courts in all civil cases involving these two sets of litigants. As Figure 9.4 documents, the states vary substantially along this dimension. In general, state supreme court decisions are skewed against have-not victories; individuals win less than half the time in all but nine states in cases involving more powerful litigants. Have-nots are most unsuccessful in Minnesota, Wyoming, and Florida, where have-nots win less than 25 percent of the time in these cases. However, have-nots have a slight advantage in Tennessee, Delaware, Washington, Michigan, New Hampshire, Missouri, Arizona, and Nevada.

Figure 9.5 examines who wins in criminal cases, revealing some intriguing patterns. State supreme courts vary tremendously in their willingness support defendants in criminal cases, either by reversing convictions or sentences. Concerning convictions, in Colorado, Kansas, Arkansas, Wyoming, and Ohio, for example, defendants prevail in about 5 percent or less of their appeals, while in Oregon and New Mexico they are successful in about 40 percent. Concerning sentences, many states are more likely to reverse sentences than convictions, with Oregon really standing out by overturning just over 60 percent. In fact, states like Oregon can be viewed as being quite active in supervising the decisions of the lower courts in matters of criminal law and, more broadly speaking, in checking the power of government to deprive individuals of important rights and freedoms.

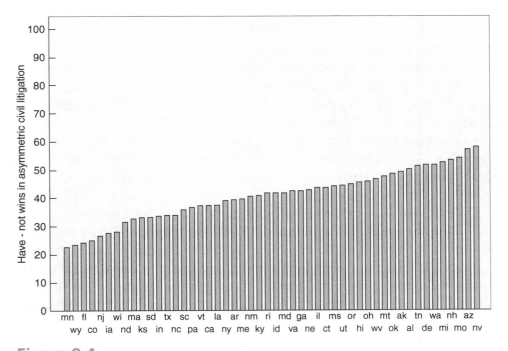

Figure 9.4

SOURCE: State Supreme Court Data Project 1995–1997.

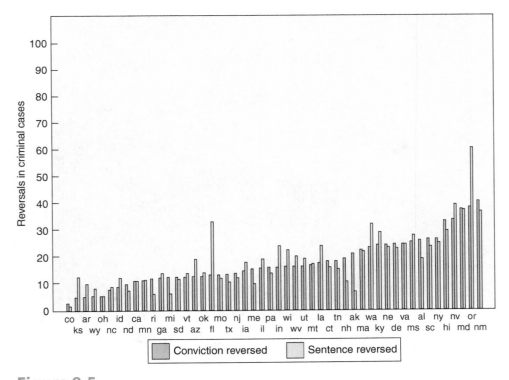

Figure 9.5

SOURCE: State Supreme Court Data Project 1995–1997.

Supervision of the Lower Courts

Concerning general propensities to reverse the lower courts, Figure 9.6 illustrates these tendencies among state supreme courts. Like the previous figures describing other dimensions of state supreme court decision making, Figure 9.6 portrays the incredible variation among courts of their willingness to reverse, along with the somewhat surprising result of the extent to which they do so. In this and all subsequent graphs, the two supreme courts in Texas and Oklahoma are considered separately. The civil courts of last resort, the Texas Supreme Court and Oklahoma Supreme Court, are designated as "txs" and "oks" in the graphs. Similarly, the criminal courts of last resort, the Texas Court of Criminal Appeals and the Oklahoma Supreme Court, are labeled as "txc" and "okc."

As Figure 9.6 illustrates, twenty-six state supreme courts reverse the lower court, either fully or in part, in at least half of the cases on their dockets. The Texas Supreme Court leads the pack with a reversal rate of almost 90 percent, while Wyoming secures the opposite end of the spectrum with a reversal rate of about 22 percent. Clearly, the supervisory role of state supreme courts in the state judicial system differs considerably from state to state. Also fascinating are the differences between the civil and criminal courts of last resort in Texas and Oklahoma. While the Texas and Oklahoma Supreme Courts have the highest lower court reversal rates of all state courts of last resort, the two criminal courts of last resort in these states are below the median. In fact, the Oklahoma Court of Criminal Appeals has one of the lowest reversal rates. Obviously, much is at play in these two sets of courts to produce such different outcomes on this crucial dimension of judicial decision-making.

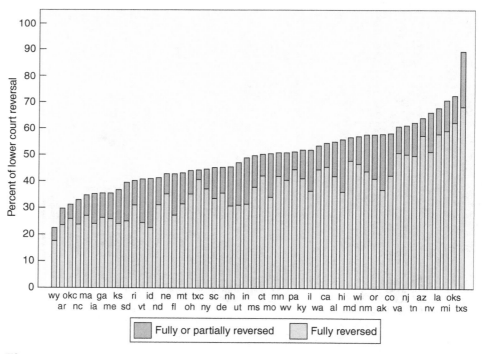

Figure 9.6

SOURCE: State Supreme Court Data Project 1995–1997.

State Supreme Courts in the System of Separation of Powers

Figure 9.7 displays the percentage of cases on each court's docket involving constitutional challenges under the state or federal constitution to a statute, executive order, or ballot initiative. In most courts (forty-seven of fifty-two), these cases do not occupy much docket space, constituting 10 percent or less of the overall docket. However, some states decide substantial proportions of these cases. At the extreme, about one of every five cases in Missouri and Illinois asks the court to rule on the constitutionality of the actions of other actors in the political system. Keep in mind, however, that these are likely to be highly salient cases politically, so that even a few of these per term can place the state high court in the political spotlight.

How do other actors fare in constitutional litigation? Figure 9.8 presents these data, which are in some sense quite surprising. Although most states have few of these cases on their dockets, in some states the tendency to invalidate on constitutional grounds is significant. Fifteen state high courts invalidate in at least 30 percent of the cases raising issues of constitutionality. Clearly, in a sizable proportion of states, supreme courts are very active players in the system of separation of powers. From a different perspective, when one considers states like Missouri and Illinois with relatively larger proportions of these cases on their dockets, a reversal rate over 20 percent, which both of these courts have, means that the supreme court is spending a considerable amount of time taking on the legislature and voters, even though the court does not have a general tendency to invalidate on constitutional grounds. Considering the exercise of judicial review as a counter-majoritarian action, these data reveal that courts in some states are most willing to perform this function.

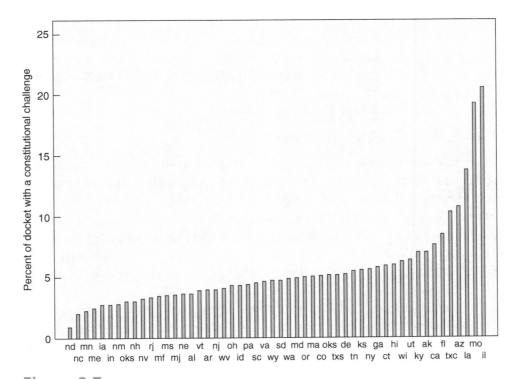

Figure 9.7

SOURCE: State Supreme Court Data Project 1995–1997.

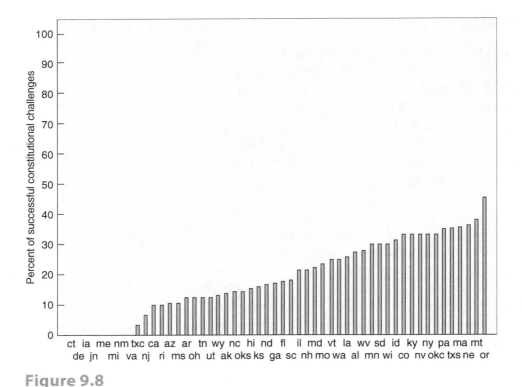

Figure 9.8

SOURCE: State Supreme Court Data Project 1995–1997.

On the other hand, the courts in some states did not invalidate on constitutional grounds at all during the period being considered. The high courts in Connecticut, Delaware, Indiana, Iowa, Maine, Michigan, New Mexico, and Virginia failed to find constitutional fault with any statute, ordinance, or ballot initiative from 1995 through 1997.

Factionalism in State Supreme Courts

Finally, the degree of dissent in state supreme courts is considered. Dissent rates are determined by a number of factors, including, but certainly not limited to, ideological disagreement among the justices of a court. However, dissent can have political consequences. Unanimous decisions may be perceived as more legitimate and, for the individual justice, can shield an unpopular decision with the power of the court. Dissent, on the other hand, represents factionalism of some sort and has the opposite consequences of those just described. Thus, dissent can be problematic for a court or for individual justices, depending on the extent to which it occurs, and in which cases.

Figure 9.9 illustrates dissent rates in state supreme courts from 1995 through 1997. As these data document, most states have unanimity rates that exceed 70 percent, demonstrating a high level of formal consensus in these courts. Only three courts (Texas Court of Criminal Appeals, Michigan, and the Oklahoma Supreme Court) have dissent in more than half their cases. Thus, in most state supreme courts, many decisions do not reflect the kind of factionalism that can raise issues of legitimacy for the court or cause difficulty for individual justices who deviate from popular decisions, but there certainly are exceptions to this general rule.

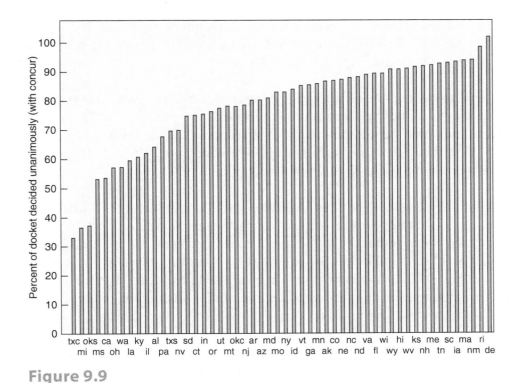

Figure 9.9

SOURCE: State Supreme Court Data Project 1995–1997.

Democratic Processes and State Supreme Courts: The Special Case of Electing Judges

One intriguing way in which democratic processes and courts clearly intersect is in the realm of judicial selection. In the American states, most judges are elected and must face voters regularly to retain their seats. While debates over judicial selection are complicated and cannot be summarized effectively in a single essay, one important concern is whether electing judges undermines judicial legitimacy by requiring judges to raise campaign funds and engage in other activities that mar the image of impartiality. There is another perspective, however, that suggests that elections might serve to enhance the legitimacy of courts by giving voters control over the composition of the bench and by serving to sensitize judges to the preferences of constituencies on those matters of law that more clearly involve public policy making than application of settled rules of law. Regardless of which system of selection might be best overall, there are numerous ways in which elections interject democratic pressures into the process of judging and complicate the normative goal of judicial independence.

As studies of elections to many different types of offices have established, electoral competition forges observable linkages between citizens and government, enhancing the representative function. Among other things, incumbents chosen in relatively competitive races are more likely to defer to the preferences of their constituencies when casting votes on controversial issues rather than choosing policy alternatives that better reflect their own personal preferences. Moreover, tighter margins of victory increase the likelihood of future electoral challenge and possible electoral defeat, thus promoting another cycle of competition to enhance the incumbent-constituency connection. Finally, some challengers actually do win, and the resulting turnover in personnel can serve to bring the institution more in line with public preferences generally.

Regarding judicial elections, one of the most important questions about this relationship between democratic processes and judicial decision making is whether judicial elections really have the sort of competitive nature that could provoke such a response. Some basic information about state supreme court elections from 1990 through 2000 provide some preliminary answers. Generally speaking, there are lots of reasons to think that they might.

Consider, for instance, reelection rates over the past decade for the United States House of Representatives, United States Senate, statehouses, and state supreme courts. From 1990 through 2000, reelection rates were, respectively, 94.1 percent, 89.3 percent, 85.1 percent, and 84.1 percent.[19] Thus, the likelihood of electoral defeat in state supreme courts is on average at least equivalent to, if not higher than, the electoral threat for other important state and federal offices. In fact, seats in the House of Representatives, the quintessential representative institution, are considerably safer on average than seats on state supreme courts.

Further, competition in the form of challengers has been increasing in state supreme court elections, particularly in nonpartisan elections. In 1990, only one of every three justices (37.5 percent) in non-partisan states was forced face challengers, but by 2000 two of three (68.0 percent) were challenged for reelection. At the same time, partisan elections have a challenge rate of 81.2 percent and now are virtually guaranteed to produce challengers for justices seeking reelection to the state high court bench. Thus, while there are differences between partisan and nonpartisan elections regarding competition, both potentially could serve to interject democratic politics into judicial decision making.

Finally, although state supreme court justices are more likely to be challenged in partisan elections than nonpartisan elections, in contested races the margins of victory are about the same in these two types of elections. The average percentage of the vote in contested nonpartisan elections from 1990 through 2000 is 57.08 percent (n = 74) while the average margin in contested partisan elections is 55.04 percent (n = 65).[20] Generally speaking, elections won by 60 percent of the vote or less are considered marginal, and a substantial portion of contested supreme court seats can be so classified. Thus, overall, electing judges might not only give voters direct control over the composition of the bench but also might have substantial consequences for the choices justices make under competitive electoral conditions. Whether this is a desirable or undesirable consequence is left to the evaluation of the reader.

A Note on Membership Change

Aside from elections, frequent membership change is the norm on the state high court bench. In fact, it is critical to observe that state courts differ dramatically from their federal counterparts in this respect. Consider, for example, that the last appointment to the United States Supreme Court was Stephen Breyer in 1994. However, from January 1994 through May 2000, nine justices in Nebraska left the bench (representing complete membership replacement), while New Mexico and West Virginia each had eight turnovers. On average, from January 1994 through May 2000, each state supreme court had between seven and eight natural courts (i.e., periods of stable membership).

Stated differently, a time span of approximately six and one-half years (January 1994–May 2000) produced substantial changes due to death, resignation, retirement, and electoral defeat in state supreme courts, resulting in *385 natural courts* in the fifty-two courts of last resort during that period. This is a period in which there were only *two natural courts* on the United States Supreme Court. Because of the high turnover on these courts, short periods of time nonetheless produce membership changes comparable to many decades on the United States Supreme Court. This extraordinary rate of change has consequences relevant to the courts' legitimacy and connection to democratic majorities. Generally speaking, courts should be kept in line, or brought back into line, with majority preferences through the process of membership replacement, and it appears that substantial opportunities for this important process exist in state supreme courts.

Conclusion

This theoretical and practical look at state courts has highlighted their critical importance to American democracy and, more specifically, to the maintenance of order and stability in the United States. At the broadest theoretical level, state courts remove choices from majoritarian politics and thus curb the kind of instability that can result from unrestricted agendas.

Similarly, state courts, particularly state supreme courts, engage in politics in different ways and thus influence political access and outcomes in different ways. While all courts are a forum for dispute resolution and generally enjoy a great deal of legitimacy with the public, courts vary in the extent to which they are able or willing to consider certain types of issues, provide access to particular groups, rule in favor of certain classes of interests, supervise the lower courts and thus control outcomes within the state judicial hierarchy, take on legislatures and voters in the game of separation of powers, and demonstrate factionalism within the ranks of the justices. Further, courts are connected to democratic processes to varying degrees through various alternative processes for selecting and retaining judges, and through the incentives or disincentives for service on the bench. In other words, courts not only serve democracy, courts also are controlled to varying degrees by democratic processes, normative ideals of judicial independence aside.

Given the incredible variation among the states' highest courts, one scarcely can imagine how a single court system could provide the sorts of democratic alternatives described while simultaneously responding, at least to some extent, to political pressures that promote legitimacy and guard judicial power. Regarding courts, one size does not fit all, and the republic has survived in part because federalism allows these critical variations.

References

Cardozo, Benjamin. *The Nature of the Judicial Process.* New Haven, Conn.: Yale University Press, 1921.

Condorcet, Marquis de. *Essai sur l'application de la analyze à la probabilité des decisions rendues à la pluralist des voix.* Paris: De l'Imprimerie royale, 1785.

de Tocqueville, Alexis. *Democracy in America.* Edited and translated by Harvey C. Mansfield and Delba Winthrop. Chicago: University of Chicago Press, 2000.

Friedman, Lawrence M. *A History of American Law.* New York: Simon and Schuster, 1973.

Hall, Kermit. *The Magic Mirror: Law in American History*. New York: Oxford University Press, 1989.

Hamilton, Alexander, James Madison, and John Jay. *The Federalist Papers*. New York: New American Library, 1961.

Horowitz, Morton J. *The Transformation of American Law, 1780–1860*. Cambridge, Mass.: Harvard University Press, 1977.

Nelson, William E. *The Legalist Reformation: Law, Politics and Ideology in New York, 1920–1980*. Chapel Hill: University of North Carolina Press, 2001.

Riker, William H. *Liberalism Against Populism: A Confrontation between the Theory of Democracy and the Theory of Social Choice*. San Francisco: W. H. Freeman, 1982.

Schattschneider, E. E. *The Semi-Sovereign People*. New York: Holt, Rinehart and Winston, 1960.

Skowronek, Stephen. *Building a New American State: The Expansion of National Administrative Capacities*. New York: Cambridge University Press, 1982.

Tyler, Tom. *Why People Obey Law*. New Haven, Conn.: Yale University Press, 1990.

End Notes

1. Alexis de Tocqueville, *Democracy in America*.
2. Stephen Skowronek, *Building a New American State: The Expansion of National Administrative Capacities* (New York: Cambridge University Press, 1982).
3. Morton J. Horowitz, *The Transformation of American Law, 1780–1860*, 1.
4. Ibid., xvii.
5. Kermit Hall, *The Magic Mirror*, 107.
6. Kermit Hall, *The Magic Mirror*.
7. 7.Ibid., 227.
8. Benjamin Cardozo, *The Nature of the Judicial Process* (New Haven, Conn.: Yale University Press, 1921).
9. William E. Nelson, *The Legalist Reformation*, 345.
10. Lawrence M. Friedman, *A History of American Law*, 333.
11. William H. Riker, *Liberalism against Populism*, 49.
12. Marquis de Condorcet, *Essai sur l'application de l'analyze à la probabilité des decisions rendues à la pluralist des voix* (Essay on the Application of Analysis to the Probability of Majority Decisions). Dennis R. McGrath, "James Madison and Social Choice Theory: The Possibility of Republicanism" (Ph.D. diss., University of Maryland, College Park, 1983).
13. Alexander Hamilton, James Madison, and John Jay, *The Federalist Papers*, 26.
14. E. E. Schattschneider, *The Semi-Sovereign People: A Realist's View of Democracy in America*.
15. Deborah Goldberg, Samantha Sanchez, and Bert Brandenberg, eds., *The New Politics of Judicial Elections: How 2002 Was a Watershed* (New York: Justice at Stake Campaign, 2002).
16. James L. Gibson, Gregory A. Caldeira, and Vanessa A. Baird. "On the Legitimacy of National High Courts," *American Political Science Review* 92 (June 1998), 343.
17. Tom Tyler, *Why People Obey Law*.
18. Ronald Weber and Paul Brace, "States and Localities Transformed," in *Change and Continuity in American State and Local Government*. edited by Ronald Weber and Paul Brace (New York: Chatham House, 1999).

19. House and Senate data are calculated from Paul R. Abramson, John H. Aldrich, and David W. Rohde, *Change and Continuity in the 2000 Elections* (Washington, D.C.: CQ Press, 2002), for gubernatorial elections from Richard M. Scammon, Alice McGillivray, and Rhodes Cook. *America Votes 24: A Handbook of Contemporary Election Statistics* (Washington, D.C.: CQ Press, 2001), and for judicial elections from Melinda Gann Hall and Chris Bonneau. "Does Quality Matter? Challengers in State Supreme Court Elections," *American Journal of Political Science* 50 (January 2006), forthcoming.

20. Melinda Gann Hall and Chris Bonneau. "Does Quality Matter? Challengers in State Supreme Court Elections," *American Journal of Political Science* 50 (January 2006), forthcoming.

CHAPTER 10
LOCAL GOVERNMENT

TAX INCENTIVE COMPETITION AND ECONOMIC DEVELOPMENT

CLINT PEINHARDT
University of Texas at Dallas

All over the world, governments are interested in improving their economies and providing jobs to their citizens. As a result, those governments are often willing to offer incentives for businesses to operate locally. Investment incentives are "targeted measures designed to influence the size, location, impact, or sector of an investment project—be it a new project or an expansion or relocation of an existing operation" (Tavares-Lehman et al. 2016, p. 3). Incentives can take the form of reduced taxation, subsidized land for a factory or office or subsidized education for workers, and frequently even lump sums transferred directly to the business. Many governments have established investment promotion agencies (IPAs) that coordinate the recruitment of these firms, manage incentives, and advocate for policies that entice new firms into the area. The State of Texas has many such programs, of which the Texas Enterprise Fund (TEF) is the most prominent. Most municipalities in Dallas-Fort Worth also have investment promotion arms, whose recruitment activities are coordinated regionally by the Dallas Area Chamber of Commerce.

Recruiting Toyota's North American Headquarters to Plano, Texas, demonstrates how investment promotion works. Toyota hired a site selection firm to assist in finding a new location, which allows the company to remain anonymous until the later stages of the process. Site selection companies use existing databases and personal networks to advertise that a major headquarters wants to relocate, and they collect data on workforce, costs of living, and standards of living, among other factors. They also collect offers of investment incentives from the interested municipalities, so IPAs sometimes submit initial offers without much information about what they are recruiting. In the case of Toyota, the site selection firm evaluated about 100 possible locations.[1] Plano won the investment owing to the geographic location of the site, local amenities for workers, the cost of housing, and other factors in addition to their incentives. The announcement came in late April, 2014, and the city council of Plano then approved a $6.75 million incentives package from its $30 million Economic Development Incentive Fund. About half of that money will go directly to Toyota if the company completes construction and creates or moves 2,900 jobs by the end of 2017. Another $2.2 million will reimburse the company for construction and permitting fees. Just under $1 million is for reimbursement of relocation expenses, and a final $750,000 is a direct cash grant if the company adds another 750 jobs by the end of 2018. Aside from the direct rewards, the company receives a 50% reduction in property taxes through 2027 and reduced taxes for the following decade as well. Even with those payouts, the city still expects to gain upwards of $70 million in property tax revenue and a similar amount in sales tax revenue, so if these estimates are accurate, Plano benefits much more than the cost of these incentives.

Despite the importance of economic growth and employment opportunities, the proliferation of investment promotion activities may not be good news if that proliferation leads to bidding wars for jobs that would have materialized anyway. This article will review the academic literature on the topic, focusing particularly on the political logic of investment promotion and on efforts to improve its practice.

The Political Economic Logic of Locational Incentives

Whether incentives improve such outcomes in practice is a different question, and it revolves around the notion of *redundancy*. An incentive is redundant if a business would have relocated without it (Tavares-Lehman et al. 2016, p. 7). Evaluating redundancy is difficult, but existing evidence suggests that incentives usually play a marginal role in the location decisions of most businesses. Krakoff and Steele (2016) summarize the existing literature, and they point to other factors as more important to most businesses, including infrastructure, local market size, and the skills of the available workforce. Importantly, they highlight that state and local taxes amount to about 1.1 percent of total costs on average (Krakoff and Steele 2016, p. 127). For the largest investments, which Mattera and Tarezynska (2013) refer to as "megadeals," incentives are more likely to influence the location decision, but even in those cases other factors play a role.

Local incentives competition is not constrained to megadeals or even to competition for new business. If a longstanding business can credibly threaten to move, it might receive new tax breaks for staying in place. UTD professor Stephen Guisinger (1985) was the first person to recognize (at least in print) the strategic dynamic of the competition in investment incentives. Each individual municipality or state government would prefer to offer fewer incentives to get the same benefits. Indeed if they could coordinate to cap the amount of incentives any one municipality could offer, they would be better off, since many municipalities would offer the cap but none could offer more. The sheer number of municipal and regional governmental investment promotion agencies makes such coordination extremely difficult, and even if successful it would incentivize one IPA to break the pact and offer more. The strategic interaction is clearly that of the Prisoners' Dilemma, when all parties are stuck at a suboptimal outcome.[2] Governor Joseph E. Kernan of Indiana pinpoints the heart of the problem: "I understand the argument that taking jobs away from Boston and putting them here is nationally a zero-sum game. But Indiana, like virtually every other state, is not going to disarm unilaterally" (New York Times, 10 November 2003).

Given the weak evidence that competition via tax incentives improves local economies, why does it persist? Political scientists have recently begun to examine the political benefits of the process. Jensen, et al. (2014) use a survey experiment to examine individual attitudes toward investment promotion. They find that voters, particularly independents, are more likely to support incumbent governors that use incentives, whether or not those governors are successful in attracting new business. In a companion paper, Jensen, Malesky, and Walsh (2015) compare local political institutions and their effect on the use of incentives. They find that municipalities with elected mayors use more incentives than municipalities run by appointed city managers. The two findings together provide strong evidence that elected leaders use incentives as a political tool that improves their own chances of reelection.

Those findings are in keeping with recent events in the state of Texas, which has been quite success-ful in recruiting businesses from elsewhere in recent years. Governor Rick Perry famously used radio advertisements to reach out to California businesses.[3] Perry's successor, Greg Abbott, threatened to veto the entire budget during the 2017 legislative session if it did not fund the Texas Enterprise Fund. In response, the legislature reinserted $48 million in funding for the TEF. Clearly, governors of Texas relish their role in investment promotion.

TEF is not their only tool for providing material incentives to businesses to operate in Texas. At the state level, a whole host of programs engages in investment promotion of one type or another. In addition to the Texas Enterprise Fund, the state of Texas has a Research and Development Tax Credit, an Emerging Technologies Fund, the Moving Image Industry Incentive Program, an Events Trust Fund, and the Texas Economic Development Act (sometimes referred to as Chapter 313).[4]

Over the last three years, TEF helped to recruit dozens of businesses to Texas, many of them funded by foreign investments. During that same time, however, hundreds of firms made new investments. From 2014 to 2016, *The Financial Times'* FDI Markets database documents over 400 new or expanded business operations through foreign investment. Only six of those received state-level incentives via the TEF, but many more received incentives from local municipalities. Not all cities were equally likely to get foreign investments, though—they are heavily concentrated in major urban centers. Houston (not including suburbs) got 142 of the 406 foreign investments, followed by Dallas (61) and Austin (56). San Antonio was a distant fourth with only 16 projects over that three-year period. Thus, just a few local entities successfully recruit new businesses in volumes big enough to have a large impact on the local economy. That result runs directly counter to the original economic logic for incentives—that they would help to attract businesses to places they might not otherwise go.

Policy Solutions

Other countries have enacted politics to reduce the costs to local governments of the incentives game. Canadian provinces frequently restrict municipalities from offering incentives, and the European Union regulates how much "state aid" that local governments can offer to businesses (Thomas 2011). One solution in the United States would clearly be for Congress to limit such com-petition, and occasionally local governments have demanded such actions. In 1996, for example, the state senators of Ohio voted unanimously for such a request (Thomas 2000, p. 171). Could Congress one day act to restrict incentives? Some believe that the Constitution's Commerce Clause, or at least the way it has been used makes any such solution difficult (Enrich 1996).

In the absence of a national solution, NGOs like Good Jobs First and think tanks like the Brookings Institution have proposed ways of improving the outcomes of the incentives game as it currently exists. They focus predominantly on keeping incentives transparent, making sure that taxpayers know what their governments are doing. Another recommendation is measuring the outcomes when public resources are used to attract businesses. Initial estimates of jobs produced by a given investment are often overblown, and sometimes even the level of investment falls well short of what is promised. In such cases, IPAs should use "clawback" provisions to recoup public moneys. According to The Pew Charitable Trusts (2017), "more states are evaluating incentives, with far more rigor and policy impact, than were doing so just a few years ago." Texas currently ranks in their middle category of accountabil-ity, and the state has made strides in recent years improving the TEF along these lines. In 2015, the legislature audited the TEF, and required greater disclosure in tax abatements via GASB 77. Currently all TEF disbursements (and clawbacks, if any) are available via the website of the Governor's office, so Texas has become more transparent and more focused on accountability.[5]

Perhaps such efforts will serve to reduce the most egregious examples of incentives. Even so, the game is likely to persist in its current form as long as local autonomy overrides the Federal Government's ability or willingness to intervene.

References

Enrich, P.D., 1996. Saving the states from themselves: Commerce clause constraints on state tax incentives for business. *Harvard Law Review*, pp. 377–468.

Guisinger, S.E., 1985. A comparative study of country policies, in Guisinger, S.E. and Associates, *Investment incentives and performance requirements*. New York: Praeger.

Jensen, N.M., Malesky, E., Medina, M. and Ozdemir, U., 2014. Pass the bucks: credit, blame, and the global competition for investment. *International Studies Quarterly*, 58(3), pp. 433–447.

Jensen, N.M., Malesky, E.J. and Walsh, M., 2015. Competing for global capital or local voters? The politics of business location incentives. *Public Choice*, 164(3–4), pp. 331–356.

Krakoff, C. and Steele, C., 2016. Incentives in the United States. In Taveres-Lehmann et al, eds. *Rethinking Investment Incentives: Trends and Policy Options*, pp. 122–152. New York: Columbia University Press.

Mattera, P. and Tarczynska, K. 2013. Megadeals: The largest economic development subsidy packages ever awarded by state and local governments in the United States. Washington, DC: Good Jobs First.

Peinhardt, C. and Sandler, T., 2015. *Transnational cooperation: An issue-based approach*. New York: Oxford University Press.

Pew Charitable Trusts, 2017. How states are improving tax incentives for jobs and growth: A national assessment of evaluation policies. Available at http://www.pewtrusts.org/en/research-and-analysis/reports/2017/05/how-states-are-improving-tax-incentives-for-jobs-and-growth.

Tavares-Lehmann, A.T., Sachs, L., Toledano, and P., Johnson, L. 2016. Introduction, pp. 1–16. In Taveres-Lehmann et al., eds. *Rethinking investment incentives*. New York: Columbia University Press.

Thomas, K., 2000. *Competing for capital: Europe and North America in a global era*. Washington: Georgetown University Press.

Thomas, K., 2011. *Investment incentives and the global competition for capital*. Basingstoke: Palgrave Macmillan.

End Notes

1. All of the details about Plano's incentives package are from *The Dallas Morning News*, 11 May 2014, "Plano approves $6.75 million grant and other incentives for Toyota."
2. The Prisoners' Dilemma is a game in which the players would achieve better results by cooperating with one another but have difficulty doing so in a finite number of interactions. See Peinhardt and Sandler (2015, pp. 20–26) for an extended presentation.

3. For an archived example go to http://www.youtube.com/watch?v=oGTEGfEoEJo.
4. See House Select Committee on Economic Development Incentives (2015), available at http://www.house.state.tx.us/_media/pdf/committees/reports/83interim/House-Select-Committee-on-Economic-Development-Incentives-Interim-Report-2014.pdf.
5. http://gov.texas.gov/files/ecodev/TEF_Listing.pdf

CHAPTER 11
PUBLIC POLICY IN THE STATES

MEASURING PUBLIC SUPPORT FOR ENVIRONMENTAL POLICIES IN THE STATES

ROBERT C. LOWRY

University of Texas at Dallas

State governments have become increasingly important players in environmental politics in recent years (Konisky and Woods 2018; Rabe 2016; Rosenbaum 2017). States have always had the option of assuming responsibility for many implementation and enforcement activities under federal anti-pollution laws, and many of them have done so. In more recent years, states have become much more assertive in developing their own environmental policy agendas. This is part of a more general trend toward decentralization under American federalism. With regard to environmental policy in particular, some states have acted out of frustration with gridlock in Congress, while others have opposed regulations adopted by the Environmental Protection Agency or the management of public lands owned by the federal government. A pattern has developed where opposing coalitions of states seem to be perpetually locked in litigation to either prevent the federal government from taking some action or require it to take action.

What explains differences across states in their positions with respect to environmental policy? One obvious factor is environmental conditions and the nature of specific problems in each state. Another factor is the degree of public support for government policies affecting the environment. While we might hope that state government agendas and actions are responsive to the preferences of their constituents, are they?

In order to answer this question, we first need to measure public support for environmental policies at the state level. Ideally, we would like to identify valid, reliable measures for all 50 states that are not too difficult to obtain and update over time. A measure is valid if it accurately captures the concept we want to measure; it is reliable if repeating the measurement gives the same answer over and over (Shively 2013). It turns out that this is far from easy.

Two other concepts we would like to measure are environmental conditions in each state and the policies pursued. These present their own challenges (Konisky and Woods 2018), but are beyond the scope of this article.

This article discusses five potential approaches to measuring public support for environmental policies at the state level: opinion polls, voting by the state's congressional delegation, membership in environmental interest groups, counts of the number of environmental organizations, and campaign contributions to political action committees advocating for the environment. It concludes with some thoughts on which approach is most appropriate depending on the specific research question we want to answer.

Measuring Public Support Using Opinion Polls

At first blush, it may seem like the answer to the question, "How should be measure public support?" is easy: Just use an opinion poll. Isn't that what opinion polls are for?

The main problem with this approach is that if we want to compare public support across states and time we need multiple polls at different points in time that cover the whole country. Most national polls based on random sampling aren't reliable at the state level because they only have a few respondents per state. The norm for telephone polls is about 1,100 respondents—enough to give us a 95 percent confidence interval of plus or minus three percent.[1] With a sample size of 1,100, we might have only two or three—or possibly zero—respondents from states like Rhode Island, North Dakota, and Wyoming, and maybe only 100 or so from California or Texas. That's not nearly enough to generate statistically reliable estimates at the state level. Some internet polls have much larger sample sizes, but scientific internet polls are a relatively recent phenomenon and even they may not have enough respondents from smaller states.

One approach to this problem was developed by Wright, Erickson and McIver (1985), who measured the percentages of Democrats, Republicans, liberals and conservatives in each state by aggregating the responses to many national polls taken during 1974–1982. This gave them a total of over 76,000 respondents. They assumed that the percentages they wanted to measure stayed constant over the years covered by their data.

Of course, if we want to consolidate results from many different polls and possibly measure shifts in opinion over time, we need to have substantially the same question asked over and over again. Most opinion polls dealing with politics and public policy ask background questions like whether the respondent identifies as Democratic or Republican and considers themselves to be liberal or conservative, but finding multiple polls that ask the same policy question(s) is another matter.

The Gallup Poll has asked two questions regarding environmental policy repeatedly. They have asked whether Americans think "government" is doing too much, too little or about the right amount in terms of protecting the environment at least 11 times since 1992. They have asked whether environmental protection or economic growth should have higher priority almost annually since 1984 (Gallup Poll 2018). Plots of national data show significant shifts over time, so it wouldn't be reasonable to assume responses by state are stable, and no one poll has enough respondents to generate reliable state-level estimates.

A more recent approach is to use a technique with the imposing-sounding name of multilevel regression with post-stratification, or MRP. The idea (skipping over lots of technical details) is as follows (see Lax and Phillips 2009):

- Aggregate data from national public opinion surveys.
- Estimate a model predicting the probability an individual gives a certain response as a function of the individual's demographic characteristics, aggregate state characteristics, and year (that's the multilevel regression part).
- Generate a predicted probability for each permutation of individual characteristics, state and year; for example, Hispanic women age 18–44 in Texas in 2018.
- Estimate state-level public opinion as the weighted sum of the predicted probabilities using the percentages of the population with each permutation of individual characteristics for each state and year (that's the post-stratification part).

Lax and Phillips (2009) argue that one can generate reliable estimates of state opinion from even a single national survey by using this technique.

Howe, *et al.* (2015) use MRP to estimate public opinion regarding climate change for states, counties and congressional districts. They compare their estimates to the results of polls taken at the state or local level, and conclude that the estimates are reliable. Maps showing estimated public opinion at the state, congressional district, and county level for a variety of questions related to climate change can be seen at the website of the Yale Program on Climate Change Communication (2018).

The obvious limitation of this technique is that we still need to have access to data from appropriate national opinion surveys—preferably several surveys that all ask the same question in the same way. Another limitation is the individual demographic characteristics are limited to those that are included in the surveys and for which we have aggregate data at the subnational level. In addition, proper execution requires a fairly high level of sophistication with statistical methods.

Finally, interpretation of the results from any opinion poll requires close attention to the exact wording of survey questions. For example, one of the questions Gallup has used repeatedly over time asks respondents whether

> protection of the environment should be given priority, even at the risk of curbing economic growth (or) economic growth should be given priority, even if the environment suffers to some extent? (Gallup 2018)

It is not surprising that answers vary with the state of the economy, as the question asks about the *relative* importance of environmental and economic issues. Higher percentages of respondents give priority to the environment when the economy is doing well than when it is in recession. We should not necessarily interpret trends in these responses to indicate a shift in underlying values with regard to the environment (Boyd and Kousky 2016). The same holds true for comparisons across states at any given point in time.

Measuring Public Support Using Votes in Congress

A different approach might be based on a technique developed by Berry *et al.* (1998) for measuring state ideology. Their underlying assumption is that votes cast by members of Congress on legislation faithfully represent the opinions of voters who support them. Thus, public support for public policies in each state can be measured by the votes cast by members of Congress from that state on relevant legislation.

Again skipping over the technical details, Berry, *et al.* (1998) start with scores assigned to members of Congress by the Americans for Democratic Action (ADA) and the AFL-CIO Committee on Political Education. These scores measure the percentage of times each member of Congress votes for the "liberal" position on selected roll call votes chosen by those organizations. They then estimate ideology in each congressional district as the weighted average of the incumbent's score and the average score for all incumbents from the same party as the challenger in the most recent election, using the percentages of votes cast for the incumbent or challenger.[2] Finally, they use the average across congressional districts as their measure of statewide ideology. Berry *et al.* refer to this as "citizen" ideology, but the weights are all calculated from percentages of voters. They also produce an estimate of state government ideology by using the party of the governor and the percentages of seats in the state legislature controlled by each party. These measures have been widely used in the state politics literature and are available for 1960 through 2013 from Professor Richard Fording's website (Fording 2018).

One potential limitation of using interest group scores is that they are based on a relatively small number of roll call votes in each year, and the specific issues that come up for a roll call vote vary from year to year. Thus, a score of X percent in one year does not necessarily indicate the same underlying ideology as a score of X percent in a different year. Having said that, the same members of Congress do tend to score high or low year after year. Berry, *et al.* (2010) apply their method to NOMINATE scores, which are calculated by political scientists based on all roll call votes cast in a given Congress and scaled so that they are comparable over time (see Lewis, *et al.* 2018). They conclude that their original measure is slightly better for citizen ideology, although NOMINATE scores may be better for calculating state government ideology.

How can this approach be applied to public support for environmental policies? The League of Conservation Voters (LCV) is part of a network of environmental groups that focuses, among other things, on congressional elections and policymaking in Congress. It has assigned interest group ratings based on roll call votes on environmental legislation to all members of Congress since 1971 (League of Conservation Voters 2018). We could apply Berry, *et al.*'s technique to LCV scores and have measures of public support for every state and year since 1971.

But perhaps we are making this too hard. Don't liberals generally support strong environmental laws, while conservatives oppose them? If so, why can't we just use the Berry *et al.* measure of citizen ideology as a proxy for public support of environmental policies?

It turns out that general liberalism is a reasonable proxy for environmentalism as measured by LCV scores in recent years, but the relationship breaks down as we go back in time. Figure 11.1 shows the ADA scores and LCV scores for United State Senators during the 111th Congress, covering 2009–2010. Data are

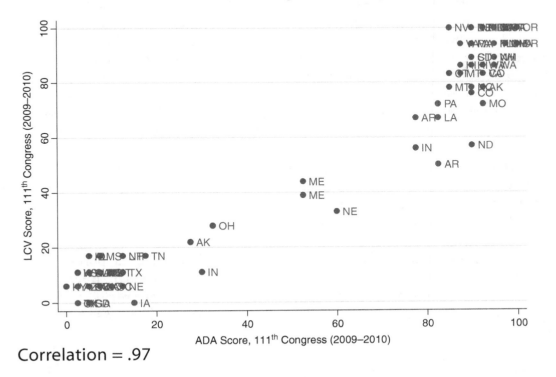

Correlation = .97

Figure 11.1 Voting in the U.S. Senate, 2009–2010

SOURCE: Robert Lowry

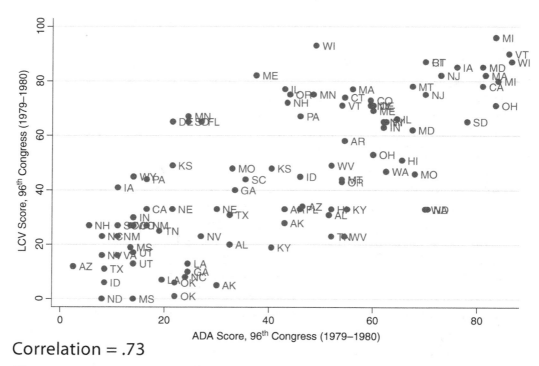

Correlation = .73

Figure 11.2 Voting in the U.S. Senate, 1979–1980

SOURCE: Robert Lowry

publicly available from Americans for Democratic Action (2018) and the League of Conservation Voters (2018). Scores were calculated using two years' worth of data to increase the number of votes and the range of issues included. Each data point represents an individual senator; senators who did not serve the entire two-year term are excluded. It is obvious that the two sets of scores are very closely related (r = .97)[3], and senators are clustered at the extreme values for both measures. Figure 11.2 shows the equivalent scores for the 96th Congress, covering 1979–1980. The relationship is still positive (r = .73), but not nearly as tight as in later years. Also, there are many more senators with moderate scores for one or both measures. A comparable analysis using NOMINATE scores rather than ADA scores shows the same pattern.

This is consistent with more general trends in American politics, where Congress has become increasingly polarized and environmental policy has become increasingly partisan (Rosenbaum 2017). Kraft (2016) argues that the shift with respect to environmental policy began with the 1994 congressional elections and has continued ever since.

This quick-and-dirty analysis implies that if we want to analyze public support of environmental policies for recent years, the Berry *et al.* measure is probably good enough. If we want to analyze data from the 1970s or 1980s, or if we want to examine trends over a long period of time, it would be better to generate a measure using the LCV scores. It may be best to use LCV scores computed for a full, two-year session rather than individual years.

Measuring Public Support Using Interest Group Membership

Another measure that may be used as a proxy for public support is membership in organizations that advocate for environmental policies. In particular, researchers sometimes use state membership per

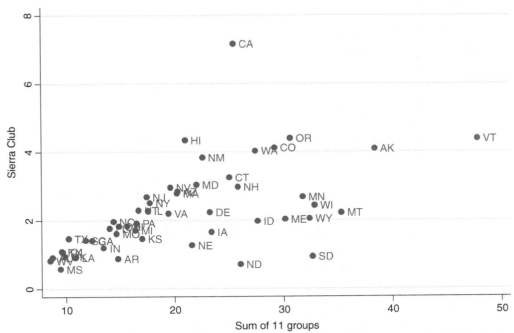

Data measure the number of group members per 1,000 state residents age 16 and above.

Correlation = .56

Figure 11.3   Environmental Group Members, circa 1992

SOURCE: Robert Lowry

capita in the Sierra Club (Konisky and Woods 2018). The Sierra Club is one of the oldest and largest membership-based environmental organizations in the country, and one of the most politically active. It is a safe bet that people who join the Sierra Club support strong environmental policies. Nonetheless, the Sierra Club is just one organization. There are dozens of membership-based environmental organizations active at the national level and hundreds (at least) active at the state and local levels. The reason researchers tend to use the Sierra Club is very simple: It is willing to share the data, and in fact used to publish state-level membership totals every year in *Sierra* magazine. Many other national organizations are less willing to share their membership data, and it would be next to impossible to obtain state-level totals of all members in state and local environmental organizations.

Using data from the early 1990s, we can see that Sierra Club membership is almost certainly a biased proxy for membership in all environmental groups. Lowry (1998) obtained state-level membership data for 11 environmental organizations active nationally or across several states. They include the Sierra Club, the Environmental Defense Fund, Friends of the Earth, the National Audubon Society, National Parks and Conservation Association, National Wildlife Federation, Natural Resources Defense Council, The Nature Conservancy, Wilderness Society, Ducks Unlimited, and the Rocky Mountain Elk Foundation. Figure 11.3 shows Sierra Club members per 1,000 state residents age 16 and above on the vertical axis, and the sum for all 11 organizations (including the Sierra Club) on the horizontal axis. Membership data are for 1990, 1991, 1992 or 1993, depending on the organization; population data are for 1992. The two membership rates are positively related, but the correlation is only .56. If we look at the Sierra Club alone California has by far the most members per capita, but if we use the sum for all 11 organizations, California ranks just 15th. This is not surprising, as the Sierra Club was founded in California and until the 1950s was an actual club for people who wanted to enjoy and protect the Sierra Nevada Mountains (Fox 1981).

Of course, the sum of all 11 organizations is not necessarily a valid measure of public support for environmental policies either. Some very prominent organizations like the World Wildlife Fund and Greenpeace are not included in the data, and the groups that are included do not necessarily share the same attitude towards public policy.

For example, Ducks Unlimited and the Rocky Mountain Elk Foundation are organizations of hunters who focus on preserving and restoring land that provides natural habitat for migratory waterfowl or elk, respectively. They account for many of the total members in states like Montana, Wyoming and North Dakota. While they clearly do promote conservation of natural resources, their members might have very different attitudes toward specific public policies than do members of the Sierra Club or the Environmental Defense Fund (Lowry 1998).

This suggests that we may need to distinguish between support for environmental values and support for public policies that rely on government regulation. Most measures that have been developed of public support for environmental policies are focused on the latter, but it is certainly possible for someone to consider themselves to be an ardent conservationist and yet be opposed to "big government" solutions.

If we drop Ducks Unlimited and the Rocky Mountain Elk Foundation from the data set, the relationship between Sierra Club members per capita and total members per capita in the remaining nine organizations is tighter ($r = .77$), but California still only ranks ninth in total members per capita. California is greatly overrepresented by Sierra Club members, while the New England states are underrepresented.

This exercise illustrates the problem with relying on incomplete data just because it's easy to obtain. Some public opinion surveys include questions on whether the respondent belongs or contributes to an organization advocating for the environment. Keeping in mind that different respondents may have very different perspectives on advocating for the environment (are the Boy Scouts an environmental organization?), these could be analyzed using the MRP technique described above. Using membership data for one or a few specific environmental organizations as a proxy for public support, however, is not a good idea.

Measuring Public Support by Counting Organizations

If we cannot feasibly count the number of members or supporters of state and local environmental organizations, can we at least count the number of organizations? The answer is yes, or at least we can get a close approximation. Most organizations that might be considered interest groups in some sense (as opposed to individual business firms) qualify for tax-exempt status under the Internal Revenue Code. Organizations with at least $25,000 in annual revenues must apply for tax-exempt status and provide some description of their activities in order to show that they fall under one of the relevant sections of tax law. Data for these organizations, including the state where they are incorporated, are available back to 1989 from the National Center for Charitable Statistics (2018). Lowry (2005) analyzes the number of organizations focused on "conservation, environment and beautification activities" by state in 1990 and 1998. We could, perhaps, use the number of such organizations relative to the state population or economy as a measure of public support.

As usual, there are several caveats. The data do not include information on how many individual members or supporters a group has, or the specific focus of its activities. While the data do include various financial variables that can be used as measures of size (the data are more detailed for more recent years), these may be distorted by organizations like the Sierra Club that operate nationally or even internationally but are incorporated in one state.

Perhaps less obvious, the number of organizations in a state may depend on economies of scale. As the size of a population grows, the number of organizations needed to serve the interests of the population does not necessarily grow proportionately (Gray and Lowery 1996).[4] This implies that public support measured by the number of organizations relative to state size will be overstated for small states compared to large states.

Measuring Public Support Using Campaign Contributions

I have consistently used the term "public support" rather than "public opinion" because the two are not quite the same. In particular, public support depends on the intensity of opinion as well as its direction. None of the methods described above do a good job of accounting for intensity.

Economists frequently invoke the concept of revealed preferences, which comes from the idea that we should pay attention to what people do, not what they say. We should focus on actions that require some actual cost to the person who takes them. We can infer that the greater the cost someone is willing to bear, the stronger their opinion. If someone responds to an opinion survey by saying they "definitely agree" with a position as opposed to "agree," it doesn't cost them anything to say so. Similarly, the fact that a member of Congress casts a roll call vote in favor of legislation tells us little about the strength of their support. It is safe to assume that people who join environmental organizations feel more strongly than those who don't, but satisfying the minimum requirement for membership (which varies from group to group) is a pretty crude measure.

One way to measure intensity might be to look at campaign contributions. Data on contributions to individual candidates don't give us information on support for particular issues, but a number of environmental organizations operate political action committees (PACs). These are organizations that raise money to make contributions to congressional campaigns. The largest environmental PAC is operated by the League of Conservation Voters; others include the Sierra Club, Ocean Champions, Natural Resources Defense Council, and Environmental Defense Fund (Center for Responsive Politics 2018). The Federal Election Commission (FEC) makes data available on contributions by individuals to PACs for every year since 1974, although data are available online only since 1993 (U.S. Federal Election Commission 2018). We could use total contributions from each state and year to environmental PACs as a proxy for public support that incorporates intensity.

One potential objection to using campaign contributions to measure public support is that dollar amounts may be distorted by the contributions of one or a few wealthy individuals. However, each individual can only contribute a maximum of $5,000 during a calendar year to any single PAC (Code of Federal Regulations 2017, Title 11 § 110.1(d)). Thus, the impact of any one individual on aggregate state contributions will be limited.

Unfortunately, we may not be able to observe the state of origin for a large enough share of all campaign contributions to generate valid measures of public support. PACs are only required to report information on individual donors if they contribute more than $200 during a calendar year (Code of Federal Regulations 2017, Title 11 §§ 104.8 (a), 104.8(b)). This means that we have no information on the state of origin for "small" donations. "Itemized" contributions—those individually reported to the FEC—often make up less than half the total dollars contributed. In 2004, for example, 45.8 percent of all dollars contributed by individuals to all "issue advocacy" PACs were itemized, whereas 54.2 percent were small donations (Lowry 2013). If the ratio of small to itemized donations was approximately the same for every state and year this would not be a concern, but that seems extraordinarily unlikely.[5]

More generally, the trend in campaign finance is for money to flow outside of traditional channels and go instead to "super PACs" that spend money independent of candidates and parties, and nonprofit "social welfare" organizations not regulated by the Federal Election Commission (Chand, 2015). Thus, contributions to traditional PACs are likely to become less valid as a measure of public support over time. Aggregate state contributions to super PACs may be dominated by a few, very large donors, while contributions to social welfare nonprofits are generally not subject to public disclosure.

Discussion

By now it should be obvious that the holy grail of a measure of public support for environmental policies that is valid and reliable, available for all 50 states across a number of years, and relatively easy to obtain and update does not exist. It therefore becomes a question of which imperfect measure is best under a given set of circumstances.

When it comes to measuring public opinion, multilevel regression with post stratification (MRP) is the state of the art. Subject to the caveat that opinion polls do not adequately capture intensity of preferences, MRP is probably the best alternative if we want to analyze support for specific kinds of policies and can get access to appropriate national survey data.

The citizen ideology scores produced by Berry *et al.* (1998, 2010) are likely "good enough" measures of support for activist environmental policies since about 2000, and are readily available for all states and years from 1960 through 2013. If we want to analyze data from before 1995 or over long stretches of time, we could apply their technique to League of Conservation Voters voting scores. This would require a large initial investment, but the data are all publicly available and, once assembled, would be relatively easy to update.

Using membership data from one or several national environmental interest groups is probably not a valid measure of public support due to differences in their geographic and programmatic focus, and it would be virtually impossible to obtain data from the full population of relevant groups. Using MRP to estimate participation in environmental organizations by state may be worth pursuing.

Another alternative is to use the number of organizations in a state, although the subject matter classifications used in the tax data are broad. Moreover, the number of organizations relative to state population or the economy may overestimate public support in small states compared to large states.

Finally, analyzing campaign contributions to pro-environment PACs seems like a promising way to capture intensity at first blush, but data on the state of origin are not available for small donors. Moreover, recent trends in campaign finance suggest that contributions to traditional PACs will become less valid as measures of public support over time.

These kinds of issues may seem dry and technical at first, but getting the measurement of key concepts right (or as right as we can) is critical to doing social science research that can withstand scrutiny and give us answers to the questions we care about.

References

Americans for Democratic Action. 2018. "ADA Voting Records." https://adaction.org/ada-voting-records/. Last accessed April 22.

Berry, William D., Evan J. Ringquist, Richard C. Fording, and Russell L. Hanson. 1998. "Measuring Citizen and Government Ideology in the . American States, 1960–93." *American Journal of Political Science* 42(January): 327–348.

Berry, William D., Richard C. Fording, Evan J. Ringquist, Russell L. Hanson and Carl Klarner. 2010. "Measuring Citizen and Government Ideology in the American States: A Re-appraisal." *State Politics and Policy Quarterly* 10(Summer): 117–135.

Boyd, James W. and Carolyn Kousky. 2016. "Are We Becoming Greener?" *Resources* 191(Winter): 26–33.

Center for Responsive Politics. 2018. "Political Action Committees." https://www.opensecrets.org/pacs/. Last accessed April 22.

Chand, Daniel. 2015. "Anonymous Money in Campaigns: Is Sunlight the Best Disinfectant?" *The Forum: A Journal of Applied Research on Contemporary Politics* 13(July): 269–288.

Code of Federal Regulations. 2017. Title 11, "Federal Elections." Washington, DC: U.S. General Printing Office.

Fording, Richard C. 2018. "State Ideology Data." https://rcfording.wordpress.com/state-ideology-data/. Last accessed April 23.

Fox, Stephen. 1981. *John Muir and his Legacy: The American Conservation Movement*. Boston: Little, Brown, and Company.

Gallup Poll. 2018, March 29. "Americans Want Government to Do More on Environment." http://news.gallup.com/poll/232007/americans-want-government-more-environment.aspx?g_source=link_NEWSV9&g_medium=TOPIC&g_campaign=item_&g_content=Americans%2520Want%2520Government%2520to%2520Do%2520More%2520on%2520Environment Last accessed April 23.

Gray, Virginia and David Lowery. 1996. *The Population Ecology of Interest Representation: Lobbying Communities in the American States*. Ann Arbor, MI: University of Michigan Press.

Howe, Peter D., Matto Mildenberger, Jennifer R. Marlon, and Anthony Leiserowitz. 2015. "Geographic Variation in Opinions on Climate Change at State and Local Scales in the USA." *Nature Climate Change* 5(June): 596–603.

Konisky, David M. and Neal D. Woods. 2018. "Environmental Policy." In Virginia Gray, Russell L. Hanson and Thad Kousser (eds.) *Politics in the American States: A Comparative Analysis* 451–477. Thousand Oaks, CA: CQ Press.

Kraft, Michael E. 2016. "Environmental Policy in Congress." In Norman J. Vig and Michael E. Kraft (eds.) *Environmental Policy: New Directions for the Twenty-First Century* 103–127. Thousand Oaks, CA: CQ Press.

Lax, Jeffrey R. and Justin H. Phillips. 2009. "How Shall We Estimate Public Opinion in the States?" *American Journal of Political Science* 53(January): 107–121.

League of Conservation Voters. 2018. "National Environmental Scorecard." http://scorecard.lcv.org/ scorecard/archive. Last accessed April 13.

Lewis, Jeffrey B., Keith Poole, Howard Rosenthal, Adam Boche, Aaron Rudkin, and Luke Sonnet. 2017. "Voteview: Congressional Roll-Call Votes Database." https://voteview.com/. Last accessed April 13, 2018.

Lowry, Robert C. 1998. "Religion and the Demand for Membership in Environmental Citizen Groups." *Public Choice* 94(March):223–240.

Lowry, Robert C. 2005. "Explaining the Variation in Organized Civil Society across States and Time." *The Journal of Politics* 67(May): 574–594.

Lowry, Robert C. 2013. "Mobilizing Money: Political Action Committees and Political Participation." *American Politics Research.* 41(September):839–862.

National Center for Charitable Statistics. 2018. "National Center for Charitable Statistics Data Archive." http://nccs-data.urban.org/index.php. Last accessed April 23.

Rabe, Barry G. 2016. "Racing to the Top, the Bottom, or the Middle of the Pack? The Evolving State Government Role in Environmental Protection." In Norman J. Vig and Michael E. Kraft (eds.) *Environmental Policy: New Directions for the Twenty-First Century* 33–57. Thousand Oaks, CA: CQ Press.

Rosenbaum, Walter A. 2017. *Environmental Politics and Policy.* Thousand Oaks, CA: CQ Press, 10th edition.

Shively, W. Phillips. 2013. *The Craft of Political Research.* Upper Saddle River, NJ: Pearson, 9th edition.

U.S. Federal Election Commission. 2018. "Quick Answers to Disclosure Questions." https://classic. fec.gov/ans/answers_disclosure.shtml#historicaldata. Last accessed April 22.

Wright, Gerald C. Jr., Robert S. Erikson, and John P. McIver. 1985. "Measuring State Partisanship and Ideology with Survey Data." *Journal of Politics* 47(June):469–489.

Yale Program on Climate Change Communication. 2018. "Visualizations and Data." http://climate-communication.yale.edu/visualizations-data/. Last accessed April 18.

End Notes

1. A 95 percent confidence interval of plus or minus three percent means that if we took 100 samples from the same population and calculated the percentage of respondents giving a certain answer for each sample, 95 of them would be within three points of the percentage we would get if we surveyed the entire population. The rule of thumb for a random sample is the confidence interval is approximately equal to 100 divided by the square root of the sample size.

2. If a state's congressional delegation has no members from one of the major parties, they use the scores for that party from neighboring states. In the case of an uncontested congressional election, they interpolate the percentages of votes received by the challengers in the previous and next contested elections (Berry et al. 1998, p. 331, notes 3, 4).

3. r is the symbol for the statistical correlation coefficient, which measures how closely the values of two variables are related. It can range from -1 to 1, with 1 representing a perfect, positive relationship, -1 a perfect, negative relationship, and 0 representing no statistical relationship at all.

4. Gray and Lowery (1996) analyze the number of organizations registered to lobby in state capitals for various years. They break the data down by economic sector, but the closest they come to environmental organizations is "social" interest groups. It may be possible to get more specific information on group focus from the original data sources.

5. The threshold for itemizing donations is not adjusted for inflation, so the definition of a "small" donor in real terms changes over time.

U.S. PUBLIC HEALTH SURVEILLANCE SYSTEMS IN RESPONSE TO DISASTERS: PROCESSES AND CHALLENGES

DANIELLE ZAYCHIK AND DOHYEONG KIM
University of Texas at Dallas

Abstract

Public health surveillance is important to ensuring the health of the US population. The current surveillance system requires the coordination of several levels of government. Surveillance efforts are particularly important during and after a disaster since they help us understand the impact of a disaster and plan for future disasters. In particular, targeted surveillance systems, such as shelter, sentinel, syndromic and active mortality surveillance, are important for guiding an effective emergency response. However, disaster mortality surveillance data collected by the state is oftentimes problematic. This is evidenced by discrepancies in mortality surveillance data between different agencies, which may directly or indirectly affect disaster-related policy. State data may be flawed because of the structure of the reporting system, which varies by state. In some states, administrative barriers make coordination and standardization difficult. Additionally, both in cases of direct and indirect disaster mortality, medical examiners or coroners may not attribute deaths to a disaster on death certificates.

Public Health Surveillance in the U.S.

Public health surveillance is the system by which health data is collected, analyzed, interpreted, and disseminated (Nsubuga, 2006). It is the process by which health information is transferred, used, and made useful by different local, state and federal actors. In the United States, a federal agency, the Center for Disease Control (CDC), is primarily responsible for coordinating these aspects of public health surveillance, but this process spans many levels of government. For instance, when clinicians working in hospitals and clinics diagnose a patient with a contagious disease that requires reporting, this data is passed on to the local health department, state health department, and the CDC. Clinicians and hospitals also report vital statistics data, including births and deaths, to the state. After analyzing data and shaping strategies that maximize population health, the CDC establishes guidelines concerning different conditions for state and local health departments.

This process is important for several reasons. Firstly, public health surveillance serves as an early warning system during health emergencies. An effective surveillance system should make it possible to identify an infectious disease outbreak before it affects a large portion of the population. Information about the outbreak and demographics of the population are used to guide policy and prevent the spread of disease (WHO, 2018a). Secondly, good public health surveillance is used to identify and track health trends, which may ultimately shape healthcare policy and practice that promote a healthier society. Monitoring health trends may help policymakers and public health officials prioritize specific health conditions or geographic regions based on need. For instance, tracking when and where cancer rates rise or fall may lead to a better understanding of the risk factors for cancer. Tracking obesity rates may help policymakers identify regions that would most benefit from programs that promote healthy living. Finally, surveillance data can be used to assess the effectiveness of various healthcare programs and interventions.

There are four primary types of surveillance: passive, active, sentinel and syndromic (Stone and Horney, 2017). Passive surveillance is the system by which hospitals, clinics and other facilities submit health data to the local Department of Health. For instance, the National Notifiable Disease Surveillance System (NNDSS) is the system for reporting cases of notifiable diseases—those diseases that must legally be reported to the government- such as cholera and malaria. This system relies on hospitals and doctors to report all cases of notifiable diseases. Additionally, state governments maintain vital statistics registries, which track life events, such as birth and death. These registries have health-related functions as well as legal functions that include issuing documents attesting to individuals' rights and status. The CDC facilitates the exchange, compilation and sharing of state-level vital statistics data with the National Vital Statistics System (NVSS) (CDC, 2018). This system connects state health departments with the National Center for Health Statistics at the CDC. These data are then analyzed to better understand trends such as infant mortality, teenage birth rates, and leading causes of death.

Active surveillance occurs when public health agencies seek out information about a specific condition. For instance, officials at the Department of Health and Human Services (DHHS) may inquire about patients and scan medical records in order to identify potential cases of a condition of interest. If cases are found, they are explored, analyzed, and monitored (WHO, 2018b). In the US, the CDC runs the Foodborne Diseases Active Surveillance Network (FoodNet), an active surveillance network employed in 10 states in different regions of the country. The purpose of FoodNet is to detect new cases of foodborne illnesses. In order to do this, network employees regularly review laboratory records in the participating states for relevant diagnoses of infections and illness (CDC, 2016). Although active surveillance systems often produce better data, they are more expensive and labor intensive.

 In sentinel surveillance health agencies are charged with collecting high quality information on certain conditions from designated hospitals, labs, or regions. Based on samples collected, public health analysts can make inferences about the entire population's health. Sentinel surveillance, which can be either passive or active, is used when the existing passive surveillance system cannot provide all necessary information about a specific condition and widespread active surveillance may be too expensive or impractical. Finally, in syndromic surveillance, case definitions and reports of symptoms- rather than medical diagnoses- are monitored. For instance, public health officials may monitor fever or shortness of breath. In this system, all cases matching the symptoms being tracked are reported; the resulting information allows for the early detection of outbreaks.

While maintaining effective surveillance systems is always important, it is particularly important during manmade or natural disasters. Not only do these events produce mass injuries and fatalities, but emergency responses are oftentimes dependent on accurate and timely surveillance data. Below, we explore public health surveillance during natural disasters.

The Impact of Natural Disasters on Public Health

Natural disasters include a wide range of weather- or geologic-related events that adversely impact human beings. These include floods, hurricanes, earthquakes, volcanoes, tornados, heat waves, extreme cold, and droughts. Throughout the 20th century, an average of 275,000 people died per year worldwide due to natural disasters (Bryant, 2005, p. 9). Excluding famines, natural hazards were responsible for an average of 140,200 deaths per year globally. Weather related deaths claimed more than 2,000 lives per year in the U.S. between 2006–2010 (Berko, 2017). The 21st century has seen an intensification of natural disasters, which may be a result of climate change. In 2017, 16 extreme weather events in the U.S.- including Hurricanes Harvey, Irma, and Maria- caused a record-breaking $308 billion in damage, costing the country more in disaster damage than any other year on record (Berko, 2017). However, the extent to which these events become "disasters" depends on the vulnerability of the proximate human population. While we may not be able to prevent a hurricane or earthquake, we can curb the impact of the event with proper preparation and response.

Noji (1997) outlines many ways in which disasters impact public health. Most directly, they cause large numbers of deaths and injuries. However, they may also have less direct effects. For instance, many disasters destroy healthcare infrastructure, making it difficult to provide healthcare. Certain groups that need regular medical care, like the elderly or chronically ill, may experience interruptions in care. Because disaster response may require increased levels of medical attention, infrastructure damage to clinics and hospitals may impede the ability of emergency responders to assist the affected population. Also, disasters can impact the mental health of a community, causing widespread panic, anxiety or depression. Finally, some disasters spur the movement of large populations. At times, populations move to regions that are unable to support their medical needs, causing a secondary medical crisis.

Given these effects, maintaining accurate public health surveillance during and after a disaster is of particular importance. Responding effectively to public health needs requires monitoring health through various public health surveillance systems in order to thoroughly understand the community's changing health status. During a disaster, it is important to maintain existing surveillance systems and continue to effectively monitor the health of the population. However, it is oftentimes necessary to enhance existing systems in order to adapt them to the changes and needs in the affected region.

Surveillance Before, During and After the Disaster

Before a disaster, surveillance systems are maintained as usual, in order to track the general health of a population. The data collected in these systems may also assist in preparing adequately for disaster response. A study by Ford et al. (2008) shows how using pre-disaster surveillance data would have helped responders better understand the needs of Katrina victims during and after the hurricane. The authors show that the Behavioral Risk Factor Surveillance System (BRFSS), an ongoing surveillance system in which the CDC collects information about individuals' health through phone interviews, could have been used to estimate the number of people in the hurricane-affected region with chronic conditions (Ford et al, 2006). For instance, according to pre-Katrina data, approximately 9% of people in the region reported having diabetes. Knowing this information would have helped policymakers and responders prepare to deliver appropriate food and medications to the region during and after the disaster. Additionally, before the disaster, efforts should be made to plan for disaster surveillance. Although a disaster surveillance system must remain flexible and adapt its goals to the situation at hand, laying the groundwork for such a system is important nonetheless. This includes defining the goals of the system, sources of data, method of analysis, and plan for communicating results (CDC, 2016b).

Surveillance during and after disasters gives a better understanding of the impact of a disaster and helps to plan for the future. Additionally, surveillance facilitates and guides the emergency response, so that necessary resources can be directed where they are most needed. The CDC's *Primer for Understanding the Principles and Practices of Disaster Surveillance in the United States* stresses that "information collected from a surveillance system must serve to facilitate action (CDC, 2016b, p.3)." According to the CDC's primer, one of the primary goals of disaster surveillance is to detect outbreaks and health problems. Detecting outbreaks of communicable disease is particularly important when large populations may be living together in shelters. However, tracking other illnesses is also crucial, particularly as the health of chronically ill patients often deteriorates during and after a disaster, due to interruptions in care or medication, and changes in diet and living conditions. In addition, surveillance is used for a host of other reasons during the disaster response. This includes (CDC, 2016b):

- determining the nature of injuries, illnesses, and deaths
- preventing adverse health effects;
- identifying health problems and evaluating their scope;
- identifying vulnerable populations and regions;
- guiding emergency response and monitoring the effectiveness of relief efforts; and
- planning effectively for future disasters.

In order to accomplish these goals, disaster surveillance systems collect both morbidity and mortality data. Morbidity data tracks the incidence and prevalence of illness in the population. It plays an important role in the disaster response and allocation of resources. Mortality data tracks the time, location, and manner of death, as well as demographic characteristics of the deceased. This information is useful in evaluating policy effectiveness, determining the magnitude of the event, and preparing to mitigate damage in the next event (CDC, 2016b).

During a disaster, active surveillance is often used to characterize the health of specific populations and identify needs. For instance, if there is extensive damage, large numbers of people are housed in temporary shelters. In this case, it is important to establish a centralized shelter surveillance system. Tracking the health status of the sheltered population is critical in order to identify the health needs in a particular shelter, monitor trends across all shelters, properly allocate health resources, and monitor infectious diseases, which are easily spread in communal living conditions. In order to get a complete picture of the health needs of the sheltered population, healthcare personnel may initiate active surveillance, in which a healthcare or public health employee goes cot to cot inquiring about the medical history of individuals. They may also implement passive shelter surveillance, in which relevant medical information concerning patients who sought care in the shelter in passed on to Department of Health (Heick, 2017).

Additionally, sentinel and syndromic surveillance often become important, particularly if traditional surveillance systems are interrupted. For instance, after the 2010 earthquake in Haiti the National Sentinel Site Surveillance System was formed to track the health of the affected population (Stone and Horney, 2017). Under this system, specific hospitals and clinics submitted daily reports for 25 different conditions for three months. The CDC also runs a National Syndromic Surveillance Program (NSSP) Biosense Platform that facilitates the coordination between local, state, and federal agencies in monitoring health effects after a population is exposed to hazardous materials or conditions. After the 2007 wildfires in near San Diego, California this platform was used to track specific conditions of concern, like asthma (CDC, 2016b).

During disasters of unprecedented scale, epidemiological research and surveillance become critical in identifying health risks and establishing policies that protect first responders and residents in the affected area. Thorpe et al (2014) show how epidemiological research was used to understand the behaviors and health risks faced by first responders to the World Trade Center attacks on September 11, 2001. Epidemiological research and data collected while monitoring the response was used to identify ways to better protect and train first responders in future disasters, identify exposure to hazardous materials, and map the health and mental health needs of various demographic groups after the attack.

Ambiguities of Disaster Mortality Surveillance

After Hurricane Ike ripped through Texas and Louisiana in 2008, the Federal Emergency Management Agency (FEMA) reported 104 hurricane-related deaths, the active mortality surveillance system established during the crisis reported 74, the Red Cross reported 38, the National Ocean and Atmospheric Agency (NOAA) reported 20, and the vital statistics records of the state government showed just 4 (Rocha et al, 2017). There are several factors that may explain the variation in reported deaths.

The National Center for Health Statistics (NCHS) at the CDC assigns a code, according to the *International Classification of Diseases, 10th Revision* (ICD-10), that attributes a death to a specific cause, based on what is written on the official death certificate. The state's vital statistics records track deaths by these codes. If there is no disaster-related information on the death certificate, a disaster-related ICD-10 code will not be assigned. Sometimes the district medical examiner or coroner neglects to reference the disaster on the death certificate, which leads to an underreporting of deaths at the state level. For instance, in deaths related to Hurricane Ike, words like "Ike," "hurricane," "flooding," or "natural disaster" often did not appear on death certificates (Noe, 2017). Thus, locally-issued death certificates with missing information can significantly skew surveillance data at the state and national levels.

Furthermore, Noe (2017) of the CDC writes that because accurate mortality surveillance requires data sharing and cooperation by many government agencies, administrative barriers may hinder the process. The structure of the medical examiner system varies by state. In some states, there is a state-wide centralized system, while in other states, the system of medical examiners is decentralized, with each jurisdiction operating independently (Fierro, 2003). Furthermore, on the county-level, some states use medical examiners while others use coroners. While medical examiners are typically appointed officers with medical degrees or training in forensic pathology, coroners or Justices of the Peace are elected and often are not required to have medical knowledge. Many states also use a mix of country-based medical examiner and coroner systems (CDC, 2016c). States may encounter administrative barriers to data sharing if they operate decentralized medical examiner systems and or have not integrated the vital statistics department into the public health department (Noe, 2017).

Furthermore, there is debate about which deaths should be attributed to disasters. Deaths can either be directly or indirectly related to disasters. Direct deaths occur when death is a result of the forces of the disaster. These may include drowning in flood waters, getting crushed by a falling building, or being burned. However, many of the deaths that occur during and after a disaster are less easily classified. Combs et al (1999, p. 1126) suggests asking three questions in order to identify indirectly-related disaster deaths:

- Did the environmental forces of the disaster lead to unsafe or unhealthy conditions that caused a loss or disruption of usual services—and did these loses or disruptions contribute to the decedent's death?
- Did the environmental forces of the disaster lead to temporary or permanent displacement, property damage, or other personal loss or stress—and did these losses or disruptions contribute to the decedent's death?
- If the disaster had not occurred, would this decedent still be alive?

Based on these questions, we see that indirect deaths may include varied circumstances. For instance, somebody who dies of a chronic condition because they are unable to get routine healthcare due to infrastructure damage after a disaster is an indirect disaster casualty. However, various agencies and medical examiners may report this death differently. Some may attribute the death to the disaster, while others may not.

Such discrepancies in mortality reporting may lead to skewed assessments of the impact of a disaster. In addition, omissions of disaster-related data from death certificates may have direct policy implications. For instance, FEMA provides funeral benefits, including paying for a casket, burial plot, and headstone for those who die in disasters. In order to be eligible, relatives of the deceased must have formal written documentation that attributes the death to the disaster (FEMA, 2016). Thus, the information on the death certificate may either hinder or facilitate claiming these benefits.

References

Bryant, E. (2005). *Natural Hazards, Second Edition.* New York, NY: Cambridge University Press.

Berko, J. (2017). Deaths attributed to heat, cold, and other weather events in the United States, 2006–2010. *Health.*

Centers for Disease Control and Prevention (CDC). National Vital Statistics System. Retrieved from http://cdc.gov

Centers for Disease Control and Prevention (CDC) (2016a, March 17). *Foodborne Disease Active Surveillance Network.* Retrieved from http://cdc.gov

Centers for Disease Control and Prevention (CDC). (2016b). A Primer for Understanding the Principles and Practices of Disaster Surveillance in the United States. *Atlanta (GA):* CDC.

Centers for Disease Control and Prevention (CDC). (2016c). *Death Investigation Systems.* Retrieved from http://cdc.gov

Combs, D. L., Quenemoen, L. E., Parrish, R. G., & Davis, J. H. (1999). Assessing disaster-attributed mortality: development and application of a definition and classification matrix. *International journal of epidemiology, 28*(6), 1124–1129.

Cookson, S. T., Soetebier, K., Murray, E. L., Fajardo, G. C., Hanzlick, R., Cowell, A., et al. (2008). Internet-based morbidity and mortality surveillance among Hurricane Katrina evacuees in Georgia. Preventing Chronic Disease, 5(4).

Federal Emergency Management Agency (FEMA). (2016, August 9). *Disaster Funeral Assistance. Retrieved* from http://fema.gov

Fierro, M. (2003). Comparing Medical Examiner and Coroner Systems In Institute of Medicine (US) *Medicolegal Death Investigation System: Workshop Summary.* National Academies Press, United States.

Ford, E. S., Mokdad, A. H., Link, M. W., Garvin, W. S., & McGuire, L. C. (2006). PEER REVIEWED: Chronic Disease in Health Emergencies: In the Eye of the Hurricane. *Preventing Chronic Disease, 3*(2).

Heick, R. J. (2017). Applications: Shelter Surveillance. In Horney (Ed.) *Disaster Epidemiology* (pp. 41–47). Academic Press.

Murray, K. O., Kilborn, C., DesVignes-Kendrick, M., Koers, E., Page, V., Selwyn, B. J., et al. (2009). Emerging disease syndromic surveillance for Hurricane Katrina evacuees seeking shelter in Houston's Astrodome and Reliant Park Complex. Public Health Reports, 124, 364e371.

Noe, R. S. (2017). Applications: Disaster-Related Mortality Surveillance: Challenges and Considerations for Local and State Health Departments. In Horney (Ed.) *Disaster Epidemiology* (pp. 55–63). Academic Press.

Noji, E. K. (1997). The nature of disaster: general characteristics and public health effects In Noji (Ed.), *The Public Health Consequences of Disasters* (pp. 3–20). Oxford University Press, Oxford, United Kingdom.

Nsubuga, P., White, M. E., Thacker, S. B., Anderson, M. A., Blount, S. B., Broome, C. V., . . . & Stroup, D. F. (2006). Public health surveillance: a tool for targeting and monitoring interventions.

Rocha, L. A., Fromknecht, C. Q., Redman, S. D., Brady, J. E., Hodge, S. E., & Noe, R. S. (2017). Medicolegal death scene investigations after natural disaster-and weather-related events: a review of the literature. *Academic forensic pathology, 7*(2), 221.

Stone, K. and Horney, J. (2017). Methods: Surveillance. In Horney (Ed.) *Disaster Epidemiology* (pp. 55–63). Academic Press.

Thorpe, L. E., Assari, S., Deppen, S., Glied, S., Lurie, N., Mauer, M. P., . . . & Trapido, E. (2015). The role of epidemiology in disaster response policy development. *Annals of epidemiology, 25*(5), 377–386.

World Health Organization (WHO). (2018a). Public Health Surveillance. Retrieved from http://who.int

World Health Organization (WHO). (2018b).Accelerated Disease Control. Retrieved from http://who.int